THE PEACE PROCESS

Afif Safieh

The Peace Process

From Breakthrough to Breakdown

SAQI

ISBN 978-0-86356-422-2

First published by Saqi Books 2010

A full CIP record for this book is available from the British Library.
A full CIP record for this book is available from the Library of Congress.

Manufactured in Lebanon

SAQI
26 Westbourne Grove, London W2 5RH
2398 Doswell Avenue, Saint Paul, Minnesota, 55108
Verdun, Beirut, Lebanon
www.saqibooks.com

To my daughters, Diana and Randa

To my daughter, Diana and Karen

Contents

Introduction

As a diplomat, I have had the rare opportunity, if not the unique privilege, of being the Head of Mission in London, Washington and Moscow, this in addition to the Netherlands and The Holy See. My personal itinerary within the Palestinian National Movement will be the subject of my next book, *Anatomy of a Mission*.

Here I am presenting the reader with a selection of lectures, speeches, articles and interviews ranging from 1981 to my farewell speech in London in 2005. Most were unwritten, taped and transcribed later. There are lectures at Harvard, MIT, Oxford, the Royal United Services Institute for Defence Studies (RUSI) and the Royal Institute for International Affairs (Chatham House). They constitute a Palestinian perspective on the unfolding reality as well as trace the evolution of Palestinian political thinking.

I have included two documents of special value to me. In April 1991, just after the Gulf War, I was invited for a hearing by the Select Committee for Foreign Affairs in the House of Commons. Palestinian diplomats rarely, if ever, got that type of invitation. The hearing gives a 'flavour' of the era and shows the importance and the difficulties of Palestinian diplomacy in the quest for independence and sovereignty.

In 1987, while a visiting scholar at Harvard University, I interviewed Gene Sharp, an expert on non-violent struggles. That interview was published in the autumn 1987 edition of *Palestine Studies*, and was translated into Arabic and distributed in the Occupied Territories when the first intifada erupted in December that same year.

The Palestinian people are not offered the luxury of choice between resistance and non-resistance. The choice is between the different modalities of expression of our rejection of the prevailing unacceptable status quo. Reproducing this long interview is, I hope, a modest contribution towards the formulation of a concerted and cohesive approach in the phase to come.

What has happened since 2005 is not addressed in this book. Today it is almost nineteen years since the Madrid/Washington Peace Conference, and almost seventeen years since the Oslo breakthrough. Instead of a durable peace, it is the process that became permanent – a succession of spectacular non-events.

How can one summarise the situation?

1. The Nakba was not a frozen moment in History that happened sometime in 1948–9: the Nakba remains, alas, an ongoing process;

2. The aim of successive Israeli governments has been constant: how to acquire as much of Palestinian geography as possible with as little of Palestinian demography as possible;

3. During the years of theoretical peace-making, what we witnessed was not Israeli withdrawal but rather the expansion of the Israeli occupation through the elastic growth of the illegal settlements;

4. Today, with ceasefires observed in both the West Bank and the Gaza Strip – at least from the Palestinian side – it is obvious that it is territory and not terrorism which is the obstacle to peace;

5. With the Arab Peace Initiative on the table since 2002, the deadlock is surely not due to an Arab rejection of Israeli existence but due to an Israeli rejection of Arab acceptance;

6. Unfortunately, the Quartet has turned out to be a 'one-*tête*' operation. Because of its self-inflicted impotence when dealing with Israel, the USA seems to have the political weight of a

Luxembourg, or even worse, Lichtenstein. In their confrontation of wills, President Obama has lost the first round with Israeli Prime Minister Netanyahu. Will there be a second round? Will there be a second Obama mandate? Too early to say. Yet knowing the flaws and the reasons of failure of the peace process, I deeply believe that, if ever we are to achieve peace, what is really needed is an elegantly imposed solution that is mutually unacceptable. The concept of mutual unacceptability carries more potential than the eternal and elusive search for mutual acceptability by two unequal negotiating partners left to themselves to sort it out. Bearing in mind the psychology of belligerency, the fact that the other side does not like the proposal on offer either makes it ... less unattractive.

In international relations, in matters of war and peace, the international will should prevail on a national whim.

I wish to express my indebtedness to my wife Christ'l – a Palestinian by choice – for shouldering, for over thirty years, many of the responsibilities I have had to cope with. I am deeply grateful to my daughter Diana for her invaluable assistance in preparing the material for this book. It was a joy to work with her. It was also a privilege to work with Saqi, most notably with Lynn Gaspard and her team, who have shown great competence coupled with profound decency.

Afif Safieh
London, March 2010

I

The PLO

The challenge and the response[1]

Strategically located at the crossroads of three continents, Palestine was throughout the ages coveted by external powers. During the twentieh century, British colonialism was only a transition beween Ottoman (Turkish) domination and Zionist penetration.

Yet Zionism has its specificity. Unlike previous occupations, it has imposed on Palestine a double human migration: the massive expulsion of the Palestinians to the periphery of their homeland was coupled with the massive arrival of settlers to replace them.

It is an irony of history that all settler colonies were demographically composed of persecuted individuals and groups who migrated in search of more hospitable shores. They were Catholics from predominantly Protestant societies or Protestants fleeing an intolerant Catholic environment. They were republicans from the European monarchies or royalists from newly born republics. To take Algeria as an example, the *pieds-noirs* were mainly the descendants of migrants from regions of Alsace and Lorraine annexed by Prussia (i.e. nationally oppressed), or descendants of the defeated revolutionary communards from Paris (i.e. economically exploited or ideologically persecuted).

---

1. This paper was presented in a United Nations symposium held in Colombo, Sri Lanka in August 1981 and was first published in *Monday Morning*, a Lebanese weekly. I was then staff member in President Arafat's office in Beirut, in charge of Europe and UN institutions.

In each case, a reversal of roles was operated, the needs of the newcomers gradually trespassing on the rights of the indigenous population until totally negating their existence.

Israel is no exception. Zionism has transformed the oppressed of one continent to the oppressors of another continent. The State of Israel to which it gave birth had, from its very first day, an elastic conception of its frontiers resulting from an insatiable territorial appetite. Ben Gurion, Israel's first prime minister, explaining the absence of a constitution and any delimitation of frontiers, stated that the borders of Israel will go as far as 'the Israel defence army' will reach.

Today, the Palestinians are the heirs of the Jewish sufferings, the sufferings of Treblinka, Dachau and Auschwitz. The Jews were the direct victims of Nazism. The world recently discovered that the Palestinians were the Nazis' indirect victims. Zionism took advantage of the Nazi atrocities and from a minority tendency within the Jewish communities, it emerged as a hegemonic organisation systematically exerting moral and intellectual terrorism on reluctant Jews.

But each hegemonic movement secretes its own dissidents. I should say fortunately, because Jewish, and later on Israeli, dissidents helped the Palestinian people to reject all the theories abusively assimilating Zionism with Judaism. The role of those dissidents, in spite of their numerical weakness, is potentially great. By denouncing the long-term strategy of the State of Israel as well as its daily practices, they prove that there is no Jewish collective guilt vis-à-vis the ordeal of the Palestinians and thus they save the future possibilities of pacific cohabitation.

Pacific and harmonious cohabitation in Palestine has been the objective of the Palestinian revolution since its inception. Rebellious against the intolerable prevailing situation in which the Palestinians had become 'the Jews of the Zionists', the Palestinian freedom fighters pledged that the Jewish community would not, when the balance of power inevitably changed, be transformed into 'the Palestinians of the Palestinians'.

This is how the project of a democratic, secular, pluri-confessional and multi-ethical state in Palestine should have been perceived. By recognising the accomplished demographic fact, the PLO demonstrated that it was not seeking any historical revenge but, on the contrary, was sincerely yearning to break the dialectics of oppression.

Arnold Toynbee has explained human history in its unity and in its diversity through the individual and collective responses to the challenge of the environment, the natural and the human environment.

A homeland occupied, a people diasporised, a capital, Jerusalem, mutilated, a civilisation at the same time denied and plundered, an Arab nation balkanised, into multiple states which imperialism constantly tries, often successfully, to antagonise; these are the challenges that the PLO has to cope with.

From 1948 until 1965, the Palestinian people resorted to what can be called the arms of criticism. But their complaints, expressed through petitions or street demonstrations, gave birth only to compassion and charity. It is only when the Palestinians opted for armed struggle, criticism by arms, that their national identity and aspirations were recognised and the claim for their necessary satisfaction endorsed by the international community.

The battle of Karameh in March 1968 was a turning point. Only months after the humiliating defeat of 1967 and the Arab armies' discredit because of their poor performance, the Palestinian resistance movement proved its military credibility by heroically facing a massive Israeli attack intended to wipe it out of existence.

The next day, *Le Monde*'s main article was on the political resurrection of the Palestinians. In fact, that very day the people joined its vanguard. In February 1969, even the classical political elite admitted that radical changes had occurred in the Palestinian scene, and Yasser Arafat, leader of the major guerrilla movement, Fateh, was elected chairman of the PLO. The Palestinians had recuperated the historical initiative; no more a mere object of history whose destinies were decided upon in foreign capitals, they had become the subject of their own history.

Before seeking international recognition, the PLO had already obtained internal legitimacy. It unified the political expression of a geographically/demographically dispersed people and began channelling their struggles towards the common goal: the right of return and independent statehood. If the intoxicating Israeli propaganda has emphasised the military aspect of the Palestinian struggle, the PLO's non-military fields of interest are not of lesser importance in the Palestinian revival, survival and – some day, hopefully soon – victory.

Today, the PLO is a pre-governmental organisation which is already assuming the responsibilities of a state. Each Executive Committee member is in charge of a specific department: the political department, economic department, information department, health department, cultural department, department for the occupied territories, etc.

As a political system, the PLO carries the following characteristics: it is a multi-party system, with freedom of expression for all its components, in which eventually internal opposition is not only tolerated but legal. It is to be noted that decisions are rarely adopted by a unanimous vote. The supreme decision-making organ in the PLO is the Palestinian National Council (PNC), the parliament-in-exile.

Its last session, the 15th, was held 11–20 April 1981 in Damascus. Its current composition is as follows:

Guerilla movements: 94 members
- Fateh: 33
- Saika: 12
- Popular Front: 12
- Democratic Front: 12
- Arab Liberation Front: 9
- Popular Front-General Command: 8
- Front of Palestinian Struggle: 4
- Palestinian Liberation Front: 4

Mass movements and trade unions: 60 members
- General Union of Palestine Workers: 21
- General Union of Palestine Women: 8
- General Union of Palestine Teachers: 7
- General Union of Palestine Students: 7
- General Union of Palestine Writers and Journalists: 3
- General Union of Palestine Lawyers: 3
- General Union of Palestine Engineers: 3
- General Union of Palestine Medical Professions: 5
- General Union of Palestine Youth: 2
- General Union of Palestine Artists: 1

Representatives of the Palestinian communities in the diaspora: 62 members
- Jordan: 17
- Lebanon: 9
- Syria: 7
- Kuwait: 9
- Saudi Arabia: 8
- The United Arab Emirates: 2
- Qatar: 2
- Iraq: 1
- The American continent: 7

Personalities expelled by Israeli occupation authorities: 20 members

Scientist and intellectuals of international reputation: 13 members

Independents: 66 members

Total: 315 members, including 32 women

The representatives of the guerilla movements, of the trade unions and of the Palestinian communities in the diaspora (i.e. 207 members) are directly elected by their respective constituencies. The others (108 members) are co-opted by the elected members of the PNC.

There are 122 additional members from the occupied territories. The Israeli military governor having threatened each of them with expulsion if they ever took part in any session of the PNC, the Palestinian leadership advised them not to attend. However, they regularly send their evaluation of the prevailing situation to the leadership and petitions are addressed to the United Nations and other intergovernmental organisations, reaffirming that the PLO is the sole legitimate representative of the Palestinian people. This unfaltering national unity has foiled all the attempts aimed at promoting an 'alternative leadership' for the Palestinian people.

If, and perhaps I should say because, Zionism as a colonial movement had its specificity, the Palestinian national liberation struggle is unique. In the game of nations, until recently monopolised by states and only states, the PLO ('a non-territorial state' – Hisham Sharabi) emerged as a dynamic actor. Contrary to the claim of the Zionists, the PLO was not propelled on the international arena by the energy crisis but because it had proved, on the terrain, that it was an irreversible political and military factor.

It is today a full, active and effective member in the League of Arab States, in the Conference of Islamic States and in the Movement of Non-Aligned Countries. All the socialist countries have officially recognised the PLO, and successive presidents of the European Council of Ministers, in preparation for an eventual European initiative, met with the chairman of the PLO as a major party concerned in an endeavour for the solution of the Middle Eastern crisis. Last but not least, the PLO enjoys an observer status in the United Nations Organisation and in its specialised agencies, having all the privileges of a full member except the right of voting and of directly submitting project-resolutions or amendments.

In the last four sessions of the Palestinian National Council (1974, 1977, 1979, 1981) resolutions were adopted calling for the implementation of international legality. Regarding the international body as capable of reconciling ethics with politics, the PLO considers that the United Nations is the most adequate forum for the solution of the conflict.

Today, it seems to me that an acceptable mechanism could be the following three-phased formula:

1. The speedy withdrawal of Israel from all the territory occupied in 1967;

2. In the Palestinian territories evacuated, and in coordination with the PLO, the sole legitimate representative of the Palestinian people, the United Nations assumes responsibility for an interim period between Israeli occupation and Palestinian sovereignty;

3. An international conference is convened under the auspices of the United Nations to which are invited all the parties concerned, including the State of Palestine, to agree upon all pending issues.

But the desirable is still impossible, and the possible (Camp David) totally unacceptable.

One might wonder why the PLO, which has already achieved national consensus, then international consensus, has not yet succeeded in materialising its political objectives on the geographical map.

Alas, the impotence of the United Nations on the one hand, and first the complicity, then the complacency, and now the abdication of Western Europe on the other hand are part of the answer. So is the insufficient mobilisation of Arab potentials. But the unlimited and so far unconditional support, military and financial (from flour to Phantoms), abundantly delivered to Israel by the United States remains the determining factor. Israel is in crisis. The Promised Land has not kept its promises. But the economic and social vulnerability of Israel is for the moment largely compensated for by an overwhelming military superiority.

Yet just a few weeks ago, the Palestinian guerrilla forces, in a direct Palestinian-Israeli war (10–24 July 1981) successfully confronted this huge war machine equipped to defeat all the Arab armies combined. One might now expect the American administration to draw some evident conclusions, and this dialogue by arms to inaugurate another phase in the confrontation, that of the arms of dialogue.

All Middle East specialists and observers have underlined the realistic approach of the PLO. The Israeli leadership knows by now that it is totally erroneous to confuse realism and resignation. My personal hope is that the international community, friends and foes alike, will act in a manner to contradict Hegel's pessimistic vision – pessimistic yet so often justified: from history we learn that we have not learned from history.

II

One people too many?[1]

Vivant Univers: What does it mean to be Palestinian?

Afif Safieh: You know, there is a popular saying, 'happy peoples have no history.' The Palestinian people – should they congratulate themselves, or should they be regretful? – are burdened by a history several thousand years old.

To be Palestinian today means to have been deprived of the elementary right to live in one's country. It means having been displaced by force, time after time, from one place to another, and under conditions of complete destitution. It means having lost one's property, the plot of land which one cultivated, and the home one lived in. It means helplessly witnessing the gradual Judaisation of one's homeland, and the removal of the Arab influence and presence from it.

It means having no identity papers like all the other citizens of the world have. It means having administrative problems throughout one's life, from birth to death, a death which is often caused by arms and bombs which have been prohibited by international law but which have been discharged indiscriminately, with a preference for civilian targets, in order to terrorise the population. It means unimaginable complications when one sets out to search for a job, and interminable waits in airports and at borders.

To be a Palestinian means belonging to a family which has been

---

1. Translated from French, this interview was first published in the September 1985 issue of *Vivant Univers,* a Belgian journal.

broken up and scattered to all corners of the world. My family, for example, which consists of five people, lives in three different continents. My parents and one sister are in Jerusalem, my brother in Brazil and I am in Belgium. At the time of my father's death two years ago, I could not return to his side because of the military occupation.

Those who have been able to remain in the country feel unwanted there. They are subjected to daily harassment; they are pushed into an emigration which has nothing voluntary about it. Juridicial harassment (expropriation), economic harassment (unbearable taxes, pillage of hydrological resources), police repression . . . The overwhelming majority of Palestinian adults have already been imprisoned at least once by the occupation authorities. In the prisons, the practice of torture is frequent. When there are protest demonstrations, it often happens that the forces of 'order' which 'officially' receive orders to fire into the air, prefer to aim at the air which is to be found in the lungs of the demonstrators . . .

Vivant Univers: How many Palestinians are there today? Where do they live?

Afif Safieh: There are about five million Palestinians. Seven hundred thousand are in Israel, within its pre-1967 boundaries. One million live in the West Bank and 700,000 in the Gaza Strip; these two territories having been under Israeli military occupation since 1967. One and a half million live in Jordan, 400,000 in Lebanon, 300,000 in Kuwait and 250,000 in Syria. Half a million Palestinians are spread throughout the two Americas. In every country of the world you will find Palestinian communities of different sizes.[1]

But whether they live in occupied lands, are stuck in refugee camps or are experiencing exile in a far-off country, all Palestinians

---

1.   Figures stated are for the year 1985. It is estimated in 2009 that there are around 10.9 million Palestinians worldwide.

share common sufferings and aspirations: to be able to exercise their right of return, their right to self-determination and to national sovereignty.

At the crossroads of three continents (Asia, Africa and Europe), Palestine has been throughout time the object of external desires. My father's generation, for example, witnessed three distinct and successive phases of national oppression: Turkish domination until 1917, followed by the British Mandate (1917-1948) which then favoured Zionist penetration (1948). But the last distinguished itself from the preceding aggressions. Zionism, an imported ideology, also recruited its followers abroad. With the aim of transforming Palestine into 'a country just as Jewish as England was English', it could not succeed in its enterprise except through the subordination or expulsion of the indigenous population. The Zionist movement, and then the State of Israel, imposed a double human migration on Palestine: on the one hand, the massive expulsion of the Palestinians to the periphery of their national soil and, on the other, the arrival – just as massive – of settlers to replace them. In this way then, Israel constituted the last colonial project – accomplished paradoxically in the age of decolonisation.

Vivant Univers: But a certain 'History' insists on presenting Palestine as 'a land without a people' which was to have been offered to a 'people without a land'. What truth is there in this? Was Palestine really nothing but an uncultivated and arid desert?

Afif Safieh: The Zionist movement is a master in the art of fabricating myths and it appears that the Palestinian people were condemned, not only to have their rights despoiled, but to be systematically denigrated as well. It was in order to *legitimise* its visions regarding this monstrosity; that is, the 'demographic vacuum' in the country, which would therefore be colonisable without injustice and without remorse. This is a conceptual genocide.

As a matter of fact, many Zionist colonisers left Palestine once they discovered a people like any other, made up of city-dwellers, countryfolk and nomads, all of whom aspired to independence. But that was nothing but the reaction of a tiny minority.

The majority, with full prior knowledge, were to pursue their colonial project and continue to attract new waves of immigrants. And this with the support of Great Britain. Lord Balfour, Minister for Foreign Affairs, was to write, 'in Palestine we do not envisage undertaking the consultation of the will of *the present inhabitants*,' explaining that Zionism was, for Great Britain, of greater importance than 'the desires and prejudices of 700,000 Arabs who *now* live in this ancient land'.[1]

As acknowledged by the British themselves then, 700,000 Palestinians lived in Palestine in 1917. On such grounds as these and according to this logic, how many states which are today members of the United Nations, could be considered 'lands without people', available for enterprises of domination and monopoly?

An Israeli intellectual, Saul Friedlander, unable to deny the demographic evidence, was to speak of the confrontation between the 'subjective right' of the Jews to Palestine and the 'objective right' of the Palestinians in Palestine.[2] Interesting formulation! Yet, while I might understand what an 'objective right' is, I cannot keep from finding the notion of a 'subjective right' strange and even dangerous. It paves the way for so many crimes.

As to the second formula, 'the people without a land,' would require a lengthy elaboration the limits of this interview render difficult. Nevertheless, permit me to dissipate and refute some of the 'admitted truths' which are the most contestable. Above all, the majority of today's Jews cannot be among the descendants of the ancient Hebrews of Palestine. Many of them converted to other religions. On the other hand, many people and tribes converted to Judaism. The best known example is that of the Khazars, a tribe of half a million people who massively adopted Judaism in the seventh century.[3] Is the argument of 'the historic right' valid then? Is the colonisation of Palestine really 'the return after two thousand years of exile'?

Now, many scholars, such as Maxime Rodinson to cite only one of them, inform us that the present Palestinians have more 'Hebrew blood' in their veins than most of today's Jews.

As to the notion of 'divine right', since there has been the 'divine promise' made to the 'chosen people', I – like many Jews moreover – cannot admit this image of a God who would commit the sin of 'favouritism', of a God who would be a 'discriminator'. I prefer to refer to what Golda Meir says to us in her memoirs: 'The Jews were the first to have chosen God.' She has not always shown such subtlety and sophistication, but I must admit that this interpretation is by far preferable to that of the 'chosen people', keeping in mind that it was in fact the dignitaries of Pharaonic Egypt who were the first to preach monotheism.

Finally, anti-Semitism is above all a Christian and essentially a European phenomenon. The solution to it must be sought in the same countries where it rages, through the struggle for equal rights and responsibilities, through the fight for the right to be different and for freedom of religion, and through inter-community integration. But anti-Semitism and Zionism are two currents which go together and feed each other reciprocally. Thus Israel, through its practices and alliances – which often go so far as to include active support for bloody dictatorships – has come to reinforce if not to arouse anti-Semitism in regions where it was almost nonexistent, for example in the countries of Latin America or the Arab World. Now, both anti-Semites and Zionists try to lead us to believe that anti-Semitism is an uneradicable and eternal feeling. I dare to believe, I dare to hope that it is not.

But let us go back to the alibi of the barren, uncultivated

Palestine. It is necessary to read the accounts of the Crusades. In them we learn that the Crusaders admitted having learned enormously from the techniques of agriculture and irrigation used in Palestine in that epoch. It would be necessary to look at the figures for external commerce before the twentieth century, where we would see that Palestine was not only self-sufficient in food, but exported fruit and vegetables to Europe. That Israel would have increased the agricultural capacity of the country is not surprising considering the enormous injection of foreign capital and the superior qualifications of the Zionist settlers who came from Europe. But here a great moral question is posed: in the name of what, and since when, does the planting of a tree justify the uprooting of a human being? Since when does the decision to plant a forest justify the uprooting of an entire people?

Vivant Univers: What do you think of the attitude of international public opinion towards the Palestinian problem?

Afif Safieh: I would limit myself to Western opinion. Lately it has evolved considerably. It finally recognises that the Palestinians have suffered an historic wrong and wishes to see them recoup *certain* rights previously trampled on. But its vigilance and the pressure which it sometimes decides to exercise, are well below that which could be expected of it.

The Palestinians cannot but remember with sadness and bitterness that the enterprise which led to their dispossession and their dispersion was followed by Western public opinion with an admiring, never reproving, regard towards Israel. Insensitive to the trials of the Palestinians, it applauded the exploits – above all the ones of war – of Israel.

This can be explained by the painful and sometimes guilty memories of the atrocities committed during the Second World War. But if the Jews were the direct victims of Nazism, then the

Palestinians are its indirect victims. Without Hitler, Zionism would have remained a minority current within the Jewish communities. Without Hitler and his attempts at exterminating the Jews, the Zionist movement would not have benefited from this capital of sympathy which it has used and abused. From this indulgence, this complacency touches on complicity.

It is important to point out that the first in the West to dare to rebel against Israel's false propaganda were Jews: Maxime Rodinson, Ania Francos, Alfred Lilienthal . . . They believed themselves safe from intellectual terrorism and the accusation of anti-Semitism, but they were mistaken: they were harshly attacked, reviled and threatened. They were accused of 'self-hatred' and betrayal.

Over the decades, solving the 'Jewish problem' was a high priority objective for Western opinion, even if it meant paying for it with a 'Palestinian problem'. One would have wished that the Palestinians did not exist, that they would have disappeared before the arrival of the settlers. In short, they had committed the wrong of existing.

The Zionist colonisation of Palestine enjoyed great popularity in the West and it was the resistance of the people who were the victims of this dispossession which was to be condemned. The Palestinian was to be described as a brute, a fanatic and a terrorist. At best, a potential terrorist.

Paradoxically, the Zionists themselves judged this resistance to be normal. Jabotinsky, the master thinker of the Israeli right, was to write, 'has any people ever been seen to give up its territory of its own free will? In the same way, the Arabs of Palestine will not renounce their sovereignty without violence.'[4]

Ben Gurion said to Nahum Goldmann: 'If I were an Arab leader, I would never sign an agreement with Israel. It is normal, we have taken their country. It is true that God promised it to us, but how could that possibly interest them? Our God is not theirs.

There has been anti-Semitism, the Nazis, Hitler, Auschwitz, but was that their fault? They see but one thing: we have come and we have stolen their country. Why would they accept that?'

In the West, on the other hand, this clarity of perception was forbidden. Phillipe de Saint Robert tells us that a reader reproached him for his 'impartiality which is intolerable when Israel is in question.'⁵ Jean-Paul Sartre was to write, 'Without a doubt they (the Arabs) are right, but can they keep these Israelis from being, for us, also Jews?'⁶ This is why impartiality becomes intolerable and objectivity unwelcome.

Vivant Univers: Why have many Palestinians left their country and their lands?

Afif Safieh: You have probably asked me this question because there are those who claim that the Palestinians left their country of their own accord. This is absolutely contrary to historic reality. But it seems to me that they who have propagated this version as well as they who have let themselves be convinced by it, have never asked themselves the following question: do the civilian refugees coming from combat zones in other conflicts equally automatically lose all rights to return and their property? Of course not!

Thus at the time of the German invasion of France in 1940, thousands of French people left. Once the fighting had ended, they were able to return to their homes, their towns and villages. In Palestine, the civilian population was a privileged target for the Zionist troops who sought to conquer *the maximum of territory with a minimum of demography*. This is what profoundly differentiates this war in the Middle East from any other conflict.

While the massacre at Deir Yassin (1948), in the course of which 254 peaceful villagers were liquidated in a single night, is the most well known, it was unfortunately not the only one. Menachem Begin, the one politically in charge and who gave the orders for this carnage, was often to boast loudly claiming that without Deir Yassin, there would never have been an Israel. In his memoirs, he wrote, 'the Jewish forces advanced in Haifa like a knife in butter. The Arabs fled in panic, crying Deir Yassin.'[7] It was necessary to terrorise the population in order to encourage them to flee.

It is useful to remember that according to the cutting up of Palestine contained in the Partition Plan adopted by the United Nations, there was to be a small Jewish minority in the Arab state, while in the territory granted to the Jewish State, the Arab population was equal in number to the Jews who had installed themselves there. For a political movement, Zionism, which wanted 'an Israel as Jewish as England is English', the presence of these Arabs was inadmissible, intolerable! In 1948, the State of Israel was admitted to the United Nations but in a conditional manner. It had to permit the return of all the refugees which its violent and brutal birth had flung out along the path of exile.

This resolution had been submitted to a vote by the United States and each year since then it is once again voted on and adopted by the international community. But it has never even begun to be applied. On the contrary, new refugees have regularly come to join the previous ones.

Vivant Univers: There is often talk of the 'settlement colonies' in the occupied territories. What do these implantations represent?

Afif Safieh: A first remark is called for: it was under the aegis of the Israeli Labour Party that the policy of creating settlement colonies in the occupied territories was begun in 1967. General Dayan, to whom we must grant the merit of frankness, called this process 'rampant annexation'. Under Menachem Begin and the Likud, it just galloped. But the main difference resides in nothing more than the rhythm.

It is this process of the gradual nibbling away of Palestinian territory which has permitted the creation of the State of Israel: a succession of *fait accomplis*, legitimised afterwards by the always favourable balance of military power.

Since the first hours of its creation, Israel has shown itself to have an insatiable territorial appetite. Its leaders start out from a very elastic conception of the frontiers of the State which they themselves have carved out. For Israel, right follows from *fait accomplis* on the ground, both military and demographic.

The peace camp in Israel defends the idea that it is necessary to 'liberate Israel of these occupied territories' in order to disentangle itself from this interminable war. Unfortunately, this current is very much a minority. The overwhelming majority of Israeli voters pronounce themselves regularly and democratically in favour of annexation and the denial of the minimal national rights of the Palestinians.

Yet they would have been well inspired to recall the words of Rabbi Heschel, who had declared, 'in a free society, if a few are guilty, all are responsible.' Perhaps one day we might be told in order to justify the oppression of the past that 'we did not know.' This talk will be no more credible tomorrow than it was yesterday.

Vivant Univers: What does the PLO represent for the Palestinian people?

Afif Safieh: Put simply, it represents them. Before 1964-5 the Palestinians were threatened with oblivion – because of their dispersion, their lack of organisation. The PLO gave them back both hope and initiative. From objects of history, they have become once again subjects of their own history. The PLO is the incarnation of their aspirations; it is a vehicle and channel for their fight for a concrete objective. With modest means, the PLO has worked on the restructuring of this torn and 'diasporised' people.

The mass media have, unfortunately, focused on the military

aspect; they have bluntly hidden the immense work which the PLO carries out on a sanitation, educational and economic level in order to preserve the national identity, dignity and cultural patrimony of the Palestinian people.

The PLO is perceived of as a pre-governmental organisation which is already assuming state responsibilities. The Palestinians have chosen it, and designated it to be their spokesman and their negotiator in the search for the peace they long for so much. I would not dodge the problem of violence. I know some identify the PLO with terrorism.

Believe me, the dominated peoples are always the first to wish that an end be put to their suffering, without bloodshed, and the first to hope that their liberation will be accomplished through peaceful mechanisms and institutional channels. But, in reality, no other choice was left to them but to resort to armed struggle in order to confront the state terrorism which they had to face. Remember that Israeli violence has left more Palestinian victims in three days than Palestinian violence has left in three decades. The Palestinians have been sent into mourning a thousand times more than the Israelis.

Why does Western opinion demonstrate such selective sensitivity, especially when, in such and evident manner, the sufferings are disproportionate to such an extent?

Vivant Univers: Now, what future awaits Palestine?

Afif Safieh: Today, there is no 'just solution' for Palestine or the Palestinians. Too many disruptions have been imposed by force. The Palestinians, who are today 'the Jews of the Israelis,' do not wish to see that tomorrow the Jews of Palestine become in turn the Palestinians of the Palestinians.

We do not seek historic revenge. On the contrary, we want to smash this infernal dialectic of oppression. If a 'just solution' is inconceivable at the present time, an 'acceptable peace' is nevertheless always possible.

The formula of two neighbouring states on Palestinian territory would render partial justice to the Palestinians. Moreover, this solution conforms to the wishes of the international community and the resolutions of the United Nations. Unfortunately, two dissident states – Israel and the United States – render the international consensus inoperable.

How could this Palestinian state be born? Three courses are possible. First of all, a profound change coming from inside Israel. I am among those who had bet on this course and who acted consequently. This way had my preference, essentially for ethical reasons.

If the Israelis, without having been forced to do so militarily or diplomatically, were to restore the territories conquered in 1967 to the Palestinians, or if they were to come back to the United Nations Partition Plan, that would facilitate both authentic pardon and reconciliation. Unfortunately, the 1984 Knesset elections reveal nothing but a further slide towards annexationism or, at best, immobilism.

The second possible course would be a new Israeli-Arab war according to the model of 1973, in order to seriously reactivate the diplomatic front and the search for peace. Besides the fact that war is never a desirable eventuality, the state of the Arab World, with its present divisions and the resulting impotence, render this hypothesis improbable, at least in the short term.

Finally, the third course envisagable, taking into account the fact that the *status quo* is showing itself to be intolerable and highly explosive, and that Israeli intransigence on one hand and Arab *powerlessness* on the other do nothing but perpetuate this situation – I am personally in favour of a peace process actively stimulated (I would even say *imposed*) by the international community, on the basis of the whole set of United Nations resolutions.

The United Nations is still the only framework in a position to reconcile politics with ethics. It could temper the arguments of force, reminding the protagonists of the force of arguments. If that fails, the spiral of violence would experience an uncontrollable escalation. And the conflict could burst out of its regional framework.

In the Middle East, *we have either one people too many, or one state less than what is needed.* It is for each of us to pronounce himself. Must we allow the annihilation of this one people too many? Or must we work to make possible the birth of the State which is missing?

Notes

1. In a letter to Lord Curzon, cited by Gilmor D., in *Dispossessed: The Ordeal of the Palestinians.*
2. Friedlander, S. *Reflexions sur l'Avenir d'Israel,* p. 11.
3. Koestler, A., *La Treizieme Tribu.*
4. Jabotinsky, cited by M. Rodinston in *Peuple Juif ou Probleme Juif?,* pp. 121–2.
5. de Saint-Robert, P. *Le jeu de la France en Méditeranée* p. 95.
6. Sartre, J.P. *Les Temps Modernes,* no. 253 bis. 1967, p. 10.
7. Begin, M., *La Revolte d'Israel,* Plon, 1953, p. 160.

III

Dead ends? [1]

Introduction

It seems to me that here in the United States it has become almost tradition to start a talk with a joke. The only one I have to offer belongs to what is considered *de l'humour noir*, which unfortunately I think best reflects the mood of all those concerned with the much desirable yet constantly elusive peace in the Middle East

Just before the Geneva Summit, Reagan and Gorbachev went to see God and they both asked Him, 'Will there be real détente and mutual confidence between the superpowers?' God, it seems, answered back saying, 'Yes, of course, but not during your lifetimes.' That same evening, Yasser Arafat received urgent reports on the events of the day from the PLO offices in both Washington and Moscow. In his turn, he rushed to see God (who, by the way, does not feel burdened and handicapped by dear Henry's commitment to 242 preconditions for direct and official talks) and asked him, 'God Almighty, will there ever be peace in Palestine?' God, it seems, looked melancholically at Arafat and said, 'Yes, of course, but not during my lifetime.'

The tone of my talk might be perceived as depressing. In preparing this paper, I very much hesitated between Gramsci and

1. A lecture first delivered at the Massachusetts Institute of Technology (MIT) in January 1986 and later presented during a symposium organised in the Netherlands by Pax Christi in February 1986. I was then Visiting Scholar at the Center for International Affairs, Harvard University.

Edward Said as sources of inspiration. Gramsci, from his prison cell during the gloomy period of the rise of fascism in Italy and Europe, wrote about the 'pessimism of the intelligence', which could be compensated for by the 'optimism of the will', that would be capable of changing the ethically and politically intolerable and inadmissible. Edward Said, on the other hand, writing in the end of 1983, rephrased Gramsci by alluding to the fact that we might, in the Middle East, have entered an era in which the 'pessimism of the will' also prevails. A friend told me that the question mark after the title was my only concession to optimism.

I will ask for your indulgence. Depressing I do not intend to be. Only lucid, I hope, in order to explore what can be, in the future, the adequate responses to the old and new challenges with which we have to cope.

1. Acceptable peace

In contemporary Palestinian history, conceptual aggressions often preceded demographic, military or diplomatic aggressions. In 1917, Balfour's reference to the Muslim and Christian overwhelming majority in Palestine as the 'non-Jewish communities' announced the demographic upheaval that was to occur during the following decades. After 1967 and 1973, new conceptual aggressions took birth and were propagated by the international media with little Arab or Palestinian reaction to unveil the far from innocent intentions lying behind them. 'Legitimate rights' of the Palestinian people meant that the Palestinians had some justified claims which could be satisfied one day, and excessive demands that they had to abandon. The term 'legitimate' was intended to weaken the concept of 'rights;' to shrink its extent and applicability. In the same way, the term 'just and lasting peace' invaded the vocabulary of those dealing with Middle Eastern affairs, and nobody seriously challenged the validity of the concepts.

Even official Arab and Palestinian circles have become contaminated. A 'just peace' is simply not on the agenda. The two-state solution, considered as the most realistic and least unjust of the possible solutions proposed, is and should have been qualified as 'acceptable peace'. All others being beneath the level of Palestinian acceptability, their 'lasting and permanent' character would be more than problematic. It would be improbable.

It is true that the two-state solution was not always the PLO programme for an acceptable peace. Up to 1974, a democratic state, bi-cultural, multi-confessional and multi-ethnic, was the official policy.

Unfortunately, this project was rejected and misunderstood. The enormous concession it implied, namely, the Palestinians' acceptance of the demographic accomplished fact, was belittled or ridiculed. The humanist inspiration and the ethical dimension of the equal rights and equal obligations formula in a unitary Palestine were never recognised. Seeking no historical revenge, the Palestinian intention of breaking the dialectics of oppression when the unfavourable balance of power was altered (and at the time, the Palestinians believed that the prevailing imbalance of forces was not eternally to remain to their disadvantage) and their proclaimed desire not to transform the Israeli Jews into the Palestinians of the Palestinians was totally ignored and discarded. That programme failed to materialise in the realm of the possible, but it was undeniably not incorrect on the level of principles. Even if the Palestinian national movement had to redefine the ends in 1973-4 after a better assessment of the means available in the framework of the regional and international environment, the previous finality of the Palestinian struggle was legitimate. There is no need today to rewrite history.

Is the PLO a major obstacle to peace in the Middle East as it is often portrayed? Is it rejectionist, or is it the rejected party?

One has to read Kissinger's memoirs to learn that the PLO, since November 1973, was desirous of joining the peace process and the Geneva Conference. Kissinger says that he authorised a high-level meeting in Morocco in December 1973 between General Vernon Walters – now the American representative in the United Nations, then a roving ambassador for delicate missions – and a Palestinian delegation. His Palestinian interlocutors were Khaled al-Hassan and the late Majed Abu Sharara. Kissinger, in his inimitable unscrupulous manner, recalls that he let the discussions drag on until the Geneva Conference was over, thus neutralising the mainstream PLO from actively opposing his 'peace process'. Once that objective was obtained, Kissinger boasts of having ordered the cessation of the dialogue. For a more accurate version of the substance of those talks, one has to read Alan Hart's biography *Arafat: Terrorist or Peacemaker?*, because as in many other cases, Kissinger lies shamelessly. As one can see, Kissinger who was later to prohibit any contacts with the PLO in order to eliminate it from the Middle East equation machiavellically sought the same objective when he happened to authorise direct dialogue.

Was that the only attempt made by the PLO to join the 'process', trying thus to transform it into a genuine search of peace with a 'minimum of injustice?' In the 1974 session of the Palestinian National Council, a ten-point programme calling for a Palestinian State on parts of Palestine was adopted. That was another political sign concerning the PLO's readiness for accommodation and flexibility, another message to the international community that the PLO hoped to abandon the dialogue by arms and resort to the arms of dialogue. To those hostile or sceptical, who said that a mini-Palestinian state would only be a first step in a two-phased strategy whose ultimate goal remains total liberation, the PLO answered by saying that the future Palestinian state would be willing to accept all the measures of security guarantees that the UN would ask for, rendering such an eventuality impossible, as long as these security measures did not entail territorial acquisition for Israel. But that was not all. The whole last decade has been one of unreciprocated signals. Just some examples:

1. The PLO's favourable response to the joint American-Soviet Communiqué in 1977 and in 1981 to the Brezhnez plan;

2. The PLO's meticulous respect of its commitment to a ceasefire in 1981 on the Lebanese-Israeli border;

3. The PLO's acceptance of the French-Egyptian 1982 draft resolution on mutual and simultaneous recognition;

4. Its active role in the elaboration of the Arab peace plan of Fez 1982;

5. The Jordanian-Palestinian agreement of February 1985 for joint diplomatic action. Based on the PLO's acceptance 'of all United Nations resolutions, including Security Council ones, relevant to the Palestinian question' (see Yasser Arafat's interview in *The Washington Post*, 5 January 1986);

6. The PLO's regular call, since 1974, for a 'comprehensive settlement' which would include 'all the parties concerned' on the basis of 'international legality'.

If the Palestinian polity is today fractured and the Palestinian people in disarray, it is because the realistic and moderate policies pursued by the PLO have achieved nothing. In spite of its willingness to join the 'process', it remained the rejected party. Many Palestinians now tend to look at every new policy with suspicion and distrust as if one already knows for sure that the Palestinians will be reaping the inevitable negative repercussions and that the expected positive outcome will never show up. This is why many understood the Hussein-Arafat agreement as if the PLO had, out of resignation, rallied around the previously unaccepted 'Jordanian Option'.

Palestinians wonder whether they are always doomed to accept what they have previously refused just to find that it is no more an offer – if it ever was an offer – again to be faced with new attempts to extort new concessions from them for an undefined future.

2. Jordanian options

The 'Jordanian Option' has always been a divisive and controversial issue in the Arab World. To contribute in a quiet and mature manner to the political debate on options and alternatives available, one has to bear in mind that there is not one but six different, incompatible and competing 'Jordanian options'. Each is a challenge in its own, and if only one of them is desirable, all six are plausible possibilities for the future.

There are three different Israeli 'Jordanian options':

1. Within wide circles of the Israeli right, many still believe that the Jordan River is not the ultimate frontier of *Eretz Israel*. They consider Transjordan to be an integral part of the Promised Land abusively partitioned in the early twenties by Great Britain to give Prince Abdullah a throne. An expansion in that direction is considered legitimate. Only favourable circumstances in the future are needed to render such a desirable goal possible or feasible.

2. In the same sector of the Israeli political spectrum, General Sharon (who in spite of, or because of, all the irrefutable accusations for launching an unnecessary war in 1982 and all the atrocities perpetrated during this expedition, has lost none of his tentacular influence) has often openly stated that the solution of the Palestinian problem lies beyond the Jordan River. For him, 'only the Hashemite family are foreigners in Jordan.' Jordan is Palestine. Jordan should be 'given' to the Palestinians. And those still in areas under Israeli control will have a state of 'their' own and will be 'encouraged' to settle ... there. This solution of the Palestinian problem in Sharon's vision necessitates the East Bank of Jordan and excludes the Hashemite Dynasty. (See Mohammed Hallaj

and Sheila Ryan's book *Palestine Is, But Not in Jordan*, AAUG Publications.)

3. A third Israeli scenario, abundantly studied within the Labour Party, is the 'territorial compromise' with the Jordanian monarchy. A wide variety of formulae exists for the return of densely populated areas of the West Bank to Jordan so as to avoid the 'demographic threat' to the ethnic purity of the Jewish state. The retention of more than fifty percent of its lands is 'compensated for' by the 'donation' of parts of the Gaza Strip to Jordan.

Besides these three Israeli 'Jordanian options', there are two Jordanian 'Jordanian options':

4. In certain influential circles in Amman, some think that Jordan would be better off if it were discharged of its 'Palestinian burden'. Jordan in its reduced post-1967 limits has proven to be a viable economic entity. They propose the 'Jordanisation of Jordan' in all respects; the political sphere and all the others too. Citizens of Palestinian origin (more than 1.5 million) would be offered the alternative of allegiance either to the PLO or to the Jordanian government and each would have to bear the implications of his/her political choice.

5. Another political trend promotes the idea of a 'United Arab Kingdom' on both banks of the Jordan River, wherein a post-settlement posture of a 'Palestine entity' would enjoy a certain degree of administrative-political autonomy differentiating thus the still unknown future from a past still remembered.

A sixth 'Jordanian option' emanates from the PLO:

6. Initiated by Yasser Arafat at the end of 1982, it was endorsed by the Palestinian National Council in February 1983. This policy calls for a future confederation between Palestine and Jordan. An equal partnership between two sovereign entities, an emanation of their

'free and voluntary volition' as reflected by their respective political institutions. Such a formula is seen as mutually advantageous on all levels, and it will be so if the whole issue is handled correctly. That confederation can be a nucleus for future inter-Arab integration inaugurating a new era of government by consent instead of government by coercion.

3. Possible strategies

How can the desirable target of a Palestinian State be attained? Four strategies towards this end can be contemplated: a) a political strategy; b) a military strategy; c) a diplomatic strategy; d) a combination of all three.

1. Favouring a radical change from within the Israeli society; promoting the idea of a necessary 'Israeli awakening'. This would tend to encourage the peace forces in Israel by multiplying contacts and by engaging in dialogue, of course on the clear basis of the 'acceptable peace' previously defined so as to avoid the usual pitfalls of such a slippery exercise. (An interesting article on that subject 'The pitfalls of dialogue' was written by Jonathan Kuttab in *al-Fajr*, 29 November 1985.) The peace forces in Israel might be numerically insignificant but they are symbolically important for a future of 'unavoidable co-existence'. They help the Palestinians avoid the temptations of 'collective Jewish guilt' explanations thus allowing for optimistic expectations that the future Palestine State will be rendered possible through a convergence of struggles: on the other hand the struggle undertaken by those who want 'to liberate the territories occupied by Israel in 1967' and on the other, the struggle undertaken by those who want 'to liberate Israel from its occupied territories'. This approach is intended to give more political credibility, and more numerical-electoral weight to those in Israel who know that there is a choice to be made and that 'Israel can either be in the West Bank or in the Middle East.'

Besides the necessary total mobilisation of the Palestinians in Israel around *Rakah*, of course, and now around the Progressive

List too (these two forces view each other for the moment as competitors, while in fact they are complementary), the success of this strategy depends on the receptivity of the Jewish majority component in Israel and the political courage of the 'dovish' wing of its political class.

However, the results of the last Knesset elections in 1984 tend to demoralise those who believed in such a course of action. Those elections were a historical opportunity for Israel, which has accustomed the Arabs and the world to its massive and disproportionate military retaliations, to 'retaliate peacefully' for once. Yet the Israeli voter democratically decided not to. Many a 'dove' preferred not to defy the dominant popular mood in favour of the perpetuation of the prevailing explosive *status quo* and kept silent or remained too discreet during the whole campaign so as not to endanger the chances of re-election. That was, so it seems, the price they consented to pay to democracy. The only three Jewish Knesset members who unequivocally expressed themselves in favour of total withdrawal and Palestinian self-determination – Meir Vilner, Charley Bitton and Matti Peled – were elected with Arab votes. On the other hand, the stability of *Rakah*'s representation, the emergence of the Miary-Peled list, the decision of Mapam not to join the ruling 'national unity' coalition, Yossi Sarid's 'defection' to Aloni's civil rights movement in a possible political shift inspired by Jewish ethics against actual Israeli policies. A consolation. A meagre one.

I have been using the concept of Israeli democracy deliberately. On that particular subject two schools of thought exist in the Arab world. Basing itself on the fact that Israel is the product of a colonial, theocratic and exclusivist ideology, the practices of which have resulted in the denial and the expulsion of the undesirable indigenous population and/or their subordination through second-class citizenship, the first school objects to the usage of the qualification of democracy when referring to the Israeli political system. The second school of thought, while agreeing with the above mentioned arguments, considers Israel to be an authentic and genuine Western-style democracy with a recently imported majority where pluralism and freedom are constitutionally guaranteed for its Jewish citizens. Just as South African Apartheid is undeniably a 'democracy' for its 'non-coloured' inhabitants.

That school argues that Israel, because of its 'democratic political system,' has acquired undeserved sympathies and support from Western public opinion. For that second school, this 'democracy' reveals, if anything, the massive popular support enjoyed by oppressive and expansionist policies adopted since 1947-8. The very fact 'free' elections are regularly held every four years after an unhampered political campaign where alternative political personalities and alternative political programmes are proposed to the voters, means that the Israeli 'democracy' is the reflection of the Israeli public opinion, implementing policies for which the voters have expressed a preference. Here a Rousseau-like interrogation is relevant: are the Israeli decision-makers well-intentioned innocent citizens corrupted by the exercise of power or is the Israeli citizen himself already an egoistic actor seeking to optimise territorial advantages as long as this comes at an affordable price?

Democracy means responsibility of the citizens who choose a party, a politician and a policy; the responsibility of the State, that 'neutral arbiter' which regularly has to organise elections in order to consult the people through universal suffrage; the responsibility of the political class which is accountable for its actions and has, at regular intervals, to present its balance sheet for approval or rejection.

Rabbi Abraham Heschel, during the American involvement in Vietnam, declared 'in a free society, if some are guilty, all are responsible.' I think he would agree today that the same applies to Israel and the Israelis. With Israel over Palestine and the Israelis and Palestine societies literally overlapping, telling us one day in a distant future 'we did not know' will be even harder to believe than it was forty years ago. The fact that the Israelis have demonstrated so little concern for the ordeals of their victims intrigues many an observer. Isaac Deutscher resorted to a parable of his own to summarise the Israeli-Palestinian conflict. He said it resembled the dispute between a person who jumped from the 20th floor of a building on fire in which he had lost all the members of his family and had landed safely on another person whose back he broke. Each time the latter moaned out of pain or tried to stand up again, he received a beating. How come a people so maltreated by history are now maltreating another with so much insensitivity? Should the level of tolerance for human suffering be established at six million victims? Then the Palestinians, with only five million potential victims to offer, have a hopeless case.

Today we are witnessing a huge debate on the future of the Israeli democracy threatened by the emergence and the rise of Kahanism. How do the Palestinians perceive this 'new' phenomenon? At the risk of shocking some of you, I believe that Kahanism is but the logical conclusion of the Zionist ideology. If it is only 'the tip of an iceberg', and that iceberg is not the Israeli right, but it is mainstream Zionism. The notion of Palestine being 'a country without a people' to be transformed into one 'as Jewish as England is English' pre-dates not only the birth of Kahanism as a political movement but pre-dates even the physical birth of Kahane himself, and he is not young. The scheme of absorbing the 'geography without the demography' was, for sure, not an imaginative innovation introduced by Kahane in the 1970s.

Should one also forget that as early as the 1930s a fascist trend existed as a dynamic component of the Zionist movement? The followers of Jabotinski, the *maître à penser* of Menachem Begin, used to demonstrate in the Warsaw streets with slogans such as: 'Germany to Hitler, Italy to Mussolini and Palestine to us Zionists' (see Maxime Rodinson, *Israel, un état colonial?*).

Some might wish to remind us that until 1977, the left was in control of the Jewish Agency, of the State of Israel, and that is true. But how 'left' was that left? Was it more humane in its dealings with the Palestinians? Histadrout's demand that for 'Jewish capital' there should only be 'Jewish labour' ejected the Palestinian workers from large sectors of the economic circuit. The 'idealistic' desire not to exploit Arab peasants drove thousands of peasants to unemployment in the outskirts of urban areas. The Dalet Plan of terror campaigns in 1947-8 with the objective of encouraging the Palestinians to leave (some dare still say willingly) was a Haganah plan. In the wars of 1948, 1956, 1967, mass punishment, mass expropriations, arbitrary detentions, torture, the 'creeping annexation' ... were all policies inaugurated by the Israeli left only to be pursued by their successors. The Zionist left had made Palestine unliveable for most of the Palestinians. Kahanism today might also make Israel unliveable for many Israelis.

Others might wish to remind us of those individuals or groups who, throughout the whole history of Zionist penetration, have endeavoured hard so that 'a minimum of injustice' would befall the Palestinians. That is certainly also true, but here another interrogation is relevant. Haven't those dissident voices (and many of them are becoming aware of that) unwillingly served more the Israeli establishment than its victims? With no impact at all on the unhappy fate of the Palestinians, haven't they unwillingly helped project an image of a non-monolithic Zionist movement, of a pluralistic Israel that tolerated protest and dissent, a positive image that the establishment recuperates, or rather confiscates, to harness the much needed external sympathy and support? Yet, and it must be said, those dissident voices, from Yehuda Magnes, Martin Buber and Noam Chomsky to Israel Shahak, are real strategic assets for a future of genuine reconciliation and co-existence. They know that the peace camp is in power within the PLO and that, unfortunately, the peace camp is only a minority tendency in Israel.

Today Israel has a very comfortable strategic posture. If the Israelis decide, in the absence of any serious military or diplomatic pressure, as is now the case, to withdraw and allow Palestinian self-determination in the framework of a package deal and a comprehensive settlement, they will create a psychological shock which will shatter the psychological barriers we all know exist. It will, therefore, inaugurate a new era of harmonious interstate and inter-community relations. Today, a Sadat-like initiative should and can only come from Israel. Only a Sadat-like Israeli initiative can usher a new period of (unilateral) forgiveness and (bilateral) reconciliation. Such an 'Israeli awakening', however desirable it might be, seems highly improbable and farfetched. If Peres and Shamir continue to deliberately maintain Israel's peace conditions and proposals beneath the level of Palestinian and Arab acceptability and thus perpetuate the intolerable status quo, they will be Kahanes with more historical patience and more discursive sophistication.

2. A second strategy would be one of military pressure, as in October 1973, to seriously reactivate the diplomatic front. Today one has to admit that the Arab world has lost the positive accomplishments of the 1973 initiative. Kissinger and his successors succeeded in de-linking the three major military partners (Egypt, Syria and the PLO) and in de-linking the two components of the Arab world's strategy – combining military pressure with the oil-weapon.

By itself, there is no serious Palestinian military option without a credible Arab military option. Armed struggle in the late sixties and early seventies has achieved the capital objective of salvaging the Palestinian people from political oblivion and allowing for their national resurrection, replacing the question of Palestine as a high priority on the international agenda. This is its historic accomplishment and ... limitation. In the absence of a global Arab strategy, it is suicidal. Yasser Arafat has often, and very correctly, compared Palestinian fighters to those of Sparta in Ancient Greece during the battle of Thermopylae. Their objective was to delay the advance of the Persian invading forces until the moment the Greek cities could coalesce, mobilise and advance. The Palestinian Spartans fought, and fought bravely, but the Arab states, even those with whom we were committed by 'a strategic alliance', never came to the rescue.

Such a strategy necessitates the reintegration of Egypt in the Arab League, it necessitates the mending of relations between the PLO and Hafez al-Assad or Syria, and the cessation of the Iraq-Iran war. For the Arab world, reconciled around the Fez resolutions, the ability to resort to the 'dialogue of arms', in case of continued Israeli inflexibility, should become a credible possibility and should be perceived as such, and not only as a rhetorical subterfuge to conceal political and military impotence.

3. A third strategy would be to work towards a solution which should be actively stimulated, so as not to say imposed, by the international community which has already adopted a whole

battery of resolutions dealing with all the aspects of the conflict, ignoring neither the 'facts' imposed by some, nor the trespassed 'rights' of the others. Resolutions stipulating that all the states in the area have to be recognised and have to enjoy secure borders; resolutions reminding all concerned of the inadmissibility of territorial acquisition by force; resolutions calling for the Palestinian refugees to be able to exercise their right to return to their homes and homeland and for their right to compensation; resolutions recognising the inalienable right of the Palestinian people to self-determination and sovereign statehood; resolutions considering the settlements irrevocably illegal and not at all irreversible as some wish them to be.

This strategy of revitalising the role of the United Nations will help surmount the obstacles of Israeli intransigence on the one hand and Arab impotence on the other. This approach can spare the region and the populations that inhabit it from future wars and devastations. This international legality is the only basis on which a viable and acceptable peace can be achieved. The UN remains the only forum where politics can be reconciled with ethics.

Many in the Arab world thought that Arab persuasion deployed on the American administration during a president's second mandate, a return to détente politics between the superpowers and an American-Palestinian official and direct dialogue, could give birth to a new American policy at last reconciling power and principles. Coupled with a unified Arab stand, other elements – unfaltered support from socialist countries, a non-aligned movement and a European community dynamically desirous to contribute to the settlement of a conflict in an area where all admit to have 'vital interests' – are thought to inevitably produce the desirable outcome: a Palestinian state.

The international accommodationist consensus, however, has been rendered inoperative by two notorious dissident and obstructionist actors: the United States of America and Israel. The American administration has so far refrained from exerting its 'friendly persuasion' on Israel as many have legitimately and naively expected. On the contrary, it has encouraged its territorial appetite by regularly injecting the Israeli economy with money and repeatedly flooding its army with the most sophisticated weaponry. This abundant support is given to Israel in total knowledge that its security is not threatened, if it really ever were, and that it is exploited in a strategy not of deterrence but a strategy of compellence *vis-à-vis* Israel's environment. Compellence, unlike deterrence which tends to dissuade the neighbour or adversary from undertaking any hostile action, is Thomas Schelling's under-exploited concept which refers to a strategy that tends to coerce and compel the neighbour or adversary into undertaking a course of action which is supposed to best suit one's own interest.

American policy in the Middle East, if there is one, deserves more than the limitations set for this talk. I will limit myself to some questions which are in fact answers in disguise. Does the United States of America have an interest in antagonising the entire Arab world? If so far, because of a double crisis of regimes and of oppositional movements, the Arab world was incapable of demonstrating its discontent in a convincing manner, does that mean that this policy can be a durable one? In case of serious Arab responses to the American challenge, won't Israel become a strategic burden instead of a strategic asset? Should we all wait, or prepare for that confrontation to take place or is it not better to proceed with preventive diplomacy? Why is Palestinian self-determination, a major component of any such preventive diplomacy, still a taboo? Isn't self-determination a *piece maitresse* of American political philosophy? In American-Israeli relations, who wags whom? Is it the pro-Israeli lobby that determines American policies in the Middle East or would those policies have been the same even in the absence of such a lobby? Do interests always converge or do they happen to bifurcate? Isn't the American Jewish community and its influential lobby in Washington doing a disservice to Israel's Jews by unconditionally supporting their regional ambitions? If Israel's territorial appetite in the West Bank is not surprising, what can be said of America's backing of such an expansionist policy that deals with only a few thousand square miles but can have foreseeable damaging effects on what attempts to be a global strategy? For those in favour of that third approach, the recent Geneva Summit was a monumental disappointment. The Middle

East's share in the discussion was, according to reliable sources, just a few minutes, including interpretation. Will the Foreign Minister's follow-up meetings put the superpowers' dialogue on the right track? The least that can be said is that all indications tend to prove the contrary.

4. A fourth strategy is the combination of the three preceding approached; one that would invest Palestinian potentialities in the three paths at the same time – all seen as complementary means and not as incompatible alternatives.

However, all three have produced deadlocks. All three 'paths' proved, in reality, to be dead ends, not because of Palestinian errors, shortcomings, failures or mismanagement – and there was plenty of all that. It is simply because the opponent or opponents, at any given time, could mobilise disproportionately superior forces whatever the nature of the chosen strategy: political, military or diplomatic.

The achievements of any political movement should be judged as a function of the capacities at the disposal of its adversaries. Those who, in this current mood and wave of sado-masochism, unjustifiably and harmfully criticise the Palestinian national movement for the absence of any tangible results, should bear in mind that the PLO did not have the luxury of confronting a Batista or a Samoza or even an Ian Smith. Let us compare only the comparable. I am sure that the Palestinian leadership would willingly accept an 'exchange of enemies' with any lesson-giver who thinks to be better equipped, intellectually or militarily, to cope with the Zionist challenge.

If the prevailing deadlock is perpetuated and the Palestinians left in their intolerable living conditions, with the only alternatives being politicide, genocide, Native Americanisation, Armenianisation or Bantoustanisation (as demonstrated by Ibrahim Abu Lughod's article in the *Arab Studies Quarterly* of Summer 1985), predicting that we will witness an increase of operations such as in Vienna and Rome airports is no prophecy. For the moment, such operations are being undertaken by those who intend to sabotage a peace process they suspect, mistakenly, to exist. In case of a continued stalemate many more individuals or groups, after twelve years of what has turned out to be sterile realism and moderation, will be tempted to break the rules of a game which they endlessly asked to join or even to change the nature of the whole game to which they never received admittance.

It is my intimate conviction that only those who were sympathetic and supportive of Palestinian aspirations can allow themselves today to blame and condemn such actions. All the others are not ethically qualified to issue any moral judgement.

4. The ideal coalition

Confronted with a zero-option situation, in which the management of collective survival should be on top of the agenda, one can only wish that fratricide is not added to the long list of threats to which the Palestinians are exposed. One can only wish that the political fractions will give primacy to the national interest rather than to organisational selfishness; that exasperating verbosity and ideological phraseology would finally give way to strategic thinking; that serious consideration would be given to the non-violent means of struggle; that an internal managerial revolution would be undertaken.

The problem of national unity must quickly find a satisfactory and national response. A return to façade unanimity and its paralytic consensus, the previous balance of indecision, are not adequate answers to this acute problem. It has often been said that 'all Arabs have agreed to disagree.' I think the real problem resides in the fact that we have not yet learned how to disagree. In the Arab world, there are no accepted rules to the 'political game', yet the PLO offers institutional and constitutional channels for debate, dissent and decision-making. Palestinian public opinion should rigorously demand that all factions behave respectfully of those rules and regulations. A hundred flowers can and should bloom, but in the Palestinian garden, not in somebody else's backyard. Like all other societies, the Palestinians enjoy no unanimity. They are condemned to have either unanimity but no strategy, or a strategy but no unanimity.

The ideal scenario for the coming Executive Committee would be a coalition between Fateh, the Communist Party, the Democratic Front and the independents. Occasional demagogy and systematic external interferences put aside, these tendencies, either for pragmatic reasons or for ideological considerations, share a similar point of view on problems referring to 'war, peace and negotiations'. The Popular Front, for very respectable patriotic reasons, disagrees with them. This disagreement reflects the fact that the Palestinians are not unanimous concerning the sacrifices and the concessions needed for the 'acceptable peace' and the Popular Front incarnates this legitimate, normal and authentic feeling among many. We need to rehabilitate the noble functions of a respectable opposition. Such an opposition should not be denigrated. Its existence is a necessity and the Popular Front with its historical prestige is the adequate channel for the indispensable control, criticism and counter-positions in a democracy. With such a scenario, Yasser Arafat will have the loyalists he deserves, and with such a scenario, the PLO will have the opposition it needs.

Having said all this, the region's and the world's dilemma remains the same. In the Middle East we either have one people too many, or we are short of a state which needs to be created. Today, 15 January 1986, one has to admit that history's verdict is still unclear. I am sure that Hegel hoped to be contradicted when he wrote 'from history we learn that we have not learned from history.'

IV

Palestinian peace diplomacy[1]

Chaim, I would like to welcome you here in the Centre. It was very refreshing to hear you say in your preliminary remarks that you were unequivocally in favour of Israeli withdrawal from all the territories occupied in 1967, in favour of Palestinian self-determination and in favour of each side deciding who its negotiators ought to be.

Let me first dissipate possible misunderstanding from the very beginning. This discussion is an intellectual exercise in which we will exchange our subjective perceptions of objective realities. Our distinguished audience should not perceive it as a pre-negotiation or as having any political-diplomatic implication. I hope that nobody will come out of this session with excessive and unreasonable hope that the prevailing situation does not justify at all. This is neither a morale-boosting session, nor – at least I hope not – a nerve-shattering one.

My talk will focus on one major point. In Palestine/Israel where there is, beyond a shadow of a doubt, an oppressed community that has moved, mainly since 1973, beyond double negation, toward mutual recognition; and it is the oppressive community that is still undecided. Or, to be more accurate, it has, with an overwhelming majority, decided not to move toward this desirable outcome.

---

1.   This is an edited transcript of a talk given by Afif Safieh on 1 December 1986, during a debate organised by the Centre for Middle East Studies at Harvard on the theme 'An Israeli-Palestinian Dialogue: Towards Mutual Recognition?' The Israeli panelist was Mr Chaim Shur, Editor-in-Chief of the magazine *New Outlook*.

Just a word on the pre-1948 period. During that phase, in spite of the fact that the Palestinian people considered Jewish immigration into Palestine to be against their will and their interests, the Palestinian National Movement always accepted the demographic accomplished fact. Their demand at the time was a governing council, in which also the newly arrived Jews would be represented through a process of proportionate representation. Unfortunately, this project was systematically defeated by British and Zionist insistence that the Jewish and British members of that body should always outnumber the Muslim and Christian representatives. I just mention this for the record.

In 1964 and 1965, the PLO and Fateh both emerged publicly. The National Charter adopted in 1964 has become controversial mainly for two articles it contains: 1) the aim of total liberation, and 2) that only the Jews present in Palestine before 1917 and their descendents would be allowed to remain in the future state.

Concerning the first point, you should not be surprised to learn that all Palestinians consider this target to be correct on the level of principle. Yet not so on the level of possible. However, I think that the second point was a historical mistake and a regression if compared to the previous position adopted by the Palestinian National Movement prior to 1948. But this issue became *dépassé* when, in 1968, the major component in the PLO, Fateh, adopted a programme for a democratic secular state in Palestine with equal status, rights and obligations to Muslims, Jews and Christians. It became a shared position within the Palestinian movement that beliefs and behaviours are not determined by dates of arrival or departure. The Democratic Front and the Popular Front were very close to that conception too. As for the Palestinian Communists, in that respect, they were more moderate, having accepted both, in 1947, the Partition Plan and in 1967, Resolution 242.

Anyway, the October War in 1973 was a turning point. Should

we call it Ramadan, Kippur or October War? Here in Harvard, a neutral arena, or supposed to remain so, let us call it the October War. It is from that war onwards that Palestinian peace diplomacy started manifesting itself with increasing clarity. The dates are important; 1973 was a moment of strength or perceived strength and Palestinian realism goes back to that particular moment in regional history and not to 1982 as some would like us to believe. Peace diplomacy was an emanation of the changing circumstances of 1973–4 when the Arab World had recaptured the historical initiative. There is a school of thought in Israel that explains Arab and Palestinian moderation as a result of Israeli blows. In that logic, with one more blow, maybe the Palestinian movement will accept a homeland in the other end of the Arabian Peninsula and with two such blows, it might just vanish into historical oblivion. Nothing can be more erroneous than this approach. Nothing can be more misleading than this interpretation.

Weeks after the end of the October War, Abu Iyyad-Salah Khalaf published an op-ed piece in *Le Monde* titled 'Revolution and Realism,' in which he speaks already of necessary negotiations and a two-state solution. Henry Kissinger, in the second volume of his memoirs *Years of Upheaval*, wrote that in November 1973 and in January 1974, two meetings took place in Morocco between General Vernon Walters and a top level PLO delegation composed of Khalid al-Hassan and Majed Abu Sharara, to discuss the possible participation of the PLO in the negotiating process. How an available PLO was machiavellically out-manoeuvred by Kissinger is a long story.

In the Palestinian National Council (PNC) session held in Cairo in 1974, a ten-point programme was adopted. By the way, I personally remained reluctant to accept this programme until 1977. The first article in the political platform states that the PLO rejects Resolution 242 because the Palestinian people are considered only as refugees. This formulation was adopted after lengthy debates. Only four PNC members voted against it. As one can see, another possible objection against 242 is absent from the wording. Nowhere is it said that 242 is rejected because it stipulates the recognition of Israel. As we all know, the absence of a sentence is sometimes as eloquent and significant as its presence.

In 1975–6, the Palestinian leadership authorised, even instructed, Said Hamami in London, then Issam Sartawi from Paris, to engage in dialogue with dovish personalities in the Israeli political spectrum. It was Rabin and surely not Arafat who torpedoed the potentialities of such a line of communication.

In 1977, the Palestinian polity during a PNC session again in Cairo adopted new resolutions where there was no mention of a 'two-phased strategy', in which the terms of 'National Authority' becomes 'an independent Palestinian State', and more important, in that document, and for the first time, the highest body of the PLO announced its acceptance of the implementation of international legality for the resolution of the Middle East conflict. International legality means United Nations resolutions. 242 is one of those. Fair enough. But so is 181 calling for two states in Palestine, so is 194 calling for the return of the Palestinian refugees, so is 3236 calling for Palestinian self-determination, independent sovereignty and statehood, etc.

On 1 October 1977, the PLO was the first among the parties concerned to welcome and approve the joint American-Soviet communiqué issued by Vance and Gromyko. Unfortunately, that document, which was intended to revitalise the peace process, lasted only a few days. Dayan rushed to the USA and launched what he called his Six Hours War, threatened Carter with 'domestic complications', and Carter retracted.

1977–9 were monopolised by the Sadat initiative and its aftermath. If one goes back to PLO statements during this period, one would notice that the criticism against Sadat was not for his search of peace, but against his approach to peace. His approach, bilateral and partial, was found objectionable and detrimental because it broke up Arab ranks and consensus, eroded the Arab bargaining position, etc. The PLO, Syria, Algeria and South Yemen continued to ask for a comprehensive, global and lasting peace. At the time, only Libya and Iraq had a more radical stand.

In 1980–1, the PLO constantly adopted positions encouraging the European Community finally to take a peace initiative of its own. And you very well know that the basis of such an initiative would have been self-determination to people and recognition and security to states. In April 1981, the PNC meeting held in Damascus welcomed and supported the Brezhnev Plan. Later in the year Arafat also approved, some even say inspired, the Fahd Plan which was left unadopted during the first Fez Summit not because of Syrian opposition but mainly because of Begin's immediate rejection and America's unencouraging attitude.

In 1981–2, the PLO, and by that I mean all its components, scrupulously respected the ceasefire agreement concluded after the mini Israeli-Palestinian war of July 1981. That ceasefire, sponsored by the UN, but in fact engineered by Philip Habib, was violated, as we all still remember, by Sharon's troops in June 1982.

During the summer of 1982, Yasser Arafat signed a statement to a visiting delegation of American congressmen which said 'we are in favour of the implementation of all UN resolutions relevant to the question of Palestine.' The fact that the PLO was under siege in the Lebanese capital has nothing to do with the content of that document, since as we have seen, it is simply consistent with previous PLO official positions. Arafat then welcomed the declaration made in Paris by Nahum Goldmann, Pierre Mendes-France and Phillip Klutznik calling for mutual recognition. Weeks later, the PLO supported the French-Egyptian draft resolution in the Security Council along the same lines. If that draft resolution was never adopted, it is surely not because of Palestinian but Israeli rejectionism and an American threat to veto it.

It is a secret to no one that Arafat was the major artisan of the Arab peace proposals of the second Fez Summit meeting in September 1982. I had the personal privilege of being asked to accompany Chairman Arafat to Rome on 15th September where he met his Holiness the Pope and President Pertini. I still remember his speech to the World Inter-Parliamentary Union that was holding its convention in Rome in which Arafat said, 'I come to you as a messenger of peace carrying the Arab peace proposals to which all Arab heads of state are committed.' Unfortunately, that speech coincided with the assassination of Bashir Gemayel followed by the horrible massacre of Sabra and Shatilla. This statement, which everybody expected to receive enormous press coverage, was drowned in blood, sweat and tears.

In April 1984, three months before the Israeli Knesset elections, Arafat in an interview to the *Nouvel Observateur* declared that the PLO was in favour of 'mutual recognition between Israel and the State of Palestine'. I suppose that the choice of this magazine was deliberate. It is mainly a French-Jewish-Leftist weekly. It was expected that this statement would not go unnoticed in Israel and that it would become part of the political debate. Israel, which has accustomed the Arabs to its disproportionate military retaliations, was offered thus an opportunity for a 'peaceful retaliation'. And yet dovish politicians must have considered that it would be electorally unrewarding to respond favourably to such an overture. I would have hoped that Abba Eban would reserve his beautifully worded sentence, 'they never miss a chance to lose an opportunity', to his political friends and not the Palestinian leadership.

1984 and 1985 were spent in bilateral negotiations with Jordan on ways and means of reactivating the peace process. To the distress of many Palestinians, but with the approval of the PNC, an agreement was reached calling for a future Palestinian-Jordanian confederation. Joint action was pursued up to February 1986. On 31 March 1986, the PLO published an advertisement on a full page of the *New York Times,* containing the three Palestinian proposals submitted in Amman and indirectly to the American administration. In all three proposals, the PLO states its readiness to accept Resolution 242 if ever the American administration were to commit itself to the principle of the necessity of Palestinian self-determination.

To describe Jordanian policies since February 1986, one can invoke Talleyrand who said on one occasion, 'it is worse than a crime, it is an error.' The PLO had offered King Hussein co-partnership after Israeli withdrawal. The Jordanian government seems to prefer a condominium with Israel and within a framework of a perpetual occupation. When this line of action reaches its predictable failure, maybe the Poindexters and Oliver Norths in Amman would be sacrificed for 'ill-inspired and unwise advice' and that might open possibilities for reconciliation. In any case, a Palestinian-Jordanian confederation should never be the result of a precondition, but the emanation of a volition.

I am sure, in my recapulation of events, to have forgotten many other initiatives taken since 1973. If all these steps, overtures, resolutions and policies about which I spoke are not messages sent to friends and foes alike, one wonders what are signals in foreign relations and international communications. This realism, that moderation were never reciprocated. The PLO seems to have been unreasonably reasonable, unrealistically realistic. I might be asked who in the Palestinian leadership supports the two-state solution? In 1973–5, Fateh, the Democratic Front, and – some of you will be surprised – Saika were the major forces advocating this idea. The Palestinian Communists were very supportive of that evolution since they considered that the National Movement was at last rallying what they have always called for. The Popular Front, which led a rejection front from 1974 up to 1978, made an internal self-criticism in 1978 and voted for new resolutions compatible with mainstream thinking. During the Algiers PNC session in 1983, Khaled Fahoum, then the speaker of the parliament and now the leader of the Salvation Front based in Damascus, declared that a just and lasting peace means an independent Palestinian State on the West Bank and Gaza. Mr Fahoum is even more moderate than I. I usually describe the two-state solution as just 'acceptable and lasting' but never as 'just.'

Who are the Palestinian leaders in favour of the two-state solution? To my taste, there are too many of them. I still recall a workshop organised last year by Professor Kelman. During the discussion period, a student asked me, 'If you had the ear of Arafat and Habash, what would you tell them?' I answered that I would deal with only half of the question, 'What will I tell Habash if ever I have his ear, which I don't.' I said I would ask him to remain as radical as he used to be before 1978. I could see the student's eyes popping out in surprise, so I added, let me try to explain why. If you read Nahum Goldmann's books, you will learn that he is extremely proud of the results of his negotiations with the Federal Republic of Germany concerning compensations and reparations because he knew how much this money was needed for the Israeli economy and army. He writes in his various books that an important portion of Israeli society was against his negotiations. Huge demonstrations were taking place in Tel Aviv and Jerusalem, led by Menachem Begin, against Ben Gurion and Goldmann. With his usual elegant prose, Goldmann writes that, if the Jewish people had unanimously accepted the principle of those negotiations, he would have been ashamed of himself. Yet as a politician, he knew that Ben Gurion and himself could not allow this opposition to paralyse their decisions and their negotiations with the Germans.

Each situation has its specificity and uniqueness. Yet between those two cases, the similarities are obvious. Since 1973, the overwhelming majority of the Palestinian people is in favour of a historic compromise. We need not be unanimous and I am sure Nahum Goldmann would have understood why not.

With the 1981 ceasefire agreement, the PLO has proved its credibility and capacity to abide to its commitments. If the revived peace process is undertaken under the adequate auspices of the UN and includes Syria, there will be hardly any regional forces working to disrupt it, except for Israel. National aspirations satisfied through independent statehood, the Palestinians will then become a *status quo* actor in the area.

Palestinians are often told that their positions are still ambiguous. There is always room for further clarity but that is only an easy pretext. It is my conviction that, compared with its Israeli counterparts, the PLO is an amateur in ambiguity.

Let us leave aside Kahane, Eitan, Sharon, Shamir and Begin. They are really unambiguous in the most negative sense of the word. But is Labour any better for an Israeli-Palestinian peace? I happen to think that their positive image in the Western media and Western public opinion is totally undeserved. We are often told how nostalgic we ought to be for the period when Labour or Peres were in power but nobody bothers to explain why. His Ifrane visit to King Hassan was more exercise in acrobacy than in diplomacy. Let me just remind you of a revealing incident which took place in 1974. Kissinger came to Israel and proposed to the Israeli government, composed at that time of Golda Meir, Igal Allon, Dayan, Peres, Rabin, etc to make a disengagement agreement with Jordan concerning Jericho. He told them, 'You must one day deal with Hussein, and if not, with Arafat.' Their answer was, 'We cannot withdraw from Jericho, that is contrary to our Allon Plan.' So he answered, 'Please give me a disengagement proposal compatible with your Allon Plan.' 'But our government is a coalition that includes the religious party and that party hasn't adopted this plan.' And since then, 'dynamic immobilism' continues to prevail.

The moral of this story is not that it was Israeli obstinacy that propelled the PLO to become recognised as the sole legitimate representative of the Palestinian people. The moral of the story is that the Israeli Labour Party wants to give nothing to neither. Neither to Arafat, nor to Hussein.

But, Chaim, speaking of ambiguity, I still have problems with the Israeli peace camp. If we go beyond the three to five percent of public opinion represented by Felicia Langer, Shahak, Avnery, Peled and yourself, and consider the peace camp in its broad definition and all shades of opinion it includes, what is the message we Palestinians get? That message can be summarised 1) yes, we want to withdraw, but not totally, 2) yes, we want to negotiate, but not with anybody, 3) yes, the Palestinians are a people, but we won't allow them to get the rights that are usually considered normal, natural, undeniable and inalienable to all peoples. It is a sort of Orwellian version: we are all equal but some peoples are more equal than others.

But, Chaim, for the Jews and the Israelis, we are not any people. We are not the people of Timor, of Papua New Guinea, or the Bretons of France. For you, Chaim, we happen to be that particular people that had inevitably to be dispossessed if ever the Zionist idea was to succeed. The Israelis should never forget, should never have forgotten, what price Israel was for us Palestinians. Instead of the 'sorry, please, thank you' one would have expected, not a single medium was left unused to deny our existence, suffering and rights. To mention only one example, with Joan Peters' book *From Time Immemorial,* millions of readers were told that the Palestinians were disparate Arabs who were fraudulently smuggled into Palestine in the twentieth century, attracted by the economic prosperity introduced by Zionist settlements. This nauseating hoax, Edward Said wrote, was welcomed by 'a conspiracy of praise'. Critics competed to say that the findings and revelations of that book proved that the Palestinians had neither case nor cause.

Today the Palestinian people are the Jews of the Israelis. We have become a stateless people in search of a haven and a state. Chaim, I intend soon to start exploring the possibilities of my return of Jerusalem, my home, my hometown, my homeland. My last words will sound familiar to your ears. Next year in Jerusalem, Chaim, I promise you that when we meet over there, I won't raise the embarrassing issue of who is the guest and who is the host.

V

Resurrecting the European working paper[1]

The 1975 Brookings Report was a major collective study that inspired the Carter administration during its first year's efforts toward a comprehensive settlement in the Middle East. With the American presidential elections drawing to a close, and with the likelihood of seeing a Democrat in the White House enhanced by recent events, the Brookings Institution, a Washington think tank in the orbit of the Democratic Party, is contemplating updating its analysis and recommendations. Meanwhile, across the Atlantic, the European Community, after years of relative eclipse, has lately shown renewed concern for Middle Eastern affairs.

The geopolitical situation has been profoundly modified since 1975. Nevertheless, observers agree that a solution to the apparently intractable Arab-Israeli conflict should not reflect the prevailing balance/imbalance of forces, but should seek (especially if durability is its target) to remedy, at least partially, the injustice at the root of antagonisms. For that reason, it seems relevant to remove the dust accumulated on a document which gave birth, years ago, to great expectations.

In 1980, months after the adoption of the Venice Declaration and just after the Luxemburg Foreign Minister Gaston Thorn concluded his fact-finding mission, the European Community came out with an internal working paper. This is still considered

---

1. This article was jointly written with my wife Christ'l Leclercq-Safieh and published by *al-Fajr*, a Palestinian English weekly, on 19 April 1987.

the most sophisticated document available to eventually serve as a basis for conflict resolution in the Middle East.

Through the European Political Cooperation, the four major countries of the Community – the United Kingdom, France, Germany and Italy – were each asked to prepare a study on the four most delicate problems regarding peace in the Middle East. They were Israeli withdrawal, Palestinian self-determination, the status of Jerusalem, and security guarantees. The separate inputs were then meshed together and reworded in the form of a detailed questionnaire. This was in turn submitted on behalf of the Community by Dutch Foreign Minister Christoph van der Klauw to all his regional interlocutors during his trips of early 1981. At the time, a European initiative was being seriously considered.

The document revolved around two basic principles: the right of all states to secure and recognised existence (Israel) and justice for all people (the Palestinians).

Israeli withdrawal

The Europeans reaffirmed their commitment to a fundamental principle of the UN Charter, which is also in the preamble of the UN Resolution 242: the inadmissibility of territorial acquisition by force. This meant that their understanding of that resolution was closer to its French version than to the 'highly unconstructive ambiguity' of its English formulation. The document suggested that evacuation of the occupied territories should take place during a period not exceeding two years. That time limit was seen as short enough to be acceptable to the Arabs, yet long enough to develop Israeli trust.

Two major obstacles were foreseen: Israeli settlements and Jerusalem. For the European Community, international law explicitly prohibits any modification in the demographic composition or real estate ownership in an occupied territory. They considered the dismantling of the settlements in the Sinai as a suitable precedent. Yet the Arab parties were asked if they would accept a distinction between all the settlements that would necessarily have to be evacuated and one particular settlement near Hebron, located in a place where prior to 1948 there had existed a Jewish colony. For the European Community, the settlers in the Old Jewish Quarter in Hebron would be allowed to stay on in Palestinian territory and retain Israeli citizenship if they so wished. They would, however, be subjected to legislation applying to foreigners. The idea of possible minor boundary changes, on both sides of the 1967 frontiers, if all parties agreed, was also mentioned.

For the Europeans, the principle of withdrawal also applies to East Jerusalem. The document stipulated that the status of Jerusalem could not be altered by any unilateral decision. The issue was dealt with as a separate item, because of its sentimental and religious implications. The document recalled that on two occasions the UN had decided to internationalise the city. Different formulae were explored, all presupposing free access to the Holy Places:

1. Total internationalisation of the city in line with the *corpus separatum* idea adopted for the whole city in 1947;

2. Repartition of the city with international approval;

3. Shared sovereignty between Arabs and Israel;

4. Political separation with joint municipal administration;

5. Internationalisation of only the Old City.

Palestinian self-determination

The working paper first dealt with several possible alternatives for the transition period. The options were:

1. Temporary international supervision through the UN;

2. Temporary supervision by Jordan;

3. Temporary management by the mayors and personalities of the occupied territories;

4. Management by a mixed organ representing the PLO, Jordan, the inhabitants of the territories and, the document added, perhaps Israel.

The document tried to find ways to give 'a concrete expression to the abstract right of self-determination'. For the European Community, it is not realistic that only the inhabitants of the West Bank and Gaza should have the right to express their opinions. Nor is it realistic that the vote of the Palestinians in exile should have the same weight as those of the West Bank and Gaza, since the latter will form the majority in the future Palestinian entity. Their massive approval concerning the future is essential.

A popular referendum was to enable Palestinians to choose among the following:

1. An independent sovereign state;

2. An autonomous region linked Jordan in a federal or confederal manner;

3. An entity linked with both Jordan and Israel.

The Europeans, having voted in favour of UN Resolutions 194 in 1949, did not oppose in principle the exercise by the Palestinians of their right to return. Yet they saw its implementation as subject to agreement among the parties concerned in the negotiations.

Security guarantees

The document considered Arab recognition of Israel as a valid compensation for Israeli evacuation and Palestinian self-determination. Besides mutual recognition of sovereignties within recognised borders and an end to all references to war, certain technical measures were envisaged including:

1. Demilitarised zones on both sides of the borders;

2. A network of observation posts and early warning systems by air, land and sea;

3. Establishment by the UN Security Council of a special organ for complaints on possible violations.

The working paper also announced the European Community's availability to launch a vast economic development plan for the whole area. The priorities of this plan were to facilitate the integration of Palestinian refugees returning mainly to the West Bank and Gaza, and to encourage economic and political cooperation between the Palestinian entity and its neighbours.

That was 1980–1. We are in 1987. If the PLO and the Palestinian people were given the working paper to comment upon, their unambiguous choices would be:

1. A United Nations mandate for the transition period;

2. Political separation of both wings of the city of Jerusalem, with acceptance of joint municipal committees;

3. And finally, to avoid unnecessary delay, the entrusting of the Palestinians in the West Bank and Gaza to express their collective aspirations.

The verdict – a surprise? – would be an overwhelming demand for a sovereign state. This state might, later on, seek political unification of economic integration in larger regional systems with no fear of being eternally relegated to the unenviable role of a junior partner.

The European positions were most welcome. Tribute was

paid and encouragement extended. Yet one question still begs an answer: after remaining dormant for years, why did the European Community reactivate its diplomacy? All the factors and incentives that militated in the 1970s for a European initiative have evaporated. There is no risk of oil shortages. *Au contraire!* The price of oil, as in pre-1973 period, more resembles a *bakshish* than a price. The danger of a new regional war, or of a possible superpower confrontation due to uncontrolled escalations are less likely than ever before. The Arab Orient has rarely been so disoriented. Even the occasional violent spillovers onto the European continent have fortunately ceased. So why?

Certainly the mediocrity of the American Middle East policy has exasperated the Europeans. Of course, the camp wars in Lebanon remind Europe of the urgency of a solution to the global Palestinian problem. Yet one should not disregard the major role played by Belgian Foreign Minister Leo Tindemans in this new phase of European diplomacy.

Tindemans is a talented statesman at the end of a rich political career. Several times prime minister, nicknamed in 1975 'Mr Europe' for a report he made on European unity and the need for European countries to speak with one voice on international problems and still have something to say, and a distinguished professor of international law, Mr Tindemans did not want his presidency of the European Council of Ministers to pass unnoticed. He wanted to leave his imprint – a legitimate ambition. His staff worked hard; memoranda circulated through the complex machinery of European intergovernmental coordination; and the Middle East was back prominently on the European agenda.

But Tindemans' presidency will end in June 1987. Through the rotation system, Denmark will assume the presidency. Since Denmark and the Netherlands have always made sure that the European common denominator on the Middle East was the lowest possible, one can anticipate that the Danish successor to Leo Tindemans will preside over the necessary follow-up with the enthusiasm, vitality and pace of a turtle.

After World War II and the end of the Euro-centred era in international relations, Europe became 'an actor in search of a role'. Playing an inspiring Athens to a yet unsophisticated Rome/Washington tempted it. The American political class is currently preparing itself for the 'battle of the White House' and will, in the coming two years, intensively debate foreign policy and regional conflicts. For it to take into consideration European advice, expertise and *savoir faire* is, alas, too wise a conduct to ever become true.

VI

Sources of Lebanese-Palestinian tensions[1]

I was supposed to have the less demanding task of discussant on this panel until two days ago when I was asked to replace one of the initial speakers.

With the chairman's permission, I would like to voice a concern that I have difficulties concealing. I really think that there is a panel missing over here. If I totally agree that Revolutionary Iran, the Iran-Iraq war, Lebanon and American foreign policy in the Middle East are highly relevant topics that need to be addressed, one can hardly assume that the Arab-Israeli conflict and the question of Palestine are static and stagnant and thus unworthy of further analysis in a symposium on recent developments in the Middle East. There are attempts in the media and academia to show that this endless conflict has become anachronistic, that there is around it an unjustified bibliographical explosion and that it is already over-analysed. I personally believe that it is usually misanalysed and that the universities' handling of the Middle East in general and of that topic in particular still leaves much to be desired.

The prevailing *status quo* with its 'dynamic immobilism' is in itself a fascinating field of investigation; so are the non-existent peace process, the competing approaches to conflict resolution, the modifications of the ideological constellation in Israel, the

---

1. Edited transcript of a lecture given at Rutgers University, New Jersey on 25 April 1987 during a symposium on 'Recent Developments in the Middle East – Implications for University Curriculum.'

70

evolution of the Palestinian national movement, the changing Arab balance of power with its constantly shifting alliances etc which all deserved attention and analysis.

If it is true that there is a plurality of conflicts and tensions tormenting and tearing up the area, there is nevertheless a hierarchy that cannot be ignored. Conflicts in the Middle East are not unconnected. Even the Iran-Iraq war, which has a logic of its own, is deeply affected by the Arab-Israeli conflict, as we were all reminded by what has been called Irangate. The nature of political power, the legitimacy/illegitimacy of regimes, the fate of minorities, the rise and fall of certain ideologies, oil pricing, shortages and gluts, are all profoundly influenced by that endless conflict. To take an example, closer to the topic I was asked to address, had not Palestinian demography been displaced from Palestinian geography, we would not have needed a panel on the sources of Lebanese-Palestinian tensions. Had there not been a demographic overspill to the periphery of the Palestinian homeland due to the brutal and violent birth of the Israeli State, Palestinian communities would not have had the countless problems we all know with host regimes, states and even societies.

Lebanon usually defies the analyst. The 'normal' conceptual tools, the 'habitual' theoretical frameworks, are soon found to be inadequate. Neither the class struggle approach nor the confessional approach are entirely satisfactory. Domestic struggles are constantly fed by conflicts within Lebanon's environment and internal structural disruptions are amplified by regional conjunctural influences.

I think that the tensions between the Lebanese and the Palestinians on Lebanese soil can be attributed to essentially five factors:

1. The endeavours of the resurrecting Palestinian national movement to reorganise and restructure Palestinian diaspora communities *inevitably created a dual and parallel system of authority competing*

for sympathy and allegiance. That was essentially the case in Jordan prior to 1970–1 and in Lebanon from 1969 onwards. In Syria, and for a variety of considerations, the emerging Palestinian autonomous structure remained discrete and was subjected to severe constraints that it, more or less willingly, had to accept.

2. The organisation of Palestinian communities disturbed the *unstable, delicate and fragile internal equilibriums.* In Lebanon, the alterations thus introduced were to the detriment of the Christian community and its preponderant role in the power-sharing and to the detriment of the right in general. From the late sixties onwards, the Muslim component of Lebanese society expressed its increasing discomfort with what was supposed to be its eternal junior status and this was coupled with the expansion of the Leftist trends in the Lebanese society as a whole.

3. Common wisdom in the West usually portrayed a fragmented Arab world unified only by its visceral hostility towards Israel. I personally believe that the opposite hypothesis is more accurate: Israel's creation was encouraged by the West to tear apart and break the geographic continuity of the Asian wing from the African wing of the Arab world and much of inter-Arab disputes can be traced to the *Arabs' management/mismanagement of their incompetence to cope with that external challenge.* Divergences on means of containment of Israel, attempts at conflict-avoidance are more frequent than the search of a coordinated strategy for liberation and were the source of the most bitter verbal polemics (Syria-Egypt/Libya vs almost everybody else) or bloody military show-downs (Jordan-PLO/Syria-PLO). In the absence of a clear doctrine on the inter-relationship between separate-regional security and national-global security, the 'individual Arab states' often played against the interests of the 'Arab Nation'. To come back to Lebanon, for decades the official belief was that 'Lebanon's strength resided in its weakness' and that its pro-Western orientation protected it best from Israel's expansionist drive. This doctrine surely was incompatible with the Palestinian intent of using South Lebanon as a sanctuary. Syria repeatedly left the Palestinians in a solitary and

unequal confrontation with Israel always arguing that patriotism dictated non-involvement.

4. *The American Machiavellian approach to pseudo conflict-resolution* was aimed at transforming the Israeli-Arab conflict into Arab-Arab conflicts. From 1973 onwards, by undermining the existing possibilities for a comprehensive settlement and opting for bilateral partial deals, American policy in the Middle East fuelled intra-Arab rivalries among those who hoped to be invited to the negotiating table and those who knew to be excluded. In Lebanon, besides the fact that the *reglements de compte* took place on its soil, other problems of a different nature arose. *The more remote a Palestinian entity seemed, the more precarious Palestinian presence became.* With rumours of a Palestinian permanent implantation in Lebanon, forces that saw the dynamics of the situation as detrimental were urged to seize the initiative. For the Phalangist party, two alternatives existed: either an anti-Israeli alliance with the PLO for Palestinian statehood or an alliance with Israel to crush the Palestinian presence. The second option was erroneously considered more tempting as a *solution de facilite*. One of the few things on which Yasser Arafat and Raymond Edde agree upon is Kissinger's responsibility in igniting the Lebanese civil war in 1975. In more recent years, Reagan's Plan in 1982, with a wink to the Palestinians but excluding Syria, the Israeli-Lebanese bilateral peace of 1983 excluding both Syria and the PLO, and since then frequent flirtations with Syria in the absence of any recognition of the PLO are all less-inspired continuations of the same policy of promoting intra-Arab antagonisms that translate themselves in bloody confrontations on Lebanese soil.

5. *Israel's regional strategy* is the last but not least effective of the five factors I have mentioned. The Zionist delegation gravitating around the Versailles Conference in 1919 already submitted a plan asking that South Lebanon, up to the Litani River, be included to that area to which would apply the Balfour Declaration in favour of a Jewish homeland. In the early fifties, as we learn from Moshe Sharett's memoirs, Ben Gurion was already exploring ways and means 'of provoking the Arabs into provoking Israel' so as to expand from

the 'narrow borders' it had to content itself with in 1949. On the other hand, and at the same time, Dayan, in small meetings of the nucleus of Israeli decision-makers, advocated a policy of searching for a Christian major (prophetic, if one recalls that Saad Haddad was just that), to be bribed into proclaiming a separate Christian Maronite entity. It is during that period that what is known as the 'periphery strategy' – i.e. an alliance of encirclement with non-Arab states (Ethiopia, Iran and Turkey) and alliance with non-Muslim and non-Sunni minorities – was refined. After 1969, the massive disproportionate and indiscriminate Israeli attacks by land, sea and air against Lebanese civilian targets – mainly Shia – was Israel's constant and often successful policy for instigating the Lebanese population against Palestinian presence.

I have deliberately left aside Palestinian abuses as an explanatory factor for Lebanese-Palestinian tension in spite of the fact that I do believe that there were institutional and individual abuses. Yet this theme has been so over-emphasised and seeing the way events unfolded in Lebanon after 1982 (total depreciation of the Lebanese Pound, alarming pauperisation, hostage taking, embassy insecurity, confessionalism and intolerance, etc., etc., etc.) many are expressing nostalgia for the Palestinian pre-1982 abuses which seem angelic if compared with today's utter chaos.

An actor-oriented approach could be adopted in explaining tensions involving Palestinians on Lebanese soil. The PLO has had to confront, successively or simultaneously, the Lebanese state, the Phalangist party, Amal, Syria and Israel.

The last two years were characterised by tensions between Amal and the Palestinians in Lebanon which culminated in the camp wars. It should be noted that the military confrontations opposed less than a religious community (only Amal) to an entire people (the Palestinians). With Syrian backing and aimed, among other things, at unseating Yasser Arafat with all that this implies from the presidency of the PLO, the siege of the camps resulted in reunifying a previously fractured Palestinian movement under his now unchallenged leadership. To be noted also is that the PLO has ended its immediate post-1982 isolation on the Lebanese scene. It is its opponent that now suffers from this serious handicap. Besides its traditional relations with the components of the Lebanese National Movement, the PLO enjoys a whole network of contacts paradoxically ranging from the Sunni Tawhid in Tripoli to the Phalangist Party and the Maronite Head of the Lebanese State, to Sunni upper class and have-nots in Beirut and Saida, to the Druze community and the Shia Hezbollah movement.

The Syrian regime being now a decisive actor on the Lebanese arena, allow me to say a word on Syrian-Palestinian relations. Their divergences have positioned inter-Arab relations and have added confusion to an already complicated situation. I have singled out Syrian-Palestinian relations for their importance and significance as well as because of the belief that Palestinian grievances have so far been insufficiently explained.

What is the nature of the Syrian-Palestinian dispute? Is it the result of an incompatibility of characters between Assad and Arafat or an incompatibility of strategies? Without minimising the role of psychology in politics, it is certainly a problem of divergence in strategy. Palestinian grievances against Hafez al-Assad can be summarised as such:

1. Tensions go back to the 1965–7 period. Hafez Assad then considered Fateh an uncontrolled movement close to rival Syrian officers who were hostile to his political ambitions in the power game in Damascus.

2. In 1967, the Syrian army, and Assad was then Defence Minister, gave a very poor performance withdrawing from the Golan Heights without any serious resistance, preferring to defend the regime rather than the homeland. His Egyptian homologues were taken

to court and tried for negligence and incompetence. He, on the contrary, succeeded in getting himself promoted.

3. In 1970, during Black September, the Syrian armoured brigade which intervened to help the Palestinian resistance in its fight with the Jordanian army was crushed and had to withdraw because it never received any aerial cover which Assad, then in charge of military aviation, withheld. Months later, Assad succeeded to topple the Attasi-Jedid-Zuain group under the pretext of their shortcomings towards the Palestinian cause.

4. In 1974, during Kissinger's shuttle diplomacy, Assad asked the Arab oil-exporting countries to drop their embargo, a weapon that was used at the time to obtain Israeli total withdrawal from the territories occupied in 1967 and the restoration of Palestinian national rights, and that just to obtain his disengagement agreement and Israeli withdrawal from just a few miles on the Syrian front.

5. Also in 1974, Assad unexpectedly, even for a Kissinger, abstained from asking for PLO participation in the Geneva Conference. At a time when Arabs were already asking for such a participation, he 'advised' Kissinger to meet not with PLO's chairman Yasser Arafat, but with Zouheir Mohsen of Saika.

6. Also in 1974, Assad agreed that the Syrian front would not be used for Palestinian military operations, thus not only responding to an Israeli condition but also complicating even more the Palestinians' situation in Lebanon. The Lebanese authorities and people could legitimately wonder why Lebanon was expected to be the only Arab country to tolerate Palestinian incursions from its borders and live with the massive Israeli retaliations, while the next door militant regime *par excellence* maintained its own border hermetically sealed.

7. Assad's 1976 military intervention in Lebanon against the National Movement and the PLO has also left scars still unhealed, not only within the PLO but also within the Lebanese National Movement.

8. If Carter's statement that 'no Arab leader ever asked him in private

for a Palestinian state' was proved to be inaccurate (see Carter's, Brzezinski's, Vance's memoirs and Quandt's *Decade of Decisions*), Assad never asked for one. His interpretation and version of Pan-Arabism converged strangely with Israeli *desideratas*.

9. In 1981, Hafez Al Assad deliberately sabotaged the Fahd plan which had Arafat's support and was expected to become an Arab peace plan during the Fez Summit of 1981. One has to recall that in July 1981, a two-week full-scale Israeli-Palestinian confrontation took place. It ended by a cease-fire agreement engineered by Phillip Habib and sponsored by the UN. In such confrontations, when the weak party is not defeated, it comes out to be the winner. In such confrontations, if the strong party does not win, it comes out to be the loser. July 1981 and the months that followed were the best strategic moments of the PLO. Symbolically that two-week war was the Palestinians' 'War of Ramadan'. It gave them military credibility allowing them to engage in diplomatic negotiations. Crown Prince Fahd, with Palestinian encouragement, announced a peace plan in August 1981. This was a promising period. The political, strategic and financial weight of the most conservative pro-Western country was thrown in the balance. And that was before the oil-glut and the international market turned into a buyer's market. Also before the full measure of the Iranian threat was deployed further shrinking the possible influence Riyadh could have had in Washington. That initiative had a serious chance of succeeding in 'convincing' the American administration to adopt a policy more sensitive and responsive to Arab minimal demands. If Israel's immediate rejection and the American administration's unencouraging attitude were not without impact, the *coup de grace* for the Fahd Plan came from Hafez al-Assad who blocked the necessary unanimous adoption of the plan on the grounds that he was not sufficiently consulted in advance. The failure of that Summit meant that the Palestinians had to expect a new confrontation with Israel, but on a larger scale than in 1981, again on the Lebanese arena and with no outside help.

10. on 11 June 1982, Hafez al-Assad concluded with Israel a 'bilateral cease-fire agreement' only days after the beginning of the Israeli

invasion of Lebanon. That separate cease-fire agreement, for the Palestinian National Movement, was at least as hard a blow as was Sadat's bilateral peace agreement.

11. From 1983 to 1987 Assad encouraged a dissidence movement against the legitimate leadership of the PLO, a movement that has, throughout these four years, gradually discovered that it was being manipulated for a political finality totally foreign to the Palestinian national interest and is now, especially with the success of the 18th session of the FNC, seeking ways to return to the PLO they regret having abandoned.

What is at stake is definitely not Syria's 'militancy' exasperated by Arafat's 'capitulationism' and 'deviationism'. Four major other factors have to be mentioned here:

1. When the PLO opposed Sadat's unilateral policies, that was done with the hope of recuperating Egypt which the Palestinians can never afford to lose. Assad has used Sadat's solo performances to evict Egypt from the Arab League, hoping that his regime will inherit Egypt's traditional leading role, a role he thought was looking for a new actor, a vacancy he thought he would fill. These are two different oppositions to Sadat and to Egyptian policies. These are two different perceptions of Egypt's influence and role, past or potential.

2. One would have expected Assad to seriously work, especially after Sadat's defection, at the constitution of an 'Oriental or Eastern Front' which, to be a credible deterrent, has to include Iraq. The short period of rapprochement between Syria and Iraq in 1978–9 was only used to try to rob, unsuccessfully, Fateh of the majority it detained in the Executive Committee of the PLO. Since 1980, a desirable defeat of Iraq by Iran is the policy pursued by Damascus. How that defeat will promote Arab military capacities and will help Syria achieve 'strategic balance' or 'strategic parity' with Israel still awaits a convincing explanation.

3. The third is the time factor. Assad can afford to say that since the military balance is unfavourable, peace can only be a humiliating one. He also can afford to say that because of the military imbalance, he cannot wage a war of liberation. Can the Palestinians afford that? For them, any loss of time means further Judaisation of the land and increasing migration from the occupied territories. This explains what sometimes seems to be Palestinian impatience. This explains their favouring of either a credible strategy of confrontation or a dynamic strategy of negotiation. The perpetuation of the 'no war, no peace' situation is, for the Palestinians, fatal. Not for him.

4. And last but not least Assad's quest for hegemony on a constellation in which the other actors would have a very subordinate role exacerbated the legitimate Palestinian desire for 'autonomy of decision'. In a fragmented Arab world unable to cope with external challenges, the PLO has always endeavoured hard towards better coordinated Arab policies. But it was being asked to abdicate its independence to a regime whose strategy it already found very objectionable.

The Palestinians find it only normal and legitimate to wonder whether Hafez al-Assad is an Arab Bismarck – a federator of a fragmented Arab nation – or whether he is a disintegrator of an already Balkanised Arab world?

The situation in Lebanon is now totally intertwined with the global Arab-Israeli conflict. As long as either of them remains unresolved, we should expect reciprocal violent overspills. In both cases, I personally believe that the local actors, if left to themselves, are incapable of reaching acceptable agreements.

Israel enjoys such a military preponderance that it short-sightedly considers its continued occupation of Arab territories affordable and values the *status quo* as the best possible posture. For lack of a better concept, an imposed solution through the UN and American-Soviet cooperation might be the only workable formula.

Lebanese intellectual Georges Corm has written extensively about the 'minority complex' that plagues all Lebanese communities and how each prefers to seek external backing to prevail rather than resort to internal bargaining in view of accommodation. Here too, an imposed solution, this time by the Arab League and with UN backing, might be the most desirable and efficient avenue away from national suicide.

In the first case, the prerequisites of Palestinian self-determination and statehood should be satisfied and in the second, by neutralising Israeli interference and by drowning Syrian influence, a genuine 'Lebanese option' compatible with its Arab affiliation could re-emerge and, hopefully more equitably, prosper again in a finally pacified Middle East.

VII

Interview with Gene Sharp
on non-violent struggle[1]

Dr Gene Sharp directs the Programme on Non-violent Sanctions in Conflict and Defence at Harvard University's Centre for International Affairs and is president of the Albert Einstein Institution, a foundation dedicated to research on the potential of non-violent sanctions against political violence. He is the author of numerous publications on the subject of non-violent struggle, especially *The Politics of Non-violent Action* (three volumes), *Social Power and Political Freedom, Gandhi as a Political Strategist,* and *Making Europe Unconquerable: The Potential of Civilian-based Deterrence and Defence.* Arabic and Hebrew translations of an introduction to his work *Non-violent Resistance* have been issued in Jerusalem entitled *al-Muqawamah Bila 'Unf,* published by the Palestinian Centre for the Study of Non-violence, and *Hitnagdut Lo Alima,* published by Mifras Publishing House.

This extended interview with Dr Gene Sharp was conducted in March 1986 and March 1987 by Afif Safieh, a Palestinian Visiting Scholar at Harvard University's Centre for International Affairs.

Afif Safieh: In reviews written about your books, you have been called the Machiavelli and Clausewitz of non-violent struggle. Can you comment on that?

---

1   Interview by Afif Safieh in *Journal of Palestine Studies* (Vol 17, No 1), Autumn, 1987.

Gene Sharp: I take that as a compliment. Machiavelli was attempting to deal with the world as it was, rather than imagining that some ideal world could come into existence just out of one's dreams. From the way he saw the world he drew lessons about what kind of action was practical in politics. I think his view was limited, in that non-violent struggle is a larger factor in politics than he saw it to be. Also, violence is not always as effective as it is often assumed to be. But Machiavelli also saw that without legitimacy – the perceived right to rule – and without the support of the people, a prince or a government could not last. He said specifically that the more cruel a regime becomes, the shorter is its life.

Clausewitz was not focusing on why war is noble, or even why it is supposedly necessary. Instead, his book, *On War*, is an exercise in the use of one's mind in formulating strategies to oppose the enemy. That is a lesson people of all good causes need to ponder. It is not enough simply to assert goals and objectives. We must think very carefully about how to use the available resources to give us the maximum opportunity to achieve those goals.

Afif Safieh: Your Programme on Non-violent Sanctions at Harvard has always aroused much interest but also scepticism. Much of the scepticism about non-violent methods was swept away by the success of the Filipino people in obtaining elections, in unveiling the fraudulent methods to distort the popular verdict, and finally in ousting Marcos in February 1986. How do you explain this shift?

Gene Sharp: It comes from a recognition that non-violent struggle in that particular situation was powerful. This case is not an isolated one. It is one of a series of non-violent struggles that have wielded great power in the past. They have often been forgotten and have not always become part of our historical memory, even though they were extremely important in the shaping of history.

The Philippines struggle had a number of distinct features. It was a very good example of the withdrawal of the pillars of power. The Filipino people withdrew legitimacy from the regime when it became clear that the elections were a fraud. There were plans for economic resistance and non-cooperation against the supporters of Marcos. Diplomats abroad began resigning. The population became non-violently defiant. Finally, a major part of the army and its officers in effect went on strike. They did not turn their guns in the other direction or bomb the presidential palace. They went on strike and said that they were doing it non-violently. So the army itself was taken away. Then the church called on people to demonstrate and protect the soldiers non-violently. The civilian population formed vast barricades of human bodies surrounding the mutinous officers and soldiers, in a case that probably has no historical precedent: the non-violent civilians protected the army. Finally Marcos was left with very little power. You take away the sources of power and the man who was formerly a tyrant becomes just an old man. His choice was not whether to remain in power, his only choice was how he was to leave. And so he left semi-gracefully.

That teaches us a great political lesson: that all repressive systems, all governments, legitimate or otherwise, all tyrannies, all foreign occupations are able to continue only because they receive the support of those they rule. Even foreign occupiers are supported by their own people, and frequently receive international support. If you can withdraw those sources of power, then the regime is threatened.

The beginning of all this is something else which is extremely important: the people who have seemed to be powerless and helpless learn how to act together with others to wield effective power in their own right. They thereby gain greater self-respect and are able to have an impact on the opponent group. Then the situation changes drastically.

Afif Safieh: In your opinion, which has contributed more in the production of history and events, violent or non-violent struggle?

Gene Sharp: Clearly, violence has played a major role over thousands of years in shaping political and demographical entities, as by conquests, empires and colonisation. Those results have often been tragic. But I don't fully accept your assumption that political regimes are a result of violence, because clearly historically there have been major roles played by non-violent struggle. Non-violent struggle was very important in the Gold Coast's gaining independence and becoming Ghana in West Africa. Non-violent struggle was a major factor in Indian independence from the British. Certainly, non-cooperation was very powerful in 1919–22 in the Egyptian struggle against the British. Ten years of non-violent struggle were extremely important in the American movement for independence. These are but a few examples.

Whether violent or non-violent struggle has been more important in the past is hard to say because societies that have had a major part of their history formed by non-violent struggle often have not themselves recorded that history for posterity. For example, the Hungarian non-violent struggle against Austria in the mid-nineteenth century forced the Austrian empire to recognise the Hungarian constitution and that helped to form the boundaries in Central Europe. Yet I have been told that even in Hungarian there is no good historical account of that struggle. There are many other cases of non-violent struggle which lack good historical descriptions or analyses.

One of the reasons these struggles are missing from the history books or misrepresented is that it was never in the interest of the oppressors to record and teach us that history. It is in the interest of oppressors to teach that only violence is successful because the oppressors usually have the superior capacity for violence. They will therefore have a greater chance to maintain their oppression if the oppressed also believe in violence.

The oppressed need to learn that they do not need to fight with the oppressors' best weapons. Instead of using violence, they have a greater chance of mobilising their power capacity by working and acting together using psychological, social, political, and economic weapons – weapons that enable them to become stronger. When they choose these weapons, the oppressed are mobilising their power in such a way that in the long run the forces of oppression cannot succeed against it.

History is a mixture of violent and non-violent forms of struggle, along with other types of action. We must learn from all of our history. We must learn not to repeat the disasters of the past, but instead learn how to wield these other kinds of struggle more effectively in the future than in the past.

There are choices available as to how to act, how to wage the struggle. One can do things which express one's feelings and emotions, but which may not help to achieve one's goals. Frequently people will strike out in violence because of the great anger that derives from the suffering that they, or their people, have experienced in the past. That is understandable. However, it is another and more important matter to figure out how in a particular situation – regardless of what has happened in the past – people can act most effectively to move toward achievement of their goals.

Afif Safieh: What can non-violent action offer to the Palestinian people? How can such a struggle be conducted? What is the possible outcome? What will be the challenges?

Gene Sharp: That is quite a set of questions, and I am no expert on the history of the Palestinian people or their conflict with Israel. To sketch effective non-violent strategies for any people in any situation requires such detailed, intimate knowledge of that society that an outsider really cannot do it.

On the other hand, someone from that society who does not understand non-violent struggle cannot do it either. At best, such a person starts from the beginning, re-inventing the wheel each time. It is as though someone is going to use guerrilla warfare but has to create anew the idea of guerrilla warfare, knowing nothing of past guerrilla struggles. It would be hard for someone who has never read the history of such struggles in the past, who has never read writings of the strategists of guerrilla struggle, to say how it could be used by a certain people. Any suggestions offered would be inadequate.

I think we need to recognise and learn what there is in the history of the Palestinian people that could teach us about non-violent struggle. I have been told of the great general strike by the Palestinian people in 1936 which went on for 174 days and is claimed to have been the longest general strike in human history. Certainly it demonstrates that at that time the Palestinian people were capable of using non-violent struggle, saw it to be a powerful tool, and were able to remain in solidarity during that long period of time, even though the result was not a great success. I have also heard of various other acts of non-cooperation, and of non-violent protest in recent years by the Palestinian people in all sorts of difficult circumstances.

If we are to learn from non-violent struggle, we first need to recognise that it operates from an insight into the nature of political power. Non-violent struggle recognises the crucial importance of power. In situations of great injustice and oppression – as the case in point undeniably is – there is a maldistribution of power. Some people and groups have too much power and others are relatively powerless. Even if one oppressor is removed, those people, because of their continuing weaknesses, are likely to become victims of a new oppressor.

We need to recognise that power derives from people and institutions working together toward common objectives. The power of governments derives from sources in society such as legitimacy, economic resources, skills and knowledge, submission and obedience of the population, sanctions, and others. All of those sources depend on the cooperation and obedience of individuals and institutions. When that cooperation and obedience are withdrawn, then that power is weakened in proportion to the degree that the sources are withdrawn. Sometimes you may have a dramatic, swift paralysis of the system as happened in the Philippines. And sometimes the struggle drags on for a longer period of time, while some of the forces still adhere to the old government, thereby giving it the capacity to repress. However, whether the action is fast or slow, the principle remains: shrink, withdraw, take away the sources of power. That withdrawal leads to major change.

Sometimes achieving that withdrawal means not only mobilising one's own people but doing things that have an impact on the population and society of the oppressor nation. Sometimes what is needed is to get people in the oppressor society to protest in solidarity with the oppressed. At times there may also be a role for the international community, but one needs to concentrate on strengthening one's own people. Other such influences may come later.

Afif Safieh: Can you elaborate on the different possible categories of non-violent action, relating that kind of struggle to the gradual empowerment of the people?

Gene Sharp: When one acts on that insight into the nature of power in a large disciplined movement, one creates a struggle capacity which can be greater than that of violence for achieving humane objectives. Non-violent struggle means, of course, that one does not capitulate in the face of threats. One does not run away. One does not leave one's country, or if already away, returns to it. One also chooses to fight with superior weapons, not the oppressors' violence but psychological, moral, social-economic and political weapons with which one's people can be strong.

There are several classes of non-violent weapons. First are the symbolic weapons, relatively weak ones, of non-violent persuasion and protest. They range widely, including public speeches, declarations, mass petitions, leaflets, use of slogans and symbols, posters, banners, newspapers and journals, records and cassette tapes – which were used in Iran in the struggle against the Shah. Other methods of symbolic protest include lobbying, deputations, picketing, displaying flags, putting up new signs, renaming streets, prayer and worship, and displaying portraits of national leaders. Vigils, music, and drama and singing can also be used, as can teach-ins and mass meetings. Marches, parades and religious processions are other options. Political mourning at funerals of people who have been killed has been used repeatedly in South Africa.

We then move into the whole category of non-cooperation, the withdrawal of withholding of one's cooperation from the opponent and the system that one opposes. That has happened in many, many cases in the past. Occupational group after occupational group withdraws its support.

Some forms of non-cooperation are still symbolic. These range from making as much noise as possible to having everything completely silent in a certain situation. On other occasions people turn their backs to officials who have done terrible things.

The methods of non-cooperation are divided into three categories. The first is social non-cooperation: one avoids speaking to certain people or inviting them to parties and other affairs. People may also refuse to attend certain social affairs, banquets, or meetings, and non-violent student strikes have been powerful in various parts of the world. They have been one of the major methods of struggle in South Africa in the past year. Sanctuary is another method. People go for safety into religious places, where the government has no authority to enter, and dare the troops and police to come in and arrest them.

The second category of non-cooperation is economic non-cooperation. These methods become still more powerful because they not only affect profits, but can threaten the operation of the entire economy. These economic methods include the whole sub-class of economic boycotts. Consumer boycotts are one example. They are very hard for opponents to deal with, because how can the opponents force people to buy a particular product? One can always say one doesn't need it. If the boycotted product is on the store shelf, it can simply be left there. In this way, property is not destroyed, and no one comes to any physical harm. But the action can paralyse a part of the economic system.

The second major category of economic non-cooperation is the labour strike, and it has a long history. People have learned how labourers can work together to wield power. Rather than using violence, it was far more effective for workers simply not to work. Sometimes that meant that they stayed home, sometimes it meant they went to their work places but worked very inefficiently or not at all.

Strikes should not be applied without an analysis of their relevance and probable effectiveness. It is possible, for example, that unselective Palestinian strikes could simply lead to importing Filipino contract workers (who hold many jobs in Jordan) and also convince more Israelis that the whole Palestinian population should be evicted from the occupied territories.

The last major category of non-cooperation is political non-cooperation, the application of the principle of the strike to politics.

It may be denied, for example, that the government or the head of state has legitimacy. Once legitimacy is taken away, then the obligation of the people to obey is removed. Then people can move into varying kinds of non-cooperation against the government. They may boycott elections, expecting them to be a fraud. They may refuse to work for the government. They may boycott particular governmental departments. They may withdraw from government schools and instead attend independent schools. They may withhold information from the police. If the government orders particular organisations to be dissolved, the organisations may refuse to dissolve and continue to operate, openly or later underground.

Individuals as well as groups of people have choices as to whether to obey a law or an order. The price of disobedience may often be severe punishment, but there is always a choice. People may obey, but do so very reluctantly, slowly and incompletely. Sometimes people will practise civil disobedience, a non-violent, open, flagrant breaking of the law they believe to be wrong.

When disobedience extends to government personnel, some individuals or whole departments may refuse to assist in a particular policy or help an oppressive ruler. Occasionally, police will not do their job completely because they no longer believe in the repression of non-violent resisters. On other occasions, some of the soldiers that have been ordered to shoot may aim their guns too high so that they miss. All that is affected by the fact that people are behaving in a non-violent rather than a violent way. If those same police and soldiers were being attacked and their lives threatened by people shooting at them, they would shoot to kill the demonstrators.

Sometimes the unease among troops charged with repressing disciplined non-violent resisters can lead to such disaffection and unreliability as to neutralise a whole army. This is what happened in the Philippines. Section after section of the army said they no longer recognised Marcos as president. As you take the army and other institutions away, then the power of that government is weakened. It must be emphasised, however, that this extreme response is highly atypical and must not be naively expected in most cases. When it does occur, the price already paid may have been heavy.

The last category includes methods of non-violent intervention by which people take actions that actually disrupt the operation of the system. It's a little bit like putting a wrench or some other obstruction into a machine to make it stop. The forms of non-violent intervention are sometimes psychological, such as fasts or hunger strikes. It is true that with these methods people sometimes die, but they die in all kinds of violent action. In this case fewer die, and only those who choose such action.

Another method of non-violent intervention involves physical intervention, like sitting in the office of government officials or lying down in front of tanks. Sometimes people will non-violently occupy a certain territory where they have been forbidden to enter. They simply walk in, even though they may be beaten as they enter. The Moroccan non-violent invasion of the Spanish Sahara is one example of this type of action on an international scale.

People may also intervene by establishing new economic institutions, occupying factories, practising new types of social behaviour, and so on. On the political level, people may overload administrative systems. For example, if there is opposition to a certain department that requires the reporting of all births and deaths, one might report births and deaths several times for the same people or even people that have not been born yet, so that it becomes impossible for that section of the government to function properly. Sometimes intervention means establishing a new illegal substitute government to which the population shifts loyalty and obedience, as happened in the Philippines.

These kinds of struggle are not easy to wage, but no kind of struggle is. Non-violent struggle, like violent struggle, has its requirements for effectiveness. In some ways it is very dangerous to describe this kind of a list of methods because people may act to apply it without careful thought, without considering what makes it effective or what happens next. People need to know why non-violent struggle has its own requirements for effectiveness which are different from the requirements for the effectiveness of violence.

One must choose the specific methods carefully. For example, if there are restrictions on freedom of speech, then in most situations one should fight them by asserting the right to speak freely, rather than organising a labour strike.

A great deal of solidarity is needed. People must maintain discipline and must not stop the resistance as soon as they are threatened or somebody gets hurt. It is very important that they do not shift to fight with violence because that is what the opponents want them to do. Then they must think how to develop non-violent strategies to put the greatest effectiveness into these methods in a particular situation. Their non-violence will help to split the opponent group.

Strategists and resisters should recognise that sometimes troops do shoot to kill non-violent demonstrators. It is naive not to recognise that. That often happens when there is a break in non-violent discipline, but it can occur even in the absence of such a break. However, such killings occur many fewer times than in violent conflicts. When they occur, the casualties are not part of a continually escalating pattern of violence, and the deaths of non-violent resisters can lead to increased support for the cause and reduced support for the opponents. In non-violent struggle when people die they are not forgotten; they are honoured as patriots.

Deaths and other casualties occur because non-violent struggle is powerful, able to challenge an oppressive system. That system, as long as it can, will fight back, persecute, beat, torture, and sometimes kill. That is tragic, but it is no more reason to give up the non-violent struggle than are casualties in wars regarded as reason to surrender. In fact, the evidence suggests that there are far fewer casualties in non-violent struggle than in violent struggle. In the Algerian struggle for independence against the French there are estimates that as many as one million Algerians died out of a population of between nine to ten million; in India against the British, who could be just as cruel as the French, probably not more than eight thousand out of a population of two hundred million were killed.

Afif Safieh: Can a non-violent strategy coexist with a violent one?

Gene Sharp: There have been a variety of cases in which non-violent and violent means have been mixed in essentially the same political situation. However, that does not mean that that mixture always contributes to greatest effectiveness. Here I am not talking about what is the most moral or the most immoral course of action. I am talking about what the requirements are for maximum effectiveness by the non-violent struggle.

Let us look at the situation. Suppose that we were fighting with guns, and we had enough guns for everyone, and some of our people wanted instead to continue the fighting with swords. We might try to dissuade them from that, because despite their commitment and bravery, their use of weaker weapons would debilitate our common struggle.

I would similarly argue, in even a stronger way, that for various reasons the use of guns alongside a non-violent struggle weakens the non-violent struggle. The several major advantages of non-violent struggle may be lost if violence is used along with it. For example, non-violent struggle enables every man, women, child and older person to participate in some way. Violent struggles are limited to only a relatively few people. Repression of non-violent struggle – particularly if it is brutal and appears to be unjustified – tends to arouse great sympathy and support for the non-violent resisters, and increased participation in resistance. On the other hand, bombings and assassinations produce revulsion and support for the repression, even against uninvolved people.

Non-violent struggle helps to split the opponent group, while violent struggle unites them against the resisters. Non-violent resistance helps some members of the opponent group to look at grievances and issues. Violent struggle, on the other hand, forces the people in the opponent group to unite in support of the repression and against the violent resisters.

While acts labelled as terrorism often lead to international isolation, non-violent struggle, on the other hand, contributes to arousing international sympathy and support. One can point to a whole series of cases where that has happened. Violent repression against non-violent action, particularly where the violent repression is of a very brutal type against innocent adults and children, tends to unite international opinion against the repression, and in support of the resisters.

There are therefore strong practical reasons for shifting completely to the non-violent forms of struggle. They have a greater potential for mobilising the power capacity of the oppressed against the injustices and the repression in ways that bring the resisters greater self-respect, wider recognition of the justice of their cause, and, finally, greater support. That results in greater power and an increased chance of success for their cause in ways that respect the dignity of all concerned. Non-violent struggle is the basis of a practical grand strategy for liberation.

Afif Safieh: What factors do you see as conducive to the development of a major use of non-violent struggle by the Palestinians?

Gene Sharp: Here, consideration of the role of Palestinians should come first, because their actions can be more decisive than those of the Israelis and those of the international community.

First, it appears to me that significant Palestinians are ready to consider the potential of non-violent struggle. During my visit to the Middle East in November 1986, I found an openness to discussing and thinking about non-violent struggle, even by significant Palestinians who endorsed violence. Even the people who justified violence (who usually called it 'armed struggle') often had very little confidence in it as an effective technique.

Some Palestinians are prepared to consider non-violent struggle because time may be running out, and it is silly to continue trying violence or preaching political purism when one can lose everything by doing so. It is my impression that something fundamentally different has to happen for the Palestinians relatively soon, and it needs at least to begin seriously in the next five to ten years, if Palestinian hopes are not to be dashed. If Palestinians are not to have to live indefinitely under occupation, or in a foreign country, or in one of those sad refugee camps, a break both with the policy of violence and with reliance on others to save them must come. If Palestinians are not to lose freedom as an achievable objective but are to have a chance to live in peace and safety in an independent Palestine alongside an independent Israel, a major shift to non-violent struggle is required. I think there is a widespread but rarely expressed recognition of this situation among many Palestinians. To the degree that this is true, it is an important element stimulating them to consider seriously the option of non-violent struggle.

The second factor conducive to the large-scale use of non-violent struggle by Palestinians is that many Palestinians seem to have already grasped and practised some of the fundamentals of this technique. During my visit, I heard various descriptions of unorganised Palestinian non-violent resistance by individuals or groups. People had simply refused to comply with something the Israelis wanted. People have refused to leave their homes; they have refused to abandon confiscated land that was theirs. Sometimes their tenacity has aroused Israeli sympathy, as when an eighty-year-old man had for months refused to leave his land and lived in a tent through the cold and rain, until the Israeli mayor of Jerusalem gave him an old school bus for shelter. Many Palestinians have refused to be frightened away, to become submissive, to give up, and also have refused to use violence and thereby play into the hands of those Israelis who would like to be rid of them. If a frail old man of eighty years, living alone with his dog in a tent or an old school bus can do that and make some impact, think what a whole people of several million men, women, and children could accomplish with planning, training and equal tenacity. That would be a capacity of incredible power.

That potential is a very great sign of hope, if people do something about it. But if it is left only to scattered individuals in special situations, or people whose homes are destroyed because of accusations of protests or violence by family members, then not much will change. A lot of other people will have to develop the same tenacity and combine it with a grand strategy for long-term change.

A third factor conducive to non-violent struggle by Palestinians is the high educational level of Palestinians both in the occupied territories and in the diaspora. The large numbers of students enrolled in universities is a positive sign. Even the widespread unemployment of educated young people and former students can be used positively. They can become full-time volunteers in a variety of constructive activities to improve the lives of Palestinians as well as to prepare, train, and conduct non-violent resistance in particular campaigns. Gandhi's conception of a 'constructive programme' is very important here: volunteer work to build and strengthen independent institutions to improve social life, economic conditions, sanitation, education and other components of the society.

Fourth, the Palestinians in the diaspora can be highly helpful in assisting large-scale non-violent struggle by Palestinians. Obviously, that struggle would need to be largely conducted by people living in the occupied territories. However, the immense numbers of Palestinians living elsewhere could be helpful. They are often highly educated and sophisticated. They have diverse talents and skills, often professional training and experience, and sometimes significant wealth.

A shift to non-violent struggle makes it possible to use the assistance of these Palestinians. There are several ways they could help. They could, for example, take various steps to influence public opinion and governmental policies about the Middle East in the countries in which they live. The wealth of some in the diaspora and earnings of others could be used to strengthen Palestinian society in the occupied territories, as has already happened to a certain degree. A large number of educated and talented people in the diaspora might feel a responsibility to return to live in the occupied territories in order to participate directly in improving life there. They could help provide medical services, scientific skills, educational assistance, economic improvements, improvement of the land, and assistance in agriculture and water problems. All these tasks could be part of a Palestinian constructive programme. There is a great potential source of strength there which can be used and which is likely to be more available if the struggle is conducted by non-violent rather than violent means.

Fifth, the intelligence and education of Palestinians can be used to help develop responsible, effective grand strategies for developing a free, just and democratic Palestinian nation. A major effort is needed by a handful of serious Palestinian thinkers to do that. They would need to study their own situation, Israeli society, international influences, potential supporters in Israel and throughout the world, and above all the nature of non-violent action. They could then begin to chart grand strategies for the preservation and development of the Palestinian people and for developing self-reliance, self-help and achieving increasing autonomy and independence. They would need to focus on substance and not doctrine, on the present and future rather than the past. Their aim should be to develop a comprehensive strategy and plan for practical steps for the development and growth of an independent Palestine and its positive contributions to the Middle East and the world.

Sixth, there are even signs of hope for Palestinian non-violent struggle in the fact that many young men have left homes and refugee camps to train for Palestinian military groups. These youths obviously have demonstrated great courage and commitment, even though I cannot agree with the way those qualities were expressed. Violence, however, is not the only way to express bravery and dedication.

In the context of a grand strategy using non-violent struggle, special tasks might be reserved for people of such qualities. With special training, these men could act equally courageously in non-violent ways which would bring greater chances of justice for the Palestinians. Some useful non-violent demonstrations might also be extremely dangerous. Some people might need to face machine guns, tanks or troops, or to defend holy places, without themselves using violence, as has occurred in various parts of the world. Such acts have sometimes brought victory significantly closer for the non-violent resisters, but they are highly risky. Perhaps such youths who have previously prepared for military action or other violence could apply their willingness to take risks in a new way in disciplined, trained dangerous non-violent action.

There can also be significant support among Israelis to facilitate and increase the impact of Palestinian non-violent struggle. The Israeli support for Palestinian rights and self-determination has been to this point much limited by Palestinian violence, especially the type that has threatened or taken the lives of Israeli civilians, including women and children. However, a Palestinian shift to non-violent struggle would free a significant number of Israelis to be much more supportive of Palestinian rights and to oppose brutal repression of non-violent Palestinians. It is important, however, that the shift to non-violent means be as full and reliable as possible, so that it is not seen as just a temporary change in tactics to be followed by more attacks against Jews.

I met various Israelis of different political persuasions who would be very concerned about the consequences of harsh Israeli repression of Palestinian non-violent resisters. They have strong commitments to ideals and justice and could be expected both behind the scenes and publicly to oppose brutalities and support policy changes. Some might even work with non-violent Palestinians. Palestinian non-violent demonstrations could include Israeli participants, supporters and observers, if wanted, as has already happened. Israelis could protest vigorously against brutal repression and killing of Palestinian non-violent resisters. Other Israelis could begin to question such repression and the policies against Palestinians. Reconsideration of policies against the now non-violent Palestinians might become a central focus of discussion and debate in Israeli politics. The memories of brutalities against their own people in Germany would no longer bolster support for harsh repression of Palestinians but might instead trigger sympathy for another rejected group.

Israelis could work for changes in policies without being seen as traitors supporting terrorism against Jews. Jews in other countries could support, as often in the past, a struggle for greater justice with peace, even if that meant differing with current Israeli government policies.

There is an important positive capacity among Israelis which can assist Palestinian non-violent struggle. There are positive elements in Israeli society, and the history and principles of Judaism have major stress on the importance of justice. Israelis of various religious and political views often think of themselves as very moral people. That can be very useful when Palestinians abandon violence and shift to non-violent struggle, in which their grievances rather than their violence and objectives can receive major attention. This is especially so because, in order to resolve the conflict, Israelis and Palestinians eventually will need to recognise each other and to agree to live peacefully side by side. This can only be done if they begin to understand each other, are willing to cooperate in certain matters, and also know that neither can dominate the other nor threaten the other's existence.

Very minimally, Israeli occupation, police and military officials can influence – but not necessarily determine – whether Palestinian struggle remains violent, shifts permanently to non-violent struggle, or resumes violence in a more extreme way. A major and very understandable concern of Israelis is to stop the acts of violence against their people. If Israeli repression of Palestinian non-violent resistance is very harsh, it may have the effect of driving Palestinians back to violence, perhaps in still more brutal forms. That would be tragic for all concerned, both Palestinians and Israelis. Intelligent Israeli policy, therefore, ought to be based on a careful consideration of their countermeasures.

The potential power of Palestinian non-violent resistance is widely recognised among Israelis regardless of political persuasion. When I asked various Israelis what would happen if the Palestinians shifted to non-violent struggle, without exception people answered that this would make a much greater problem for the Israeli government than Palestinian violence. However, many Israelis would welcome the shift and the problem. It would, in addition to helping to save the Palestinian people from their tragic plight, also help to save Israelis from a path which will lead to the destruction of the early dreams and ideals of an Israel which would be a place of peace, safety and justice. Many are deeply worried about the consequences of the requirements of continuing military occupation, vast military preparations, and international tensions on the nature of Israeli society and on Israeli youths who are the occupation troops. The shift by Palestinians to non-violent resistance and a peace with mutual recognition of each other's right to exist would have great benefits for both Palestinians and Israelis. I would hope that as Israelis became freed of their worst fears they, too, would become able to examine the potential usefulness of non-violent struggle for themselves. Continuing reliance on military capacity by both Israel and the Arab states can lead to disaster for everyone.

Afif Safieh: If I may interrupt your analysis, you speak of 'mutual recognition'. Attempts to achieve mutual recognition always seem to flounder on Israeli claims that an independent Palestine alongside Israel would be an unacceptable military threat to Israeli's security. How do you think this problem may be overcome?

Gene Sharp: That fear is very real, even among Israelis who think of themselves as quite liberal. Repeatedly, I heard people say that if there were an independent Palestine with Israel having the 1967 borders 'they would be eight miles from here', or a similar short distance.

I am sure discussion of the defence policy of an independent Palestine will be considered by some to be vastly premature. It may be time for that consideration, however. The reason is that a major part of Israeli opposition to an independent Palestinian state is rooted in Israeli fear that an independent Palestine might have enough military capacity to attack Israel and try to destroy it, or that a military ally of an independent Palestine – such as Libya, Iraq, or the Soviet Union – could invade Israel using Palestine as the base.

There are, I suppose, possible ways to alleviate the situation by international treaties and agreements at the time of the establishment and recognition of an independent Palestine. Austria, for example, by international treaty arrangements is prohibited from joining any military alliance. Some places might by treaty be permanently demilitarised. There could be complications in reaching such agreements, since Palestine might demand that the same restrictions apply to Israel, which might well refuse, especially in light of a perception of continuing, though probably reduced, Arab military threats. Palestinians might see such restrictions as a threat to their independence, once more preferring a pure position to a concrete political gain.

There is, however, another option. This would be especially relevant if Palestine wanted its own independent defence policy, without reliance on either other Arab states or the Soviet Union. That policy, however, could hardly be military. The military capacity of a self-reliant Palestine would be highly limited. A guerrilla warfare defence policy would likely arouse great fears in Israel of intended offensive guerrilla action inside Israel.

Another type of independent defence policy is being developed by various scholars and strategists, called 'civilian-based defence'. This relies on those same non-military forms of struggle, non-violent non-cooperation and defiance predominantly, to deter and defend against foreign aggression and internal coups. The plan is to prepare the capacity to prevent the establishment of a puppet government, to block achievement of the attackers' objectives, and to subvert the attackers' troops. By increasing the costs of such attacks and denying benefits and making political control impossible by aggressors, a substitute defence capacity would have been created without military weaponry. This policy is based in part on several improvised cases of non-violent resistance for national defence.

Palestinians who had won their independence by non-violent struggle should be able to defend it by the same means. Extension of Palestinian non-violent struggle capacity beyond liberation to defend their society by the same means might provide a solution which would respect Palestinian sovereignty, provide a deterrence and defence capacity for an independent Palestine, and also remove the Israeli fear of aggression from or through Palestine.

Afif Safieh: Don't let me distract you from continuing the discussion of conditions and circumstances favourable to a Palestinian shift to non-violent struggle.

Gene Sharp: Finally, then, there is the question whether international conditions exist which favour the development of Palestinian non-violent struggle. My answer is clearly 'yes'.

There may be exceptions and qualifications under certain circumstances, but generally speaking violent struggles – especially when they can be labelled 'terrorist' – arouse much less sympathy and support than non-violent struggles. In fact, the violence may alienate international support from the cause which otherwise would have been supported on its merits. Acts of Palestinian violence help the most extreme anti-Arab Israelis who want to annex conquered Arab land and expel all Arabs from that land and from Israel itself. Such violence alienates many Americans who generally support struggles for justice from both the Palestine Liberation Organisation and Palestinians and their cause generally. On the other hand, non-violent struggles not only do not possess the alienating factor of violence, but have various qualities of their own which bring sympathy to that cause and alienate support from the violently repressing opponent.

I think that the international community could be a source of major support and assistance to the Palestinians once they shift to non-violent struggle. There may be, however, a delay of time before such support becomes significant because of the past violent record. Many people will initially doubt the genuineness of the shift and suspect that there will be a quick return to violence. However, given that transition period, a tenacious and creative shift to non-violent struggle can open the way to a significant response of sympathy and support for Palestinians. Much sympathy and support for Israel will continue, based upon the past terrible sufferings of Jews under the Holocaust and principled support for their right to have a safe homeland. However, that support in face of the new Palestinian non-violent struggle is likely to become carefully considered and critical. Not everything the Israeli government does will be seen to be necessary, required or good. Not everything Palestinian will be seen to be violent, terrible and leading to disaster. To the contrary, positive international sympathy and support for the Palestinians and opposition to brutal repression of their non-violent movement would be likely.

One would find that world opinion would shift. The countries that have given diplomatic support to the PLO despite the violence would be likely to continue and increase that support. Arab governments could not stand aside. To these numbers could also be added those countries that have hitherto done nothing to achieve justice for Palestinians or that have actively supported Israeli policies. They, too, could become important backers of Palestinian independence.

It would even be possible for the United States government to shift its pressures and policies in the Middle East. Probably the only chance of breaking the growing identity between Israeli and American government policies is through a major shift by Palestinians to non-violent struggle. The shift by Palestinians to non-violent struggle would change the perceptions of justice and injustice for the region and make it possible for Americans to side with Palestinian national rights without believing they are supporting the killing of Jews, which the American people will rightly never justify because of the Holocaust. Americans will not support another movement which kills Jews, who have already suffered so much. But Americans could support the independence and civil rights of the Palestinians if they practised non-violent struggle.

That could then be a crucial factor in shifting Israeli government policies because of the heavy economic dependency of Israel on the US and its close military ties with the US; disciplined and courageous non-violent resistance by Palestinians, while recognising the existence of Israel and its right to security, would remind Americans of Martin Luther King Jr and the non-violent civil rights movement, of Mohandas K. Gandhi and the Indian non-violent struggle for independence, and of the non-violent insurrection for democracy in the Philippines. Repeated brutal repression of non-violent Palestinians simply asking for acceptance of their right to live their own lives on a little piece of land would not be tolerated.

There would also be a variety of arenas through the United Nations and other means to express international supportive action.

No matter to what degree one may place confidence in these kinds of responsive shifts in internal Israeli politics and government policy or in international changes in attitudes and policies, it is crucial to recognise that the key factor in achieving change is the action of Palestinians. That is rooted in a policy of self-reliance and self-determination applied to the struggle for their rights itself. This means charting a new grand strategy of change, the heart of which would be the mobilisation of all the Palestinian people – men and women, young and old – to work to enrich and preserve Palestinian society and to engage in non-violent struggle to remove the barriers to recognition of their freedom and independence.

This does not mean, however, that people should simply go out and quickly begin non-violent demonstrations. Two things are very important. First, as indicated earlier, it is very important to plan a wise strategy of how the change is to be achieved by non-violent struggle. This will make it possible to choose specific forms of action and limited, smaller specific goals, involving the activities of certain people or everyone at particular places and times. In other words, strategic and tactical planning is essential if the action is to have the maximum impact.

Second, people launching a specific demonstration must also understand the nature of non-violent struggle and its requirements for effectiveness. Courageous action, not capitulation to repression, and maintaining non-violent discipline are among those requirements. Careful specific planning is also important. People contemplating launching non-violent action should carefully study these aspects, among others, and then make preparations accordingly. They should have an effective system of training the intended participants so that they act only in ways that contribute to the success of the struggle.

This policy has the potential of preserving and freeing the Palestinians as a people, while saving the other peoples of the Middle East and the world from a wider war. I do not see any other policy which has a chance of doing that.

VIII

Minutes of evidence taken before the Foreign Affairs Committee[1]

Chairman: Mr Safieh, on behalf of the Committee I would like to thank you very much indeed for agreeing to come before us this afternoon. You are the head of the PLO London Office?

Mr Safieh: Yes.

Chairman: We are extremely grateful to you for agreeing to our invitation and for coming here to help us with our continuing inquiry into the events in the Middle East. This Committee, as you know, has been looking at the impact first of the invasion of Kuwait and its aftermath, then at the prospects for resolving both the disputes in the region and, indeed, the hideous atrocities and violence that have taken place in several parts of the region, very much in the news recently in the mountains of Iraq. Meanwhile, Secretary Baker, the American Secretary of State, has been undertaking a series of visits to the region and we would like to discuss your review of his initiative in a moment. First, perhaps as you have done us the courtesy of agreeing to come and see us, we could do you the courtesy of asking if you would like to set the scene for us?

---

1.   Given in the House of Commons, Wednesday 21 April 1991. Members present: Mr David Howell in the Chair, Mr David Harris, Mr Michael Jopling, Mr Ivan Lawrence, Mr Ted Rowlands, Mr Peter Shore, Mr Bowen Wells, Mr Michael Welsh.

Mr Safieh: I would like you to know I consider it a great privilege for me to have this opportunity of addressing your distinguished Committee, the Select Committee on Foreign Affairs. As you can expect I was given specific instructions by President Yasser Arafat and Mr Kaddoumi to establish the best possible working relationship with all organs of the UK state and society, to promote the best possible understanding of our respective positions and a mutual understanding of our interests. As you might know, my people have some serious and legitimate grievances concerning British diplomacy in the twentieth century. I am not here to speak about the grievances but about the great expectations we have for the British role in an assertive quest, a decisive and serious quest, for peacemaking in the Middle East. We believe that for four different reasons the UK is extremely well equipped to play a dynamic role and we hope it will. The four reasons are as follows.

First, the UK has been the former mandatory power in Palestine and was present at the creation of the problem. In the late 1970s – and we witnessed it with great fascination — there was an important British role in the transition from the unacceptably racist Rhodesia to majority rule in independent Zimbabwe. We have been jealous of that role, hoping we will, one day, witness the same in the Middle East.

Second, the UK is a permanent member of the Security Council and we probably share the opinion that the UN Security Council should be the acceptable forum in the search for a resolution, since it can reconcile ethics and politics.

Three, the UK is a major player in the EEC framework itself, and we are happy about it emerging powerfully as an important element in our international system. We hope to live in a multipolar international system, rather than a monopolar international system.

The last reason is the privileged relationship between London and Washington. We have witnessed with great fascination the complex relation, the sort of mother/daughter relationship between the UK and USA, and hope in the future Washington will listen to London as London listens to Washington. We hope London will be the inspiring Athens of the contemporary Rome just like in the past. Two months after the beginning of the Gulf Crisis, I received a visit from a Palestinian student, a girl of twenty-two. The Gulf Crisis had inspired in her a poster showing the Palestinians carrying an olive branch to symbolise the quest for peace. The olive tree is a Mediterranean Palestinian tree and she said, 'I see a motto on that poster saying "We too have oil; olive oil."' I looked at her with great melancholy because I believe this motto is extremely painful, because if one reads between the lines and listens between the words, what it really means, we too have rights even though we happen not to have oil. Another friend of mine told me that in the Japanese language – and you know anything Japanese cannot be ignored lightly – the same word means 'crisis' and 'opportunity', and since we live in a tremendous moment of crisis it means we are also on the verge of an enormous window of opportunity.

Sir, we believe we have become, in a way, the Jews of the Israelis in the Middle East, yet we have moved beyond demanding absolute justice, we are just asking for possible justice. We believe the two-state solution will help us to move away from the winner/loser situation, the zero sum game, to a winner/winner situation. I want to end by quoting three of my favourite authors. The first is Isaac Deutscher, a Jewish Polish historian and philosopher who summarised his views in a parable of his own. He said it is a conflict between a person who had to jump from a building on fire and landed on another person whose back he broke, and unfortunately every time that second person tries to stand up he receives a beating. I thought this parable by Isaac Deutscher summarised well the Israeli-Palestinian dilemma. The second author was Hegel who wrote in a pessimistic diagnosis of the trajectory of mankind that from history we learn we have not learned from history. The third author is another Jew for whom I have great respect and affection, Nahum Goldmann, who was the leader of the World Jewish Organisation for four decades, who was commenting critically on Kissinger's shuttle diplomacy in the middle 1970s, and who said, 'sometimes diplomacy in the Middle East is the art of delaying the inevitable as long as possible.' For Nahum Goldmann, already in the middle of the 1970s, the inevitable was addressing the Palestinian dimension, the Palestinian factor and the Palestinian actor. So, the two quotations were 'from history we learn we have not learned from history' and the second quotation was 'sometimes diplomacy in the Middle East is the art of delaying the inevitable as long as possible.' Sir, I would like you to help history, which is now hesitant and undecided, to make the right choice, and to help us prove that those two authors were wrong – and I do not think they would mind.

Chairman: Thank you for those eloquent opening words setting out your feelings on these crucial issues so clearly. I am going to begin by asking you a question which I recognise is difficult, but it puzzles many of us and we need to get it out of the way. It relates to some of the events that have been going on in other areas of the Gulf region. You have spoken both now, and indeed the PLO have spoken, about the rejection of the acquisition of territories by force, the territory where Palestinians live and which I think you believe ought to be a home, a free state for the Palestinian people. You have always rejected that very clearly and yet when acquisition of Kuwait, the annexation of Kuwait by Iraq, by the most monstrous and open force, we felt we saw in the PLO a failure to condemn that outright. Were we seeing right or could you explain to us whether there is a contradiction there?

Mr Safieh: Sir, I am very happy that you have raised this issue. I think it is very relevant and legitimate that you raised that issue and it offers me the possibility of clarifying the PLO's attitude and the Palestinian position on this question. I happen to believe that we in the PLO have been, in a way, a sort of casualty of what I have called six months ago a constant deliberate misunderstanding. I believe, Sir, we could have done better in explaining our feelings and our position, so here I am being self-critical. We could have done a better job on the level of explaining our attitudes. Yet, Sir, everybody who knows that since Moment M Day One, Yasser Arafat activated himself with discreet diplomacy from August onwards in trying to obtain the Iraqi withdrawal out of all Kuwait, and in all fora we have always stipulated that any solution should incorporate Iraqi withdrawal out of Kuwait. I can recall that on 3 August, Arafat was with President Gadaffi in Libya and then visited President Mubarak in Alexandria and then went to Baghdad and then to Riyadh to meet King Fahd and in all the ideas that he was floating, Iraqi withdrawal out of Kuwait was the first, because, as you very rightly said, we, having been victims of occupation, could not endorse other people's occupation. Yet, Sir, on the day that the Arab summit meeting met in Cairo, which was 9 August, Arafat had one suggestion which, unfortunately, was not carried, and was not voted upon. That suggestion was the following: on the basis of President Mubarak's inaugural speech, and as you know, President Mubarak was extremely critical of Saddam's entry into Kuwait – he suggested that six heads of state from the Arab world, monarchs and presidents, would go to Baghdad to convince Saddam to withdraw. We believed that there was room for giving diplomacy a chance. We believed that the two issues which were controversial then between Kuwait and Iraq, the issues of finances and frontiers, could have been solved through diplomacy, sparing the area and the world the agonies of a war, and we have conveyed to the Kuwaiti people that we cared about them, probably much more than others who favoured a military option.

I am sure, Sir, that you are tormented as much as we are by seeing what happens now in both Kuwait and Iraq, where the state and the society are really torn apart and the casualties are enormous, maybe going beyond several years to repair. We believed, Sir, maybe naively, that there was room for a diplomatic endeavour and Arafat has activated himself, not only in the Arab world but also with some European interlocutors. I think you know, Sir, that Arafat has been instrumental in the early phases of the crisis in obtaining freedom of movement for the foreign citizens that were trapped in the regional dilemma. I am not asking that we should be thanked for that. It was our duty, because we feel that our people in the occupied territories are held hostage and we are against hostage-taking. I have often said, Sir, that people on television have seen Yasser Arafat kiss the cheeks of Saddam, but they have never bothered to know or to enquire what he was whispering in his ear. And believe you me, Sir, we were always lobbying, in Baghdad and elsewhere, for a diplomatic outcome.

We have at one moment believed that the linkage idea carried potential. We thought that linkage would solve two unacceptable situations – and I insist, two unacceptable situations – in one shot, one peaceful shot. We believed that flexibility on UN Resolution 242 might obtain flexibility and implementation on 660, and we thought that it was either linkage or war. Yet unfortunately, we all know what happened two months ago. War took place. Diplomacy was the wrong horse to bet upon, but believe me, Sir, diplomacy was the only horse we had made a bet on and I do not think we should be asked in any way to regret or apologise for having made that bet on diplomacy rather than on military warfare. Having asked me this question, I still remember the very interesting interview I had with Brian Hayes, one of the knowledgeable journalists on television. He asked me this question and I told him we, the Palestinians, are in favour of Arab unity, yet we are in favour of Arab unity by consent, not through coercion, and we prefer the Jean Monet approach to the Bismarck approach. I do not know how many of my audience on television understood that allusion, but speaking to your distinguished audience. I know you are all familiar, maybe with the person, but surely with the results of that person, Jean Monet. Integration by consent through consultations, rather than by occupation and coercion. That was our position from Moment M onwards. The blur or the confusion in perception I think emanated from the two overlapping problems. There was on one side, the problem of Iraq in Kuwait, which we disapproved of, but there was also overlapping the other problem which we thought was also distinct, not only resulting from, but also distinct from, which was the rapid deployment of foreign troops in the Peninsula. We were against the Iraqi presence in Kuwait but we were not in favour of the deployment of foreign troops, for understandable reasons. I do not think you would expect a national liberation movement in the Third World to endorse or approve the rapid deployment of superpower troops in a recently decolonised area. We were against the rapid deployment of troops. We thought it was an unnecessary complication that we could have done without, if ever the Arab machinery of the Arab League was given a chance to deploy its endeavours. Things went wrong. I believe that all actors, regional and international, involved in that crisis came out damaged, not only the PLO, and when I say 'not only the PLO' I admit and confess that the PLO came out damaged and needs some damage reparation. But I believe, and you might agree, that the UN came out also discredited, because there were certain manipulations or trespassing of the mandate of the UN. Superpower relationships came out damaged because of the condescending attitude of Bush at a certain moment when the Gorbachev initiative was there. Europe was another casualty. It did not emerge as a cohesive, independent player in the game. East-West relations, the Occident and the Orient: you have seen the uproar from Morocco to Malaysia, perceiving the event as being a sort of new version of a crusading exercise. I am not endorsing those perceptions but, as you know, a perception of reality, even if it is a false perception, is part of that reality. I believe that we all have to work in damage control. We, the Palestinians, of course, but others, too, and again I believe that Palestine offers us the possibility for damage control. Just as in the Gulf Crisis, Palestine could have been the solution for once, and not the problem through the linkage approach. Again Palestine can be an opportunity for the reconciliation of the West and the East. Do not, Sir, be under the illusion that you have excellent relations with the Arab World and the Third World and the Islamic World. Good relations with rulers do not necessarily mean good relations with the people concerned, or to use a concept of Western terminology, with the civil society. I believe that Palestine is an area where the authentic, genuine reconciliation between the Christian World and Islam, the West and the East, can take place. Having seen the West go into a war to discipline a misbehaving regional actor, Iraq – and I am clear in my words, calling it a misbehaving actor – the Arab World, the Islamic World, will not understand if there is still, tomorrow, patience which resembles indulgence, which resembles and borders on complacency towards that other misbehaving regional actor – Israel – that has been tormenting the area for so long, with so many UN resolutions accumulated and unimplemented. So we believe that Palestine is again a solution for a sort of cross-fertilisation in the dialogue of civilisations, the new world order that we dream about, and we are ready to be extremely cooperative in any quest for a better world.

Mr Lawrence: You were actually asked, Mr Safieh, if you could explain the apparent contradiction between the PLO's insistence on the inadmissibility of acquiring territory by force and the PLO's failure to condemn Saddam Hussein, and I think you have explained that Mr Arafat behaved impeccably in his relationship to Saddam Hussein. Would we, therefore, be right in supposing that at the PLO Central Committee now being held in Tunis they will be commending Mr Arafat for the position that he adopted towards Saddam Hussein?

Mr Safieh: First of all, you have put words in my mouth that I have not used. I started by answering the Chairman, by saying maybe there was room for improvement in our performance, and I was being self-critical as I was ever accustomed to be. I think Yasser Arafat's leadership is very comfortable within the Palestinian people as a whole, mainly among the Palestinian people in the occupied territories, and there is no challenge, to my knowledge, nor in the meeting taking place in Tunis by Central Council members, which, as you know, is the miniature of our Parliament in Exile.

Sir, I would like you to understand how we see it. Maybe we do not see eye to eye. Arafat is our de Gaulle. He incarnates our national dignity as being the architect of our collective resurrection. He has struggled against foes and friends so as to keep the rank of Palestine and of the Palestinians undiminished. Sir, you probably know that Churchill speaking of the other de Gaulle, the first one, the real one, said, 'Of all the crosses I have had to carry, the Cross of Lorraine was the heaviest' and the Cross of Lorraine was the symbol of the French Resistance. So I guess many actors in the game sometimes find us and find Yasser Arafat difficult to deal with, yet he is like the other de Gaulle, one of the heavy crosses to bear. I believe Arafat has a historical role and is a historical necessity for the peacemaking endeavour that we are now undertaking. He is the protector of the pragmatic tendency outside and inside Palestine. The pragmatic tendency would be orphaned if Arafat was no longer the leader of the PLO. I believe that Arafat is truly committed to those statements he made in 1988 in Geneva and before that in Stockholm, and that should be music to your ears, Sir.

The challenge today is the following: when you hear that we, the Palestinians, are ready to respect our commitments stated in front of the international community, the challenge is to see whether the international community is ready to respect its commitments to us. I told you, Sir, we have tried to move beyond historical revenge. We became the Jews of Israelis, yet we do not want them to become the Palestinians of the Palestinians. We are no longer asking for absolute justice but to produce a solution which will be a winner/winner solution. We expect that Jews should be the most supportive for our quest for statehood and sovereignty. Let me be frank, and I always try to be glasnostically transparent; I am making a display of my emotions. With great fascination I have seen in recent contemporary history, Germany rightly so – and I emphasise rightly so – apologising and re-apologising to Jews for atrocities perpetrated. Then two years ago, with fascination I saw Vaclav Havel, the President of Czechoslovakia, apologise to the Germans for the maltreatment by Czechoslovakia of its German minority after the Second World War, and then I heard with fascination Mrs Margaret Thatcher apologising to Czechoslovakia because of the policy of appeasement that left Czechoslovakia to the territorial appetite of Hitler. Those were fascinating moments. I want to ask you, and you in particular, Mr Lawrence, do you not think, hopefully soon, somebody owes us – we the Palestinians – historical apologies? Do you not think the Israelis today, instead of insulting us or denying our existence, rights and sufferings, should be telling us, 'Sorry, please, and thank you'? You know, much more than I do, that Israel could not have been created without us paying a heavy collective human price. Israel was created, we have paid the price. We are not asking for revenge. We have become unreasonably reasonable; encourage us. The pro-Israelis and the

Jewish communities in the Diaspora should be the first to be the most supportive because of this factor of historical responsibility. I am avoiding the concept of guilt because I do not believe in guilt, individual or collective, hereditary or non-hereditary. It is the moment today, Mr Chairman, to have these soul-searching exercises. We are doing soul-searching exercises in Tunis, amongst others, also in London and elsewhere; others should do it too. You should encourage it.

Chairman: If you ask Mr Lawrence too many questions none of us will get a word in. Just a brief question – Mr Lawrence.

Mr Lawrence: As part of your soul-searching exercise, consistent with your peaceful inclinations, can you explain to us why Mr Arafat and the PLO still stand behind the covenant upon which your movement is based, which calls for the arms struggle in Article 7, aimed at the elimination of Zionism in Palestine. Article 15, and arms struggle is the only way to liberate Palestine? Are those still the aims of the PLO or are you renouncing the covenant which up to this moment President Arafat and everybody else, as you have called him, has upheld? Will you do some soul searching?

Mr Safieh: If we do it together, I am ready to constantly and continuously do it. Mr Chairman, I am very happy that the ball came back to Mr Lawrence because he has raised very important issues that I want to clarify in front of you.

Mr Lawrence: Can you answer it?

Mr Safieh: Yes, sure. The peaceful inclination of Arafat, which I do not doubt, having worked with him from 1978–81 as a member of his cabinet in charge of European affairs and UN institutions, and having accompanied him between 1988–90 on several of his trips, including his trip to Strasbourg where he addressed the Euro Parliamentarians, and I still remember him telling the press and the Euro Parliamentarians, 'I extend my hand in peace hoping that an Israeli de Gaulle will seize it.' Today, with regret, we have to confess not only did no Israeli de Gaulle emerge, but not even an Israeli de Klerk. A de Klerk would have been good enough to start the snowball process. Concerning the covenant, Sir, the covenant was written in 1964 and amended once, and that was it, in 1968. It is a reflection of our political culture and political thinking of the 1960s, yet as you know, Sir, in law when the same authoritative body adopts at different moments equally important documents, the most recent abrogates the one that was adopted prior to that. The most recent document which we have adopted, which for us is the most important, is our proclamation of independence which we adopted, Sir, in 1988. In that proclamation of independence in 1988, we speak of the two-state solution, so in a way every item in our charter which contradicts the proclamation of independence should be considered by you and me as being abrogated.

Mr Lawrence: Why do you not renounce it?

Mr Safieh: That is the legal interpretation, Sir, as any legal expert can tell you. I happened to be with Arafat when he visited Mitterrand in the Elysée a year and a half ago when he said that those specific items are *caduc*, which is another legal term of Latin origin to say abrogation. Believe me, I do not think that any legal document is an obstacle to peace because, as you probably know, the Herout Party, which is the major component of Likud, which is the governing party in Israel, has a party anthem, Mr Chairman, which says the following – so whenever they are assembled, the Herout Party, anywhere, like here, they sing the following song: 'The Jordan River has two banks, the West Bank is ours, so is the East Bank.' It means King Hussein's East Bank, yet I do not remember either us or King Hussein asking Mr Shamir and Mr Sharon to abandon and declare *caduc*, their party anthem, to become acceptable interlocutors and acceptable negotiating partners. Number two, Sir, concerning the armed struggle, you well know, Sir, that in our strategic thinking, we aspired for one moment to become a military actor so that we could aspire to become a diplomatic factor. The more you have of diplomatic interaction and transaction, the less you will have violence and military struggle. I hope that today we will move as far as possible, Mr Chairman, from the era of the gladiators to the era of the negotiators. We invite the other side, Sir, to abandon, like us, the dialogue by arms and to adopt the arms of dialogue; we are ready. I would like to be on record, Sir, in this distinguished gathering, I want to be on record as saying that we the Palestinian people, we the PLO, are ready for negotiations now, we are ready for peace now, and those who do not yet trust us can test us.

Chairman: I want to get on to the specific strategies and the way the PLO sees the present situation. I know Mr Shore has some questions. Mr Jopling, did you want another question on this general theme?

Mr Jopling: I want to come back, if we can, to one sentence replies and I think my question will encourage that. Could you tell me, very simply, did the PLO condemn the invasion of Kuwait, and if it did would you be kind enough to send us chapter and verse of that condemnation?

Mr Safieh: In the Arab Summit Meeting which took place on 9 August in Cairo, that is a week exactly after the beginning of the crisis and the invasion of Kuwait, Yasser Arafat expressed reservations on the resolution submitted. Apparently, the Arab League's voting behaviour is yes, no, abstention and reservation. He explained his vote by saying: 'It is because this resolution at the same time condemns Iraq and endorses the deployment of foreign forces, this is why I feel incapable of voting on it.' Sir, I will send you all relevant documents. In all the proposals, written and verbal, we have submitted, Iraqi withdrawal out of Kuwait was always item number one, we are on record on that. The one point or proposal we addressed where we addressed the territorial issue – again the acquisition of territory – we spoke of a way out through the process of leasing, renting, the Island of Bubiyan, which would remain under Kuwaiti sovereignty. So you can see implicitly, Mr Chairman, when you say, 'We would like the Iraqi withdrawal out of Kuwait and as a possible solution the sort of renting, leasing, of the island so that Iraq can have the access it wants to the open sea,' that island in our proposal would have remained under Kuwaiti sovereignty, and I think it is sufficiently convincing that at no moment did we endorse the Iraqi presence and occupation of Kuwait. As I told you, there are two overlapping problems that blurred perceptions and created the confusion that we are all now familiar with.

Mr Jopling: Can I please return to my question, which was: did the PLO condemn it? I take it from your answer that it is really no?

Mr Safieh: I think that is a very partial perception and understanding of what I said.

Mr Jopling: You said you had reservations about it. I asked you whether it had been condemned and I take it from your answer that you did not condemn it?

Mr Safieh: Sir, if I am allowed to answer in three sentences: we did not endorse it. All our endeavours tended to obtain the Iraqi withdrawal out of Kuwait peacefully, and I believe that the war that took place was, in our opinion – and I do not think we are mistaken – unwise, having left Iraq and Kuwait in very unliveable situations. We believe that we were not sufficiently helped in our diplomatic endeavours to explore every possible avenue to obtain an equitable solution on the basis of UN resolutions without going into warfare. So we never endorsed; we always wanted to obtain the reversal of the situation.

Chairman: I have a feeling we are not going to get much further on this particular point, so I will ask Mr Shore to pursue different aspects, particularly how other Palestinians have reacted to the outcome of all this, which did not turn out the way I think Yasser Arafat wanted in the first place.

Mr Shore: I would like to come to that a little bit later but I think many people have felt that at least one casualty of the Gulf War was the credibility of the PLO as an international actor, and I would like to put to you two or three points on this to have your response. Of course, Iraq did not just invade Kuwait; it did its utmost to wreak damage on the State of Israel. Indeed, both in propaganda and in actual weapons and blows, it aimed its attack at the State of Israel as well. The perception of the PLO leadership in the face of these actions by Saddam Hussein was one of approval of what Saddam Hussein was doing in relation to the State of Israel. This would seem to me to have been a total reverse of the attitude that the PLO had taken up during the past two years, in which they had said they had accepted the existence of Israel and were seeking a peaceful solution to the disagreements between themselves and the Palestinians. What do you say to that point, first?

Mr Safieh: I will try to answer you, Sir, by saying that apparently you are unaware of the endeavours deployed by the PLO so that no outside military operations take place in the European theatre and elsewhere. I am just telling you that for the record, Sir. Number two, Sir, test us and let us analyse the PLO's behaviour on matters where we were directly involved, and I would like to quote the Israeli author, the specialist, Zeev Chieef, on military affairs of the newspapers *Haaretz*, who made a whole book on the Israel/ Palestinian wars in Lebanon, or on the Lebanese theatre and mainly on the ceasefire agreement that was concluded in 1981 between Israel and the Palestinians through the good auspices of Philip Habib, the special envoy of President Reagan and the UN. There, Zeev Chieef will tell you that for a long eleven months, the PLO totally and scrupulously respected its commitment and no violation of the ceasefire took place. There were Israeli attacks to violate the ceasefire agreement, and you remember General Sharon took the incident of London, which was perpetrated by Abu Nidal, to consider it as a *casus belli* and invade Lebanon. Sir, I think that this period of 1981, the ceasefire agreement which we consented to and the scrupulous respect that we had for that ceasefire agreement because of our voluntary volition and agreement around it, is the test to see PLO credibility for now and the future. We respect commitments we make. We are not responsible for the behaviour or misbehaviour of others. We are not responsible for others. We are responsible for our behaviour and in our bipolar Israeli/Palestinian relationships you have to admit with me that we are the occupied and not the occupiers. It is Palestinian blood irrigating Palestinian soil.

Mr Jopling: I understand that. But you would say that it was unfair for international observers to say that the Palestinian movement was greatly tempted by the possible prospect of an Iraqi military success and Iraq fulfilling their own ambitions to lead to the liberation of Palestine?

Mr Safieh: Sir, I think it is very unrealistic that anyone in the Arab world would have thought of Iraqi military success. A non-defeat would have been a very superb scenario for those who supported whatever. Please allow me to explain the relationship between Palestine and Cairo and Palestine and Baghdad. For two decisive years, 1988 and 1990, we strategically cooperated with Egypt – and I happen to belong to the Egyptophile wing of the PLO – yet

Egypt, because of its vulnerabilities, economic vulnerabilities and demographic vulnerabilities, treated us the way it treated itself ten years ago during the Camp David agreement; that is, each time there was a blockage in the negotiating process it turned to us to offer the concession needed to lubricate the process of diplomatic transaction. It treated us the way it had treated itself ten years earlier. So at one moment at the beginning of 1990 we thought, that is the Palestinian political community, that the rapprochement also with Iraq, but keeping the relationship with Egypt, would be successful, so that the Israelis will see that we are looking for peace, not from a position of weakness, but from a position of relative strength, having other options available. We wanted to invest Iraqi capabilities peacefully to improve the bargaining position on the negotiating table, and I give you a proof. In May 1990 – and do not trust me, please; send one of your researchers to look at that – there was an Arab summit meeting in Baghdad after a horrible massacre in Palestine. You remember the nine workers shot by a pseudo-mentally deranged person. In that summit meeting and in Baghdad, Yasser Arafat again convinced his colleagues, the Arab heads of state and monarchs, to endorse the two-state solution for Palestine. That is my proof, Sir, to you that we wanted in a way to create a new strategic diplomatic situation where Iraqi capabilities would be invested as a bargaining chip on the negotiating table. We were not the ones that inspired the occupation of Kuwait. We were not in favour of that. We thought it was a total diversion and wanted to go to the negotiating table and wanted strategically to co-operate with Cairo and Baghdad at the same time, but apparently at moments such equidistance is difficult to achieve.

Mr Jopling: Could I ask one more question on the general attitude of the PLO and, indeed, its attitude to Saddam Hussein? All right, Mr Arafat kissed him on both cheeks but also whispered in his ear. At the recent conference now going on in Tunis, do you know whether there has been any mention at all of the plight of the Kurds? Does the PLO have sympathy for the Kurds as a suppressed people who seek autonomy and self-government, and they have made that concern articulate? They have articulated it and made it public.

Mr Safieh: Sir, I want you to know that just as for Kuwait I care about the Kurds much more than any of those in the outside world who pretend to, and I want you to know that on Arafat's specific initiative, the decision was taken for the Palestinian Red Crescent, which has enormous experience of working in disaster areas, to go immediately to Kurdistan to try to help the international endeavours, to alleviate the plight of the Kurdish populations in the mountains. So two days ago, on the initiative of Arafat, the Palestinian Red Crescent was instructed to move directly to send its medical personnel – and they have enormous experience in disaster areas – to try and alleviate the situation of the plight of the Kurdish populations. And, Sir, we are in favour of democracy and decentralisation in Iraq. We are in favour, and we would like to see a situation where the Kurdish people has the full expression of its cultural identity within the framework of the territorial integrity of Iraq. I believe they have often been victims of external manipulations, and I believe that negotiations taking place now in Iraq will hopefully bring to fruition a more liveable situation, a better interaction between the Arab population of Iraq and the Kurdish population of Iraq within the framework of a unitary state, but decentralised with autonomy and cultural expression for all communities. Yes, of course.

Mr Jopling: I am very grateful for that information and if you have got any actual statement by Mr Arafat on the problems of the Kurds and the sympathy the PLO has for them, I would be very grateful if you could send that to the Committee. I have now just one further question to put to you, and it is really in relation to the effect of the Gulf Crisis on the Palestinians in territories other than the West Bank, i.e. territories in the Middle East generally. What has been the effect on Palestinians of the Gulf War in Jordan and Lebanon, for example?

Mr Safieh: Again, Sir, extremely negative. As I told other distinguished audiences; the Palestinians have been a major casualty of that crisis in the Gulf from Moment M, Day One, 2 August 1990. Just to take the Palestinian community in Kuwait, which numbered on that day 400,000, we now have around 140,000 still in Kuwait, the remnants have already migrated, seeking more hospitable shores. Some of them are now unemployed in Jordan and many have left to go to Canada, Australia and the USA. They were a hard-working community that contributed enormously to the state building and the institution building of the Gulf and Kuwait. They took part in all areas of work, from education to medication, from culture to agriculture, they were there in the banking system and the university, the state bureaucracy and the state apparatus. 240,000 of them have left Kuwait and are elsewhere, either unemployed or still seeking jobs. They used to send remittances to the Palestinians of the West Bank, Gaza and Lebanon, which are the poorest social classes the Palestinians have. Sir, even though I am not talking in details about it, Amnesty International issued a report of some excesses, which I hope will be terminated soon, that have taken place. It is painful for me to speak about it but I am sure you are familiar with the Amnesty report. So, Sir, many institutions, also in the Occupied Territories, which used to receive subsidies either from the Palestinian Diaspora communities in the Gulf or from government or non-government Gulf institutions, up to now have been deprived of the financial aid they used to receive. You will no doubt know that we live in a situation of deteriorating economic situations under occupation, which is totally unfavourable to the process of peace that we both would like to see being triggered.

Let me tell you, Sir, I believe that our relationships with the Arab World will be improved, and much faster than many would have expected. Let me tell you that our relations with Egypt have already tremendously improved. There have been several executive committee members on our side who visited Egypt recently and had meetings with Ismat Abdul Magid, the Foreign Minister, and Ossam al-Baz, the Diplomatic Adviser to President Mubarak. We are supporting the Egyptian candidate for the Arab League's Secretary General and we think that an Egyptian now at the head of the Arab League will work seriously to heal the rift that took place in the Arab League machinery. You are not without knowing that six plus two makes only eight, and that the Arab state system is made of 21, so we are not as isolated as some would like to project the image. Six plus two makes eight out of 21; with the others we have kept excellent relations, and even with the six plus two relations, Sir, were never interrupted. I think the Cairo relations will be healed within a month and that will pave the way back to Riyadh, and access to Riyadh means the entire Gulf system.

Chairman: If the Palestinians feel sympathy for the Kurds and if, as a result of Saddam Hussein's direct action, such great suffering has been imposed on Palestinians, are some of them not a bit critical of Mr Arafat for having tried to deal with Saddam Hussein in a more gentle manner, and are people not now saying to your leadership, 'For goodness sake, let us have a firmer line against Saddam Hussein'? Are they not saying that?

Mr Safieh: Sir, we are now re-Palestinianising our thinking, our endeavour, our planning and our interaction, and I think you should advise us in that direction. Our concern, Sir, is how to find an acceptable, durable, equitable solution to the Israeli-Palestinian dilemma. To us, the entire Gulf Crisis was a diversion that made us lose time – you say credibility – and now pushes us into the process of damage control and damage reparation. You should help us, Sir, to refocus again on the Israeli-Palestinian dimension. We have to work on how to improve the economic conditions of the Palestinians under occupation, how to help trigger a peace process for which, as I told you, we are totally available to be extremely cooperative to bring it to fruition. That, we hope to put behind us. Sir, help us in that. Let us go beyond the war in the Gulf, towards the quest for peace in the Middle East.

Mr Wells: In view of that statement, in retrospect would you not have thought it best for the leadership of the PLO not to take sides in the dispute between Baghdad and other Arab countries, Syria, Egypt and Saudi Arabia in particular? Do you not think it was a mistake to side, or appear to side, with Saddam Hussein?

Mr Safieh: I think all actors in the area had very little room for manoeuvre. We live, Sir, in an era of shrinking options. I might have certain suggestions, maybe of a cosmetic nature, how our performance could have been better projected and better understood, but it took place. We are now almost at the end of April 1991, let us face the challenge of the 1990s now in the Middle East. I think a more liveable Middle East needs and necessitates a resolved Palestinian-Israeli conflict which Mr Hurd has called the 'unfinished business'. Let us, Sir, try to explore how we can address that unfinished business of Israel and Palestine. As long as that solution is not found, there will be the seeds for future frictions, tensions, instabilities and destabilisation. Sir, let us put this behind us – it took place. I think we are not the only ones that should be blushing, Sir, and I mean it; many other actors should have longer beards than Yasser Arafat to hide their blushing cheeks for what took place in that area. Let me not enter into details.

Chairman: I do not think the Committee will dispute that last remark at all. Now, we have heard as a result of questions by Mr Lawrence earlier what the PLO's current position is on the right of Israel to exist and so on, let us now turn to your strategies and then finally to the current policies and the reaction of Secretary Baker.

Mr Rowlands: If I may just ask as a preliminary: it is now quite clear that PLO supports at least an Israeli state on pre-1967 boundaries. The question that arises is what further security assurances can be given to that state? That also is much coloured by PLO attitudes in the way it now conducts its affairs from here on, in particular its belief in intifada and bringing pressure to bear on the Israeli government and, as previous questions have indicated, the whole question of whether in fact its sincerity and integrity in the security of an Israeli state can be confirmed in the strongest possible way. First of all, do you think, if there was a PLO state or homeland established on the West Bank and Gaza, it itself could be demilitarised, or with minimum military presence, and what security arrangements would you suggest and offer in any international settlement to the 1967 boundary Israeli state?

Mr Safieh: Thank you very much, Sir, for this set of questions. I believe, Sir, that once the Palestinian people obtain statehood, sovereignty and independence, we will all become a *status quo* actor in the area, because we will have an interest, and our enlightened national interest will dictate that Palestine becomes the *status quo* actor that we would like to become. Any military provocation in the future will be a re-invitation for Israel to re-occupy the Occupied Territories.

Mr Rowlands: Give us some practical thoughts on that.

Mr Safieh: Yes, Sir. Concerning the militarisation of the state, I think it would accept as a sovereign decision to have a minimum of military capability, because we do not believe any more in military options in the area. We would like to have what is needed for that state to ensure the law and order within it and not beyond. Number two, Sir, we are ready to accept the stationing of UN forces on our Palestinian territory if the other side does not want them to be also on theirs, and we will accept – so as not to fall into the trap which led to the 1967 War – that the removal of those UN troops stationed on our territory does not necessitate the demand only of the host country, but the unanimous consent of the Security Council. You know to what I am alluding. I am alluding to the 1967 period when Abdul Nasser asked U Thant to remove the UN troops from the Sinai, hoping to get 'No' for an answer, got 'Yes' as an answer and this snowballed into triggering the 1967 War. So to avoid that trajectory, that vicious circle, the departure of those troops would need more than the individual demand of the host country but the unanimous consent of the Security Council. Sir, we believe that those two countries will have to interact on the economic and cultural level enormously, and I believe that those two states will have in the future to opt for what I call vertical expansion instead of horizontal expansion, and I usually add that since both communities believe they belong to the chosen ones, maybe God will be more tolerant of our trespassing on His field! So I think the two-state solution is a wonderful idea for mutual containment. As you know, both our societies have shown extreme dynamism and sometimes excessive vitality, and the two-state solution is a formula of mutual containment. We are ready to accept any other proposal for tranquilising and securing the area that does not imply territorial acquisition.

Anyway the Scud missiles showed that territorial rectification or territorial acquisition does not give added security by giving added strategic depth. We believe that security for Israel comes not from territorial aggrandisement, but from regional acceptance, and we are the key to regional acceptance. The Israelis know that they can be either in the West Bank or in the Middle East. As long as they obstinately want to remain in the West Bank, they are not yet in the Middle East. Once they withdraw from the West Bank, they can be incorporated in the Middle East.

I believe, Sir, that also in the future we can explore formulae taken from the EEC experience or the Benelux experience for regional co-operation and economic integration in the area, and I think, to our mutual advantage, we will be also aiming for that, an Israel/Palestine/Jordan confederal link or economic co-operation as a desirable outcome. We say it proudly with self-confidence. We do not think we are destined and condemned to remain the eternal Luxembourg of the triangle, even though Luxembourg is in a very enviable situation. But we believe that having a minority in Israel and a numerical majority in Jordan, we are not condemned to remain the junior partner of any triangular exercise.

Mr Rowlands: So if I can get a summary of your response, you are saying, first of all, that an Israeli state at 1967 boundaries is accepted by the PLO, and in addition to that, that there are a variety of other confidence-building measures, if you like, that could be built upon into the agreement to ensure the security of that Israeli state, including minimum militarisation of the Palestinian homeland, a major presence which could not be removed unilaterally and other possible measures on which you would welcome suggestions? In the light of this moderate position that you offer, should not the conduct now of the PLO, as we are entering this phase of important diplomacy by Mr Baker and others now seeking to try to end the deadlock and the logjam on the PLO attitudes on the West Bank and in the Gaza, be shoring up this moderation, and violence in language or, indeed, in action at this moment in time could be totally counterproductive? Has the PLO thought through the tactics and its strategy from now on in this respect?

Mr Safieh: First of all, thank you for calling me a moderate. I personally prefer the word 'pragmatist' or 'realist' or 'idealistic realist', and I believe that peace should also be concluded one day between the immoderates on both sides. I do not believe that we are being these days vehement or vociferous. I am really surprised, as an external observer also of the realities of the Middle East, by the Palestinian self-restraint, knowing the tragic, unacceptable, inadmissible situation in which the Palestinians live, either in Palestine or in Lebanon. I am surprised by the degree of self-restraint they have exercised upon themselves, and I have not noticed either vociferation or vehemence in the literature we are producing, nor in the behaviour we are showing. Yet I agree there is a need to rework the phraseology, and I believe that in the Arab world as a whole, we need to rethink our discourse, and the phraseology of the 1950s is no more adequate to cope with the challenges and the opportunities of the 1990s. Sir, you mentioned that we recognise the State of Israel in its pre-1967 borders and I am happy to emphasise this, and we do that on the basis of mutual recognition and not unilateral recognition, as I am sure you are aware. Yasser Arafat, speaking in Geneva, spoke also on behalf of the state we proclaimed in Algeria. So, Sir, it was not only the PLO recognising the State of Israel; it was the State of Palestine, Arafat on behalf of the State of Palestine, that was recognising the State of Israel, and we are in favour of mutual recognition between the two states. It is not the national liberation movement recognising Israel, it is the State of Palestine which we proclaimed. Some say, 'You dream. The State does not in reality exist.' I know the specificity of the PLO. We are not, like others, an authority on a demography on a geography. The authority is in exile, the demography is scattered; and the geography is occupied. This is one of the reasons for our specific situation. Yet I believe that Palestine is resurrecting today and I always say to my audience, we in the Holy Land have had some previous experience in Resurrection!

Mr Rowlands: Finally, one of the additional assurances of security to Israel would be the underpinning of this whole arrangement, particularly by the United States and possibly by the European Community, but I think the United States would be the primary reinforcement of that assurance. We have talked about the UN role in any such arrangement. Would the active involvement and underwriting, even the occasional physical presence, of a US force of some kind as exists – and we have forgotten about it – in the Sinai Desert at this moment in time as a result of the Jewish settlement of Egypt – would the PLO accept that as a further underpinning and reinforcement of any security arrangement?

Mr Safieh: Sir, if this can pave the way to an acceptable peace with a Palestinian state emerging beside Israel, this would be welcomed. Let me tell you, there was a debate in the middle of the 1970s in American political science magazines on the need for a formal military alliance between the United States and Israel as a tranquilising factor concerning Israeli security. I do not know if you know that those who torpedoed that idea of a formal alliance between the United States and Israel were the Israelis themselves because, as Peres mentioned one day, both had an advantage in Israel remaining the undisciplined ally. I would welcome such a formula of an American guarantee and, if need be, an American presence as tranquilising factor if this can bring us, the Palestinians, a two-state solution in previously mandated Palestine. Why not? If that is the necessary prerequisite for peace, why not?

Chairman: Now let us turn to where we are now, which is the Baker initiative and the attempt to tackle at the same time both the Palestine issue which we are discussing and, more broadly,

Arab/Israeli relations, all within a regional conference network, hopefully with the Soviet Union and United States presiding at the top. We would like to ask some detailed questions on how you react to all that.

Mr Harris: First of all, on the Baker initiative, what is the PLO's attitude to the twin-track proposals and also to the idea of a regional peace conference?

Mr Safieh: Sir, we have enormously facilitated the Baker endeavour of 1989. If you remember, then there were the ten points of President Mubarak and the five points of Secretary of State Baker, and if you remember well, then it was the Israeli side that torpedoed them and they had a governmental crisis. The National Coalition Government made by Likud and Labour crumbled. Labour was incapable of making the coalition building, and Shamir came back to power in Israel with the indispensable coalition partners recruited from the extreme right wing. Now, again we are favourably inclined and are facilitating the quest for peace triggered by the Baker shuttle diplomacy.

You are not without knowing that he has already met three times Mr Faisal Husseini and his colleagues in East Jerusalem, and each time Faisal Husseini and his colleagues consulted with President Yasser Arafat in Tunis, and approval was given for the principle of the meeting. Instructions were given for the agenda of the meeting and for the composition of the Palestinian delegation – all this with the knowledge of Mr Baker. I have always said that the key to peace and war in the Middle East resides in Washington, and I have always said that the best American president for us would be one that combines the following prerequisites: he would have the ethics of a Carter, the popularity of a Reagan and the strategic audacity of a Nixon. From the very beginning we had a very favourable prejudice concerning Bush and Baker. First of all, they are an excellent team who work harmoniously, unlike previous administrations. Secondly, they do not owe their election to a certain lobby in Washington. Thirdly, their popularity today, whatever the nature and reason of that popularity, allows them to confront a lobby that would like to obstruct their endeavour. You are not without knowing, we in the Arab World believe, that Capitol Hill is a sort of other Israeli Occupied Territory that needs to be liberated. We believe that President Bush, secure on the level of his popularity and his electorate, could be a decisive factor.

Sir, we are favourably inclined, yet we have certain reservations. The Regional Conference now proposed is well beneath the International Conference that the UK and we have always thought as desirable. We have a favourable prejudice concerning Mr Bush and Mr Baker and we facilitated their endeavours in 1989, and we will be trying to be extremely cooperative now in the process being triggered. Yet I believe, Sir, there is a difference between the International Conference, which you and us were in favour of, and the Regional Conference idea which is now being floated. In fact three major differences, with your permission. The first one is that the UN is out, the second is that Europe is uninvolved and the third is that the PLO is not incorporated in the exercise. We believe that those three actors, their input and their presence, are of historical importance. Now, apparently, Mr Baker is talking to Mr Faisal Husseini, and they are starting to speak of a conference instead of a Regional Conference to have a sort of constructive ambiguity; they are no longer saying it is an International Conference or a Regional Conference, they are calling it a conference. I believe that Mr Baker is trying, in a way, to incorporate the European involvement, which we welcome and favour. The principle of the necessity of having the Palestinian delegation representing the Palestinian Diaspora and the Palestinians under occupation is becoming increasingly accepted by the Americans.

We believe, Sir, that the indivisibility of the Palestinian people is something sacred and for Israel the window of opportunity is not the fact that there are Palestinians ready to talk peace with them, but the entire Palestinian national movement. Palestinian nationalism as a whole is ready to move towards historical compromise. For us Palestinians, the presence of a delegation representing the occupied Palestinians and the Diaspora Palestinians is a historical necessity. Historically, symbolically, it is extremely important for Israel too. I do not believe, that he has concluded his consultations. He has already accepted the principle that the Palestinians consult with the PLO leadership since it is their political address. In a way, Mr Baker is accepting that the political authority and legitimacy stem from the inner workings of the PLO machine. Mr Chairman, I have often said the PLO is at the same time an institution and an idea. In the institution, 10,000 persons work, but the five million Palestinians are the powerful vehicles of the idea, which is extremely simple. It is our sense of identity and our ceaseless quest for self-determination and sovereignty.

Sir, let me move to another point. I believe that if the local actors are left to themselves, we will never achieve an acceptable compromise; we need external prodding. Here again allow me, Mr Chairman, to quote Nahum Goldmann who speaks in one of his books of a discussion he had with General Moshe Dayan and he tells Moshe: 'The Americans give you much aid and some advice, you take all the aid and you leave the advice aside. What will happen if America was to tell you, you can have the aid only if you take also the advice?' and apparently Moshe, with resignation, told him, 'Then we will have also to take their advice.' This is why I believe that the Americans should be more decisive and assertive than they have been up to now. If ever they were to link – and you see linkage again has potential – aid and advice, I think we would move faster towards peace. You know, Sir, it was said by political scientists that democracies have difficulties waging war and they have difficulties also undertaking peace. Israel today has an internal blockage, it is a 50/50 society, composed by half which is unwilling, and the other half which is incapable of moving towards peace. We need external encouragement which can come from Europe and the USA. I believe that when the Americans decide to couple and to link aid and advice, we will move forward much faster. I believe, Sir, that Europe has a role. You know what Dean Acheson once said after the Second World War, speaking of the UK, but it is also relevant to Europe: 'The UK or Europe has lost an empire but is still looking for a role.' We believe, Sir, that we in the Middle East have a role but are still looking for an actor. Without external intervention the local actors will not move towards peace.

If you allow me to add one sentence to Mr Rowland's question: we are ready to offer all confidence-building measures that are being asked of us reasonably. Like I said, the other side today, Sir, should offer us some confidence-building measures. Allow me to mention a few which will help facilitate the process. I believe, Sir, that the stoppage and cessation of settlement building should occur as an encouragement and inducement for peace. There should be an immediate opening of universities that have been closed for the last three years, leaving 20,000 students out of the university campuses. I believe the thousands of Palestinian detainees sentenced in court, or administratively detained without a trial, should also be released.

Sir, there is another problem that no one asked me about, and that is the problem of Soviet Jewish migration. Mr Chairman, we the Palestinians are very committed to the principles of the freedom of movement of ideas and individuals. We believe that this should be double-way traffic, also one day, hopefully, applying also to us. We believe, Sir, that the massive arrival of Soviet Jews and the installation of many of them in the Occupied Territories is damaging and harming the prospects for peace. Let me tell you, Sir, that I have confidential information that a very significant proportion of those Soviet Jews are of Christian belief. It is easy today in Moscow, with fifty roubles, because of the economic shortages and the economic uncertainties and political upheavals, to falsify forged papers showing Jewish ancestry. Today, Sir, Palestine is receiving, and when I speak of Palestine, I mean Gaza and the West Bank and East Jerusalem, thousands of Soviet Jews settling in settlements that have been illegally created contrary to the Fourth Geneva Convention. I believe that those three or four suggestions I have made would be extremely helpful as confidence-building measures, as signals coming to us from the other side.

Chairman: Those are very interesting charges and you have described the PLO's attitude both to the Baker initiative and the form of representation you would like. Do you want to pursue that, Mr Harris?

Mr Harris: Very quickly. Coming back to the PLO Peace Conference, I take it from what you said that the PLO would insist on Palestinians outside the Occupied Territories? How would the members of the Palestinian delegation be selected?

Mr Safieh: I personally believe, as I said earlier, the opportunity for peace in Israel is that Palestinian nationalism is ready for a historical compromise; you make peace with your enemy, not with your friend. I believe that diplomacy is like football, no one single side can be authorised to pick and choose the members of the competing delegation. We believe, Sir, that this is a Palestinian matter which should be decided by the PLO. Will the PLO in the beginning of those negotiations insist that Mr Arafat is personally involved? Surely not. Will we have top-level PLO officials involved in the first stage of that peace process? Not necessarily. Much depends on the composition of the other side. What we insist upon, and

I think it is an opportunity for the other side, is that the entire Palestinian people feel represented in this diplomatic interaction – the Diaspora and the Occupied Palestinians – and then it does not become problematic once that principle is adopted.

The choice of the persons is not at all problematic as long as it is a Palestinian matter. All those personalities that your colleagues who visit Jerusalem meet will be very serious candidates on our negotiating team. They are all authentic, genuine, respectable Palestinian spokespersons of the Palestinian idea, and I am happy that Mrs Saida Nuseibeh is here. She happens to be the sister of Professor Sari Nuseibeh, my friend and neighbour who is now detained in jail and who is the most prominent Palestinian Professor of Philosophy, who is detained now for three months but will be released in a matter of a week, and he is one of our most articulate spokespersons from East Jerusalem. You are not unaware, Sir, that also that negotiating team should incorporate individuals from East Jerusalem; East Jerusalem which has been occupied and illegally annexed by a unilateral decision which even the United Kingdom and the United States never recognised. You know that the Israeli position would like to see East Jerusalem inhabitants excluded because of its symbolical meaning, and I believe that the fact that we have been in a way indulged in talks about talks about talks that never took place, and we have been indulged in a way in negotiating pre-negotiations instead of pre-negotiating negotiations, means that the forum in which we meet, the nature of the participants and the number of the participants determine and dictate in a way the possible outcome.

You know that, Sir, and this is why I believe there is so much diplomatic guerrilla action now taking place because of the fact that the nature of the forum, the nature of the participants and the number of the participants dictate the possible diplomatic outcome. And believe me, Sir, I have several Israeli academics as personal friends and I would like to invoke one of them, Mark Heller, a brilliant strategic thinker, who in 1982–3 produced a book at Harvard University called *The Palestinian State: Implications for Israel*, where he studied six possible competing alternatives to come to the conclusion that the Palestinian state is in the best Israeli enlightened interests. That line of argument, which is extremely clinical, is fascinating. So I believe tomorrow the Palestinian state is in our enlightened interest and in the enlightened interest of those who have chosen to be our enemies.

Chairman: Thank you. We have one more question to ask you about who might speak for the PLO and who represent them. Mr Jopling?

Mr Jopling: In any of these negotiations which take place, I wonder if you could tell us what role the PLO would see for Jordan in that process, and to what extent Jordan might have a mediating role or a prominent role of one sort or another?

Mr Safieh: You know that we have adopted resolutions from 1983 onwards in our Parliament in Exile calling for a sort of confederal link between Palestine and Jordan, and I have always said this is a very desirable outcome that will become suspicious if ever external actors try to impose it on us as a pre-condition. It has to be the emanation of our voluntary volition, and not the result of a prior pre-condition. I think that history, geography, demography, family inter-parental relationship, dictate that Palestine and Jordan will have very intimate relations in the future and it is a desirable outcome. Yet I believe that in the interests of peace and the future, we should move towards Palestinian statehood first as a sovereign decision and towards equal partnership between the two entities, and move then towards the confederal link. I believe that Jordan has a very important regional role to play and we the Palestinians are willing to enter, as a sovereign decision, into a confederal partnership, an equal partnership with Jordan in the future. This is the dictate of geography, demography and history and we consider it desirable. Yet it should be the emanation of our voluntary volition, and not the result of a previous or prior pre-condition.

Mr Rowlands: Do you see any part of Jordan belonging to the Palestine homeland or state?

Mr Safieh: Sir, you know that Israel was supposed to be an answer to the Jewish question and now we are the question awaiting a convenient, satisfactory answer.

Mr Rowlands: So you do not?

Mr Safieh: So we should not now seek to solve our problem at the expense of the Trans-Jordanians, because then in the year 2001 we will have a session with the spokesperson of the Trans-Jordanians in his quest for a homeland for himself. As I told you earlier, we do not want the Israelis to become the Palestinians of the Palestinians.

Mr Rowlands: So the answer is no?

Mr Safieh: So we do not want it also for the Trans-Jordanians, no. So the theory, Sir, of 'Jordan is Palestine' is really a nightmare for the area and it is only caressed by a certain General Sharon.

Chairman: But there are tens, indeed hundreds of thousands of Palestinians in Jordan and in many other places in the Middle East who would find there simply was not room for them in the new Palestinian state?

Mr Safieh: I agree with you, Sir, that one of the strategic major issues of the area is, whose demography on whose geography, and I believe – and this is why I mentioned it earlier without being asked about it – I am in favour of vertical expansion in the future instead of horizontal expansion. Believe me, Sir, Palestine and Israel can incorporate many more individuals and citizens than they now hold. Not all Palestinians would like to return to Palestine. Some have settled very comfortably wherever they are, but they would like to visit, they would like to send their children to schools, they would like sometimes to retire in Palestine, they would come very frequently, and, as I told you, vertical expansion is going to solve the problem.

A Dutch friend of mine, an expert in hydrological resources, told me that in the future Israel and Palestine will have to opt for non-reliance on agriculture because of the limited nature of the hydrological resources. So all the hydrological resources available in Israel and Palestine will have to be used for domestic purposes, and so if we adopt this line of action of having an economy that does not rely heavily on agriculture, that land can incorporate many more Palestinians coming to the Palestinian state and some Jews coming additionally to the Israeli state.

Chairman: Mr Safieh, time is running out and you have given us very many thoughts. Mr Jopling has another question and Mr Lawrence has another question and then I am going to close the proceedings.

Mr Jopling: I wonder whether you believe that in the negotiations there are any problems which are insurmountable, such as the Israeli settlements in the occupied territories or the position of East Jerusalem?

Chairman: I think you did mention these things earlier, so perhaps we do not need a long answer.

Mr Safieh: I come from Jerusalem and I happen to be the son of the Member of Parliament in the Jordanian Parliament for the Christian community of Jerusalem. My father was a founding member of the Palestinian Parliament in Exile. East Jerusalem is something unique for us and for others, too, and I believe it will have a very unique status in the future. I think it will be two cities in one, two capitals for two sovereign entities, yet the city can remain undivided, and I deliberately used the concept of 'undivided' and not 'united' because 'united' was perverted by the Israeli annexationists. I believe we can explore the possibility of joint municipal committees, with each religious community managing the religious shrine to which it belongs. That would be the status for Jerusalem and it will be a remarkable place to live in or to visit, and I believe that not one single religious community or ethnic community can have a monopoly on Jerusalem. Concerning the settlements, Sir, I believe that they were created as an accomplished fact, knowing that it was contrary to international law. Number two, Sir, those who chose to settle in those settlements are not recruited from, nor do they represent the most adorable segment of Israeli public opinion. They are usually people who adhere to, who vote for, the most fundamentalist wing and the most extreme right wing of the Israeli political spectrum. Tomorrow, they have a sort of reflex of the OAS in Algeria trying to provoke tensions and frictions, hoping to invite the Israeli army back. I do not think it advisable, Sir, that we should be asked to keep those settlements and settlers. It is a recipe for friction and tension, yet I think it should be a point on the diplomatic table. Yet there are UN resolutions and Geneva conventions that regulate those types of relationships, because it was done contrary to international law, and the way they are recruited and what they represent in political terms do not make them the bridge for future harmonious relations between Israel and Palestine. I think it is a recipe for disaster.

Mr Lawrence: You mentioned just now Soviet immigration, Mr Safieh, and Yasser Arafat was reported as addressing senior Fateh military personnel in Baghdad on 6 April last year, saying, 'Open fire on the new Jewish immigrants, be they from the Soviet Union,

Ethiopia or anywhere else. I want you to shoot on the ground or in the air at every immigrant who thinks our land is a playground. It makes no difference whether they live in Jaffa or in Jericho. I give you explicit instructions to open fire. Do everything to stop the flow of immigration,' and he said, 'My decision and the decision of Fateh to use violence must be carried out in real terms.' Is that how the PLO would intend to deal with the Soviet immigration problem, and if not, will you, as a spokesman for the PLO today, take this opportunity to renounce unconditionally terrorism and the armed struggle?

Mr Safieh: First of all, Sir, I believe that this statement attributed to Arafat was published in a magazine published in Paris called *Al Mouharar*, the credibility and plausibility of which are equal to the book *Protocols of Zion*. I believe that Arafat never said that and we have already, by the way, denied the accuracy of that report. It is a magazine that resembles *Le Canard Enchaine*, which is a very adorable magazine to read, but it does not live up to its expectations. As I told you, the plausibility of that statement is equal to the book *Protocols of Zion*, and you know what I mean.

Mr Lawrence: Yes.

Mr Safieh: Having had this problem of the Soviet Jewish immigration into Palestine for the last three years, and having not seen any such butchery or massacre to which you are alluding, I would refer you to my previous answer about the Palestinian self-restraint on that issue. I promise you that there will not be such undesirable events taking place. Concerning, Sir, armed struggle ...

Mr Lawrence: And terrorism.

Mr Safieh: You know that we have criticised and denounced terrorism, be it undertaken by individuals, organisations or states. You know that the UN Charter authorises – *authorises* – armed struggle in the situation of alien occupation. Yet, Sir, I happen to belong to the Arafat school that has given instructions not to use weaponry in the intifada. We believe that the genius of our intifada is mainly its non-violent aspects. If you will allow me Sir, in my concluding remarks to say that our intifada should be defined in political terms. Our intifada is our gradual process of the exercise of Palestinian sovereignty even under occupation. Our intifada is the proliferation of popular committees that deal with all social needs. It is a message of peace and not of war. It is not only stone throwing, it is that process of the gradual exercise of sovereignty even under occupation. I well remember what Faisal Husseini told me six months ago. He told me, 'Afif, we have to keep it non-violent because if ever Tyson comes and challenges you – and you know Tyson is the heavyweight boxing champion – you do not invite him into the boxing ring, he will win; you invite him to the chess board and you might have a chance to win.' This is why we believe, Sir, the nonviolent feature of our intifada is its brilliance, it is what brought us international sympathy of which we have been deprived and we are hoping to keep it. Believe me, if there is now a diplomatic process, that will be behind us.

Sir, I hope you do not belong to the selective school that has selective sensitivities. You know that violence was accomplished by both sides and you know that according to Israeli statistics, four days of Israeli violence have created many more victims on our side than forty years of Palestinian violence against Israeli targets. I think every casualty is one casualty too many.

Mr Lawrence: If you are rejecting violence and terrorism and terrorism and violence are taking place in the name of the PLO, does that mean that you – the PLO Central Organisation – do not have control over those factions of the PLO that are committing violence against your wishes? If that is so, how could you guarantee to the Israelis that you could deliver peace in any bargain struck with them?

Mr Safieh: Sir, this is why I mentioned earlier, without being solicited, the model of the 1981 ceasefire agreement on the Lebanese theatre, where we had a semblance of control. Once we had concluded that agreement over eleven long and challenging months, everybody was asked and everybody scrupulously respected that ceasefire agreement. I believe, Sir, when you have control of a territory, and as you know, Sir, the definition of a state is an authority on demography and geography, once we have statehood in a normal manner where we have control of the territory, geography and demography, I think we will scrupulously respect any commitment we take. I ask all those who have influence on the Arab-Israeli question not to be selectively sensitive. There is violence on both sides and there is also asymmetrical violence and disproportionate violence, and to be believable and credible one should show indignation at violence whoever the perpetrator, and sympathy whoever the victim. I want you, Sir, to believe me. I think any casualty falling from now onwards in the Israeli-Palestinian arena is one casualty too many. I believe what is happening today in the area shows us that we either have one people too many – this time, we the Palestinians – or that there is a state which is missing, the State of Palestine. I told you earlier, Sir, we believe in resurrection; we did it once and we can do it again. Sir, thank you for the possibility of addressing you.

Chairman: Well, Mr Safieh, whether you have been at the chess board or in the boxing ring, you have performed with great energy and comprehensive detail and we are very grateful for your time spent here. Next week, this Committee will be holding a hearing with representatives of the State of Israel, so we will be looking at different things, maybe we will hear some common views. In the meantime we want to thank you very much for appearing before the Committee this afternoon.

IX

Superpower politics and the Middle East[1]

It was from a drab drizzly day in London that we entered the PLO delegation. We were offered coffee and Arabic newspapers in a warm, smoky waiting room. Neil Sheldon and I had had the good fortune to get to the final of the Observer Mace debating competition. Our task was to oppose the motion that 'This House believes that the power of the United States has increased, is increasing and ought to be diminished.' In order to prepare for this, Dr Buck and I had been to a meeting about American foreign policy in the Middle East, where we were lucky enough to meet Mr Afif Safieh, representative of the PLO in London. To our great surprise, he generously invited us to come and discuss the debate with him. Such opportunities are not to be missed.

The first pillar of our argument was to be that, in fact, the American economy is no longer expanding, and so its power is not increasing any more. Mr Safieh acknowledged that there are two schools of thought about superpower politics. One school of thought is called the declinists – those who advocate that over the last decade or more the relative power and influence of the USA have rather declined. They argue that during the last few years, we have witnessed an emergence of other centres of power: Japan, Europe and other countries. Even though the Americans maintain military supremacy, in a pacified world, military supremacy is not the only strategic factor for the measurement of power and

1.   Interview by M.L. Willcox in *Lancing College Magazine*, mid-1991.

influence, and you have to look at the emerging poles in the international system.

There is another school of thought which says that the American power is the hegemony – unpaired, unrivalled, unchallenged. The Soviet Union as an empire, as a pole, has been diminished after a double assault on its cohesion and strength. The first was an ideological assault during the Carter period, demanding human rights be observed. The second assault came during the Reagan period, with the arms race. This school of thought argues that America, the West, has won. We are witnessing a decline of the Soviet Union, and since all the other poles are of an economic nature, civilian powers, they don't constitute any serious competition.

I could sense that, instinctively, Mr Safieh was more convinced by this second approach. 'During the last five years, we have moved beyond the bipolar system, where you had two superpowers of equal strengths, or at least of sufficiently dissuasive capabilities on either side to create a sort of global equilibrium. We have moved from the bipolar system – not towards a multipolar system, that I for one would have preferred, but towards a monopolar system where, in a way, Washington appears to be the contemporary Rome managing the globe.'

But did the power of America really increase as a result of the Gulf War? Isn't power really shifting to the strong economics of Japan and the EEC? 'Before the Gulf Crisis, tensions were rising in relations between the USA and Japan, the USA and the EEC. Because in a period of protracted peace, it's the ally that becomes the competitor. I believe that many in Washington wanted the political confrontation in the Gulf, so that in international relations military power will again have primacy in the hierarchy of power. In periods of peace, it's the economic achievements, the productivity, and the exportation levels that obtain primacy. In periods of military confrontation the military dimension regains primacy. So I think that in decision-making processes in America, the thought of reasserting American supremacy, was not far off. In a way they made it understood to the Germans, the Japanese and the EEC countries, who is *numero uno*.'

Is it in the interests of the Palestinians that the military dimension should regain primacy? Recently, the PLO denounced terrorism. The UN Charter allows any people oppressed by alien occupation to resort to armed struggle. But the major components of the PLO to which Mr Safieh belongs have deliberately decided not to resort to armed struggle, because there are now avenues for diplomatic transactions. Mr Safieh told us, 'I am in favour of the nonviolent school because I think that nonviolence is more destabilising than violence. Since Israel is the predominant military power in the area, its strongest aspect is in the military dimension. When the intifada maintains its mainly nonviolent features, it immobilises 99.9 percent of the Israeli military capabilities. Israel can neither deploy its nuclear capabilities, nor its navy, nor its aviation, nor its tank force. They still use tear gas and bullets, which are extremely lethal, but this is only 0.1 percent of their military capabilities. Faisal Husseini once said, "If ever Tyson – the world champion in heavyweight boxing – comes to challenge you, you don't invite him to the boxing ring. You invite him to the chessboard where you have a decent chance to win." In the boxing ring, you are the sure loser.'

How does American foreign policy affect Middle Eastern affairs? Mr Safieh told us, 'I've always said that the key to war and peace resides in Washington.' There are two schools of thought again on the American-Israeli relationship. One speaks of an Israeli America, and the other speaks of an American Israel. One says it is the global superpower that dictates policies of its regional client, and the other says it is the global power that adopts the regional preferences of its client state. So does America dictate policies on Israel, or does America adopt Israeli policies?

'I believe that both those schools of thought are correct, but at different moments in history, and at different moments of that complex pattern of relations between the global protector and the regional client. I tend to believe that more frequently, it is the second school of thought which is more accurate. Because the Middle East is part of the domestic debate (and we know how strong Israel actually is in the domestic American arena), the Americans often get coaxed into adopting the Israeli strategy, policy and preference.'

This was manifest during the Reagan period, which many call the Reagan *siesta*: the Irangate event illustrates this phenomenon of America adopting the regional preferences of its client state. In Israel, the Ben Gurion doctrine says, 'Since we live in a hostile environment, we have to make an alliance with the environment of our environment.' That strategy aimed to make a network of alliances with Turkey, Iran, Ethiopia, whatever the nature of the political regime in power. It has nothing to do with the ideological policy, be it of the Shah or Khomeini. What happened in Irangate is the following: the Americans were convinced to pump arms and money into revolutionary Islamic Iran against Iraq, the regional competitor of Israel. At no moment was American strategy to help promote the chances of the Islamic revolution. Its strategy was to assist the Israelis; Islamic fundamentalism, especially if it is Iranian, clashes with Arab nationalism and Arab national states. Here is a situation where the Americans adopt the Israeli strategy and preference, even if it is in contradiction of their own national interest.

In the Gulf Crisis, Mr Safieh felt that 'Rome was in Tel Aviv, and Tel Aviv had succeeded in mobilising Washington as its own regional belligerent Sparta. The Israelis succeeded in having the

Americans in a situation where they would crush the regional competitor of Israeli hegemony, which was Iraq.'

Have USA-USSR relations affected the emigration of Soviet Jews into Israel? Mr Safieh replied, 'I believe that we the Palestinians have suffered from both Soviet strength and Soviet weakness.' At moments during the three decades of supposed Soviet strength, the Israelis convinced the Americans that they were the strategic asset capable of containing Soviet expansionism. They took advantage of the Soviet pseudo-strength, in order to be flooded with money and weaponry. Then they took advantage of the Soviet weakness by extorting from the Soviets all possible concessions, including unlimited Soviet Jewish immigration towards only Israel.

The turning point took place when Bush met Gorbachev in Malta. It is then that serious decisions concerning the Soviet Jewish migration were taken. Up to the Malta Summit, more than ninety percent of the Soviet Jews who were leaving the Soviet Union were going elsewhere than Israel-Palestine, and less than ten percent were choosing to go to Israel-Palestine. After the Malta summit, the proportions were exactly reversed: over ninety percent were ending up in Israel-Palestine, and less than ten percent were going elsewhere. The Americans were pressured by the Israelis to ensure that Soviet-Jewish emigration should be channelled only to Israel.

The freedom of choice of the country of destination has always been a Jewish concern. This concern has been violated, because now they are being channelled like cattle only to Israel. So the pro-Israeli lobby prevailed over a traditional Jewish concern, because it wanted to give an advantage to Israel: having one or two million additional citizens. The Malta Summit was accompanied by the Western countries, mainly the USA but also EEC countries, reducing their quota of reception for Soviet-Jewish migration. At a moment when it had succeeded in pressuring the Soviets to open doors and let

Soviet Jews leave if they so desired, the West closed its doors for those Soviet-Jewish migrants who would have preferred to emigrate to a Western country. 'If you go back now to the evidence and the press reporting of the day, you won't find much,' said Mr Safieh.

How do the Palestinians feel about President Bush? Mr Safieh believes that, 'We in the Arab world always prefer an American president that is strong and comfortable, whereas the Israelis prefer a vulnerable American president. This is why we are encouraged by the popularity rating of Bush, even though we think the reasons of his popularity are of a questionable nature. But we are happy that he is so popular, and that he can (if he so wanted) be decisive, assertive and confront any lobby that wants to obstruct his intentions. I have always said that the best American president for the Middle East would have the ethics of a Carter, the popularity of a Reagan, and the strategic audacity of a Nixon. But we have to make do with what we have. I don't think that Bush has the ethics of a Carter, he has the popularity of a Reagan; the question is does he have the strategic audacity of a Nixon?

'I am encouraged by one or two factors, which are the following. Bush and Baker are comfortable today, electorally speaking, and there is no serious challenge around the Democratic side. Number two, they form a cohesive team, unlike in previous administrations where there was constant rivalry between the White House, the National Security adviser, the State Department man, and the Pentagon. Stanley Hoffman spoke of "institutionalised pluralism" where an undecided President Carter was subjected to conflicting advice. But this team is very cohesive, and they owe nothing for their first election or for their reelection to the pro-Israeli lobby. So if they so wanted, they can be extremely decisive and assertive.'

Why doesn't America finish with the Israeli-American relation? 'A Zionist leader, Nahum Goldmann, commenting critically on Kissinger's shuttle diplomacy, said that "It seems to me that diplomacy in the Middle East is the art of delaying the inevitable as long as possible." Already for him in the early seventies, the inevitable was the Palestinian factor. In one of his books he speaks of a discussion he had with Moshe Dayan. He tells him, "Moshe, the Americans up to now give you much aid and some advice; you take all the aid and you leave the advice aside. What would happen if ever the Americans were to tell you, 'You can only take the aid if you also take the advice?'" and Moshe with resignation tells him, "Then we have also to take the advice." So linkage there has potential – linking American aid to American advice.'

Mr Safieh explained, 'Since we live in a monopolar world, where Washington resembles Rome, I think we all have to work as Palestinians, Arabs and the peace camp among Israelis and within Jewish communities, the Europeans and others, on the formulation and the elaboration of American foreign policy towards our area. That means that we have to convince the Americans to reconcile their power and their principles. We believe that self-determination is a cornerstone in the American political philosophy. It means the freedom of choice of one's form of government, one's governors, and government by consent, not through coercion; government with democratic representation, not through bureaucratic repression. So we have to persuade and pressure the Americans to link their aid to their advice in their relationship with the Israelis.'

If American power were to be diminished, how would it be done? Mr Safieh asserted, 'I am of the belief that the only credible alternative today to American hegemony is UN supremacy. But the UN also needs to be liberated. As we witnessed during the Gulf Crisis, the UN was very manipulated by the US. They bought votes and vetoes. When Gorbachev had his own initiative on ending the war, during the last days of the war, Bush had a very condescending attitude, and was the first to answer "No." That proposal was submitted to the international community, and to my knowledge, Bush is only the President of the USA and not yet the Secretary General of the UN.

'You have to strengthen the political philosophy on which the UN system is based, and to have actors deciding that they should play their legitimate share in international decision-making. However, some actors are very vulnerable: the Soviet Union needs economic aid, investments and capital, so you can buy its vote and its veto. China is in an identical situation. The rivalry between the UK and France often does not project an image of a cohesive Europe. It speaks with two different voices. Often British diplomacy's first aim is to topple the French initiatives and the French diplomacy's first task is to show that the British initiative is only British and not EEC. So the Americans are in a very comfortable situation. How desirable that is, is a question of personal inclinations.'

If the UN is the alternative, how in practical terms can power be transferred to the UN, given the economic strength of the US and the weakness of the USSR? Mr Safieh concluded, 'This is where I think that the second pillar of the international system is no more the Soviet Union, but the EEC. Those other pillars of the international system have to become more assertive, Europe more cohesive, Japan more assertive. Now, with the renewed attempts for the quest of peace in the Middle East, Bush has the opportunity to play statesman, and that's the challenge. He played the policeman successfully. Will he play the role of the international statesman?'

X

On the Madrid peace process[1]

I sincerely do believe that Palestine is resurrecting, and as you know, we in the Holy Land have had some previous experience in resurrection.

The Palestinian people are one of the few peoples in the history of mankind that never got their legitimate share of sympathy, solidarity and support. We have always attributed this to the fact that we have been in the Middle East, the victims of the victims of European history. In our crowded calendar, in our tormented Middle East, the date of 9 December 1987 will always be remembered as a regional historical turning point. The intifada, which has been our cry for freedom out of captivity and bondage, was a turning point. It was an eye-opener. For the first time in Western public opinion, the perception of the Palestinians in this bipolar Israeli-Palestinian relationship started to be that of an oppressed and persecuted people who had an interest in the achievement of peace. Western public opinion then began to see us as the victimised party in this bipolar relationship. People started understanding our ceaseless quest for the achievement of peace, because we were the ones whose territory was totally occupied, whose people were living endlessly under either occupation or in forced diasporaisation, whose land was being expropriated, whose water was being plundered, whose

---

1.   Transcript of a presentation delivered at a symposium sponsored by the Center for Policy Analysis on Palestine and held in Washington DC on 12 November 1991, ten days after the Madrid Peace Conference.

houses were being demolished, whose individuals were being deported, whose bones were being broken, and whose schools and universities were being closed. And I believe that this interest in the achievement of peace stems from and explains the fact that we in the PLO have been unreasonably reasonable in dealing with peace opportunities that have arisen lately.

I had the political privilege of accompanying Yasser Arafat in 1988 on several of his political trips. I was with him in September 1988 in Strasbourg when he addressed the European Parliament. I was with him again in Stockholm, then in Geneva in December 1988. Still ringing in my ears is the sentence he repeated on those occasions: 'I extend my hand in peace, hoping that an Israeli de Gaulle will seize it.' One had to wait endlessly to see that no de Gaulle emerged. Not even a de Klerk, and a de Klerk would have been good enough to start this snowball process.

In 1988, 1989 and 1990, there was already an American endeavour at peacemaking in the Middle East. The PLO and the Palestinian people were known to have been available for that exercise. We had welcomed the ten points of President Mubarak, we had welcomed and were favourably inclined to the five points of Secretary of State Baker. At that time, the diplomatic equation was the following: we were hoping that the Israelis would accept them as a basis, while the Israelis were hoping that we would torpedo them. Any serious analysis of the endeavour of 1988–90 would demonstrate that it failed then because the American administration allowed the peace process to remain a hostage of the Israeli domestic political arena, and the Israelis had a very ethnocentric conception of peacemaking. Some saw peace with us as a compromise formula halfway in between Likud and Labour. Even worse, others saw it as a compromise halfway in between Shamir and Sharon. The Israeli government then was a national coalition government described by observers as a government of national paralysis which slumbered and fragmented over differing attitudes on how to respond to the Baker initiative. Shimon Peres made an attempt at coalition-building, failed, and Shamir came back to power with indispensable extreme right-wing coalition partners. The process then was temporarily interrupted by the US administration, which had allowed the Israeli government to determine the ceiling of the possible and the permissible and had allowed the slowest actor to dictate the pace of the peace process. And as you know, a turtle compared to Shamir looks like Speedy Gonzales.

An accurate assessment of that period should be made so that we do not fall into the trap, once again, in our endeavour of 1991–92. Why was the American attempt to bring the belligerent parties together at the negotiating table successful now? I for one believe that there were three major factors.

The first was the Gulf Crisis and the Gulf War, which many thought was an unnecessary war, and during which many thought that diplomacy was not given a serious chance to bring an equitable, acceptable solution to fruition. Yet, the fact that the Americans and their allies went into war to discipline a misbehaving regional actor made inactivity on the American side toward the other misbehaving regional actor – Israel – very un-understandable. And I believe the fact that Iraq was bombed back to the pre-industrial age was a factor that motivated the administration to show assertive dynamism toward that other unfinished business of Israel/Palestine. Since no one was asking the administration to bomb Israel to a pre-industrial age, but just to exercise and exert some friendly persuasion to bring them to the negotiating table, that type of endeavour had started to be seen as possible. Inactivity on the part of the American administration toward that other misbehaving regional actor – Israel – would have been very badly perceived, from Morocco to Malaysia, because inactivity would have been seen as excessive patience, which resembles indulgence, which borders on complacency and complicity.

The second factor was the end of the Cold War and the end of the bipolar international system and their repercussions on the pattern of relations between the United States and Israel. I personally believe that Shamir is not yet fully aware of the changes that have intervened to alter the client-patron relations away from the model to which we all have grown accustomed for decades. Israel drew enormous advantage throughout the era of superpower rivalry and succeeded in convincing American policy-makers that it was capable of containing Soviet expansionism. As a result of that, it received unlimited, unconditional and unquestioning support. Now that the United States is no longer obsessed with the containment of Soviet expansionism, we should put on the American agenda the containment of Israeli expansionism. Now that the Soviet Union has been rolled back from its East European acquisitions, we should put on the American agenda how to roll back Israel from its Middle Eastern acquisitions.

There were always two schools of thought competing for the explanation of the fascinating and intriguing American-Israeli relations. The 'who wags whom' debate has occupied and preoccupied a generation of scholars. The first school spoke of an American Israel, an Israel that is a sort of belligerent Sparta at the service of the contemporary Rome. For the adherents of that trend of thought it is the United States that dictates to its local ally what should be its regional policy in accordance with the US global vision. The second school projects the image of an Israeli America, a complex relationship where the global superpower simply adopts the regional policy of its client state and integrates it in its global strategy. This is seen as a result of powerful American domestic considerations where Capitol Hill is that other Israeli occupied territory that needs to be liberated if ever we are to have an even-handed approach toward the Middle East. Both of those schools of thought are accurate but at different moments in history depending on a variety of considerations like the strength (electoral and intellectual) of the American president, on how comfortable he is in the country and in Congress and on how comfortable the United States is in the world. I believe that now a new era is being ushered in where the strategic function, utility and *raison d'être* of Israel have been drastically diminished in American eyes. The fact that the Arab world, the Palestinians included, no longer challenges Israel's existence but only its expansions has further enhanced the possibilities of American pressure on the recalcitrant Israeli leadership.

The third factor is the following: it is no longer the 1950s and the 1960s, when the Arab world was governed by militant nationalist leaders. Whether one likes it or not, in a way the regional Arab system is a moderate conservative system, and Israel, by obstinately wanting to continue its occupation of the Palestinian and Arab territories, is defying, delegitimising and destabilising a regional system that is not being a nuisance to Western perceptions and interests. It is Israeli expansionism that today is emerging as a nuisance to American global and regional interests.

We went to Madrid, and I for one believe that history is in the making. I believe that there is an enormous window of opportunity, and we, the Palestinians, have been unreasonably reasonable in order to make Madrid possible. I believe that the pride of the Palestinian people, welcoming the return of the Palestinian negotiating team back into occupied Palestine, is proof that we the Palestinians genuinely desire peace, and I fully endorse the olive branch strategy. Tomorrow the olive branch is by far more subversive than any other instrument of political expression. We were not very comfortable with the scenario that was being offered to us. We were in favour of a peaceful resolution of the Middle East conflict, yet we thought and dreamed of an international conference sponsored by the

United Nations, with the presence of the five permanent members of the Security Council, to implement, and not to interpret, the UN resolutions. That was not the negotiating process that all the belligerent parties were invited to. We felt uncomfortable, and we had many a legitimate reservation. Yet, because we had confidence in ourselves we accepted to undergo the test.

There is a need to clarify certain conceptual matters. I have always defined the intifada as the gradual exercise of Palestinian sovereignty even under continued Israeli occupation, and I have always seen the intifada as being more than stone throwing. The intifada is the parallel institution-building, it is the proliferation of popular committees that deal with all social needs, from education to medication, from culture to agriculture. I have always seen the intifada as our attempt to recuperate from the occupying authority domains and spheres of decision-making that had been usurped by the occupying authority for so long. And I believe that this definition of the intifada will prevail in the coming weeks, months and years. We have always said that it will be an intifada only towards independence.

The other definition is that of the PLO. Some Israeli commentators like to say that the PLO was excluded from the process, yet I still remember Abba Eban, whom I have encountered in one or two symposia, saying that Mr Shamir, toward the PLO, had a very ostrich-like attitude. I still remember Abba Eban saying, in his particular manner, 'and the ostrich posture is both uncomfortable and inelegant.'

What is the PLO? The PLO is more than an institution, it is an idea. The idea is much stronger than the institution. It has always been our challenge, we in the PLO, to have an institution strong enough to carry the idea. If ten thousand Palestinians work in the institution, then five million Palestinians are the powerful vehicles of the idea. Israel constantly made a mistake: wanting to crush the idea, it attacked the institution, thus reinvigorating the idea. Just as the PLO represented the Palestinian people for twenty-five years, today the Palestinian people are representing the PLO, and they are doing a hell of a good job.

Despite all the constraints that were inflicted upon us, we succeeded in out-smarting those who were putting these capricious demands upon us. They tried to exclude East Jerusalemites, and there comes Faisal Husseini as political coordinator of the Palestinian team, and there comes Hanan Ashrawi as the visible and vocal tip of that iceberg as the Palestinian spokesperson, here comes Sari Nusseibeh as the technical scholarly coordinator of the negotiating team. And they are all prominent members of the Jerusalem community. They are Jerusalem. They wanted to exclude the diaspora, and here the PLO re-smuggles back into the process Rashid Khalidi, Camille Mansour and Anis al-Qasim. Among us there was no problem of who was at the table and who was in the adjacent room. As long as we have this mutual self-confidence it becomes of such banal importance, and we have succeeded in ridiculing the capricious exigence of the other side.

The battles ahead will not be easy. Looking at Israel – which is today rich in politicians and very poor in statesmen – I often think of Nahum Goldmann, who in my opinion said in the middle of the 1970s three things relevant to our exercise today and tomorrow. Nahum Goldmann in the middle of the 1970s, commenting critically on the Kissinger approach, said, 'It seems to me that diplomacy in the Middle East is the art of delaying the inevitable as long as possible.' This definition was painfully accurate. For Nahum Goldmann, already in the middle of the 1970s, the inevitable was the Palestinian dimension, the Palestinian factor and the Palestinian actor. And tomorrow, the Israeli negotiating team will get on our nerves, and probably everybody else's nerves, trying to delay the inevitable as long as possible, while we will be

Early 1989 in The Hague with Dutch Foreign Minister Hans van den Broek, Dr Nabil Sha'ath, the Chairman of the political committee of the Palestinian National Council, and the late Mahmoud Rabbani, former Honorary Consul for Kuwait, then Jordan.

Early 1989 with Bassam Abu Sharif, then political advisor to President Arafat, at a conference I helped organise at the International Court of Justice on 'Models of Co-habitation', also attended by former Israeli Foreign Minister Abba Eban.

The Palestinian Delegation in London was instrumental from 1990 onwards in projecting the reality of the indivisible nature of the Palestinian national movement by hosting leading personalities, from both the Occupied Territories and the PLO. Here with Faisal Husseini, the Director of the Orient House in Jerusalem.

1991, with Nabil Sha'ath, today member of the Central Committee of Fateh and Commissioner for International Relations.

1991. In the House of Commons with Hanan Ashrawi, the spokesperson of the Palestinian Delegation during the Madrid/Washington talks, and MP Ernie Ross, Chairman of the Labour Middle East Council.

At the offices of *al-Sharq al-Awsat*, with Editor-in-Chief Othman al-Omeir and Palestinian author Emile Habibi and Palestinian poet Mahmoud Darwish in 1993.

With Palestinian poet Samih al-Qassim in 1995.

After 27 years of exile, I was the first PLO official in December 1993 to return to Jerusalem on a private visit with my wife and daughters. The Latin Patriarch Michel Sabbah celebrated the ceremony of First Communion and Confirmation for Diana and Randa. Several mayors from the West Bank, several Consuls General, Lord David Steele, Lord Greville Janner and Israeli Culture Minister Shulamit Aloni were in attendance.

With my mother Odette Batato Safieh at the end of the ceremony.

September 1994. First meeting with Yasser Arafat in Gaza City, after his return to Palestine, also with Mgr Robert Stern, the President for the Pontifical Mission for Palestine, and Father Dennis Madden, the head of their office in Jerusalem.

With HH Pope John Paul II in November 1995 when I presented my Letter of Credentials as First Head of Mission to the Holy See.

President Arafat arriving at the Royal Suite, Heathrow Airport.

In front of 10 Downing Street with then Prime Minister John Major.

With former Prime Minister Margaret Thatcher at the Dorchester Hotel.

Coming out of the House of Commons with Lord David Steel, Lord Paddy Ashdown and Sir Menzies Campbell, the leadership of the Liberal Democrats.

With President Arafat at the Royal Institute of International Affairs, Chatham House.

President Yasser Arafat, my wife Christ'l and the leadership of the Oxford Union.

With HRH Prince Charles.

With Amr Moussa, the Secretary General of the Arab League.

Wherever I served, I always enjoyed excellent working relations with mainstream Muslim organisations. In London, I was a frequent speaker at major events organised by the Union of Muslim Organisations.

With Prime Minister Tony Blair.

With Secretary of State Robin Cook, Mrs Gaynor Cook, Minister of State Keith Vaz, Mrs Maria Fernandes Vaz and Christ'l.

President Arafat after a working lunch with Secretary of State for International Development Clare Short.

With William Hague, then leader of the Conservative Party.

The farewell lunch in 2005 hosted by the Council of Arab Ambassadors accredited to the Court of St James with the Ambassadors of Kuwait (the Dean), Saudi Arabia, Morocco, Oman and Bahrain (now Foreign Minister).

Christ'l and my sister Diana with the spouses of the Arab ambassadors.

With President George W. Bush in the White House in 2006.

During my three years in the USA, I was constantly on the lecturing circuit in Ivy League universities or at different chapters of the World Affairs Council. Here I am lecturing at Harvard University in April 2007.

November 2007 in the White House on the eve of the Annapolis Conference, Secretary of State Dr Rice, Elliot Abrams, Palestinian Prime Minister Salam Fayyad, Nabil Sha'ath and Rawhi Fattouh.

In 2008 in the Kremlin, just after the ceremony of presentation of the Letter of Credentials to President Medvedev.

In November 2007 with former President Jimmy Carter at the Carter Centre in Atlanta, Geogria. Christ'l and I presented him with a Bethlehem passport of honorary citizenship, on behalf of Leila Sansour and the Coalition of Bethlehem NGOs, in recognition of his remarkable, tireless work for peace and justice.

seeking historical shortcuts so that we can achieve peace, for their children and ours at the earliest possible moment.

Nahum Goldmann said another thing in the middle of the 1970s that I think is extremely relevant today. He mentions in one of his books a discussion he had with Moshe Dayan, and he writes that he said, 'Moshe, the Americans give you much aid and some advice. Up to now you take all the aid and you leave the advice aside. What would happen if ever they were to tell you, you can only take the aid if you also take the advice?' And according to Nahum Goldmann, Moshe Dayan with resignation said, 'then we have also to take the advice.' And I believe there is a big historical lesson to be drawn from Nahum Goldmann, who says, 'let's make the linkage between the American aid and American advice.' And we hope that the American advice tomorrow will be compatible with universal principles of human law, of international law. Our aspiration has always been to see an American administration that reconciles its power with its own principles.

The third thing that Nahum Goldmann said, commenting on the disengagement agreements between Israel and Egypt and Israel and Syria, was that the Americans have a big reservoir of possibilities of leverage and pressure on Israel. And in his opinion they should not be wasted on marginal, peripheral issues of partial solutions, but to exercise the bulk, the capacity of this reservoir of pressure in order to obtain a solution on the crux, the central issue of controversy in the area. And I hope that tomorrow there will not be procedural battles on marginal issues, where the capital of possibilities of pressure will be wasted on a succession of small battles instead of being waged on the big battle, the central core issue.

I saw Mr Shamir on television say in Madrid that Israel had a hunger for peace. And I believe today that we the Palestinians can solemnly and publicly say we can satisfy Israel's hunger for peace if ever Mr Shamir abandons his appetite for territory.

XI

On Jerusalem[1]

The destiny of Jerusalem is surely totally tied to the fate and destiny of Palestine. The battle that took place in Palestine, all throughout the twentieth century, aiming at reducing the majority into a demographic minority and propelling the minority into a demographic majority, that battle was also waged in and around Jerusalem but in an even more acute manner.

The municipality of Jerusalem was first established in the nineteenth century, during the Ottoman rule in Palestine, in 1863. The Municipal Council was then composed of five members: three Muslims, one Christian and one Jew. At the end of the nineteenth century, there was a small Jewish community in Palestine of around 20,000 inhabitants and they were an integral part of the Palestinian social tissue. They were overwhelmingly anti-Zionist or non-Zionists. They thought that the penetration of Zionism in Palestine would complicate and poison inter-confessional relations and they also thought that Zionism would fail. History has proven them right on one point and wrong on the other. But by 1920–21, coming from Russia but also mainly from Poland, massive arrivals of new Zionist immigrants numerically drowned this indigenous Jewish community which became since then a shrinking minority within the growing Jewish community.

In 1917, at the end of Ottoman domination in Palestine, the

---

1   Transcript of a lecture given at a seminar organised in London by the Arab Research Centre in 1994.

Jerusalem Municipal Council was composed of ten members: six Muslims, two Christians and two Jews. The British authorities nominated in 1918 a new council of six members: two Muslims, two Christians and two Jews. Until 1927, Arabic was the exclusive language for the deliberations of the council's meetings.

In 1927, municipal elections were held to elect a council of twelve members: five Muslims, four Jews and three Christians. The elections organised in 1934 brought again a council of twelve members but its changed composition again reflected the alteration that had occurred in the demographic equilibrium of the city: four Muslims, two Christians and six Jews.[1]

As a result of the 1948 war, Jerusalem city came out divided in two, with the Western side under Israeli control and the East side, including the Old City, under Jordanian rule. But contrary to widespread impression or perception, in 1948 West Jerusalem was not Jewish. The massacre of Deir Yassin, which is in the outskirts of West Jerusalem, where 254 villagers were slaughtered and the blowing up of the Semiramise Hotel in West Jerusalem triggered the ethnic cleansing of West Jerusalem and of coastal Palestine. Menahem Begin, in the first edition of his memoirs in 1952 titled *The Revolt*, boasts that Zionist forces after Deir Yassin 'advanced like a knife in butter' with the Arab civilian population fleeing in panic. He was advised by more sophisticated and polished friends to remove that passage from other editions of his book. Sixty-four thousand Palestinians were driven out of West Jerusalem and the four villages in its immediate vicinity which were later annexed to its municipality boundaries, namely Lifta, Deir Yassin, Ein Karem and El Malha.

There were several Palestinian residential neighbourhoods in West Jerusalem where middle-class Palestinians, civil servants, lawyers, engineers and doctors lived and worked. To name just a few: Katamon, upper and lower Baqa'a – before 1948 my family lived in upper Baq'a – Talbieh, Mamillah, Shama'a, Musrara, Abu Tor etc. Palestinians left with only the key to their houses and one of the sad jokes among Palestinians is that their country was taken furnished. The late Professor Henry Cattan has analysed in great depth the 'legalised theft' that followed, where all these real estate properties were declared 'absentee property'.

In today's value, all these properties would amount to billions of dollars, since Jerusalem and its immediate surroundings would be the Mayfair and the Park Lane of any global Monopoly game.

Property ownership in West Jerusalem was (and is) as follows: forty percent of West Jerusalem was privately Palestinian owned, twenty-six percent was Jewish owned and the rest belonged to the Muslim Awqaf (Muslim Trust), to the different Christian Churches and to the Government of Palestine.

Let me just give a few examples as to what happened after the dispersion and dispossession of the Palestinians in 1948.[2]

The Hilton and the Sonesta Hotels are now built on the property of Lifta village (since then annexed to the municipal boundaries of West Jerusalem). So are the Knesset, the Prime Minister's office, the Ministry for Foreign Affairs and the Ministry of Interior. The Israeli Knesset is built on the property of the Khalaf family from Lifta, now residing in the East Jerusalem neighbourhood of Sheikh Jarrah, which was annexed after the 1967 war, which makes the Khalaf family very 'present absentees'. But no one ever thought of compensating them.

I share Michael Safier's hope that, in a not too distant future, there will be on one hill of Jerusalem the Israeli Knesset and on another hill the Palestinian Parliament. They will have two features in common. Both would have been democratically elected and both would have been built on Palestinian land.

The houses in the centre of Deir Yassin – the second of the villages vacated by Palestinians and annexed by the West Jerusalem

Municipality – are used today as an Israeli sanatorium for the mentally ill, run by the Ministry of Health.

The Israeli Hadassa Hospital is built on Ein Karem lands. So is Yad Vashem, the memorial for the Jewish victims of Nazism.

The stadium of West Jerusalem is built on the El Malha village and so is the recently opened Jerusalem Mall.

The Israeli Independence Park is on a Muslim cemetery in the Mamilla neighbourhood, where also a superb building, owned by the Muslim Awqaf, and which housed in the 1930s the first Palestinian theatre, has been transformed into the Israeli Ministry of Trade and Industry.

I could continue endlessly …

On the eve of the 1967 war, the West Jerusalem Municipality was composed of 37,000 dunums. The war ended, one of the first decisions of the Israeli Government was to dismiss the Arab Municipal Council of East Jerusalem headed by Mr Rouhi Al Khatib, who was then deported to Amman, and to annex East Jerusalem and much of its surroundings, up north to Ramallah and down south to Bethlehem. East Jerusalem was thus expanded three times beyond its previous dimensions and saw an additional 72,000 dunums annexed to a 'Unified Jerusalem'. Twenty-four thousand dunums of those 72,000 have since then been confiscated and a belt of Israeli settlements – fortresses that Mr Ibrahim Mattar calls 'the new walls of Jerusalem' – has been erected on those expropriated lands suffocating East Jerusalem and disarticulating the West Bank.

The choreography of the expanded and annexed East Jerusalem is both intriguing and interesting. The lands of several villages were annexed but not the villages themselves so that the demographic balance does not tilt to the Palestinians' advantage. That was the case of four villages to the East of East Jerusalem: Hizma, Anata, Bethani and Abu Dis. That was also the case of the villages of Beit Iksa and Beit Hanina to the west of East Jerusalem. To the north, Jerusalem airport was annexed but not its immediate neighbourhoods of Dahiet Al Barid, El Ram and the refugee camp of Kalandia.

Had those neighbourhoods and villages been annexed, a minimum of an additional 80,000 Palestinian inhabitants would have been added to Jerusalem.

Figures announced in August 1993 show that Jerusalem – East and West – has a global number of 564,300 inhabitants. West Jerusalem inhabitants number 260,900 and East Jerusalem 303,400, with Jewish settlers already outnumbering the indigenous Muslim and Christian inhabitants by 152,800 to 150,600.

It is highly disturbing that the international media insists on speaking of 120,000 settlers in the Occupied Territories. This shows a great degree of indulgence towards the Israeli position which tends not to include the settlers in and around East Jerusalem. The demographic balance today in the West Bank is 1,200,000 Palestinians and 280,000 Israeli settlers (over 152,800 in expanded East Jerusalem plus 120,000 in the rest of the West Bank). In the Gaza Strip, the presence of 4,000 settlers has already ruined the euphoric 'Oslo Spirit' generated in August-September 1993.

Some concluding remarks:

1. This intense and now accelerating settlement activity was conducted by successive Israeli governments, left, right and centre, since 1967. A great number of UN resolutions – at both levels in the General Assembly and in the Security Council – were adopted trying to deter and to dissuade Israel from this course of action in defiance of international law and conventions governing the behaviour of an occupying authority. All those resolutions unambiguously condemned Israel's annexation of East Jerusalem, considered it 'null and void' and declared the settlements 'illegal'.

   Because of this mercifully unequivocal legal position but also for pragmatic considerations, the settlers have to be withdrawn for the final status agreement to work. Settlers do not represent the most adorable segment of Israeli society and are not at all equipped to be the bridge for future harmonious relations between the two communities. Leaving them behind is the best recipe for failure. Any solution to be acceptable and durable has to remedy, at least partially, historical injustices inflicted. I personally believe that the settlements should be left as part of the compensation that the Israeli State owes Palestinian society, even though the architecture is of a very questionable taste. But here too, we are expected to show tolerance.

2. Since the Palestinian side has had to reluctantly accept that the status of Jerusalem be decided in the second phase of negotiations to start 'no later than the beginning of the third year' of Palestinian self-government and since the Israelis are unscrupulously multiplying *faits accomplis* that are justifiably perceived as prejudicing the outcome of negotiations, I believe that the Palestinians need to take the audacious initiative – a unilateral step – of establishing a Shadow Palestinian Municipal Council. This initiative can go parallel to the peace process and will be a collective act of non-violent defiance against a *status quo* – an established disorder – that we totally reject and that the world disapproves of.

3. We are all aware of the shortcomings and the risks entailed in the Oslo Accords but we should capitalise on the windows of opportunity that the agreements have to offer. Today many Palestinians are planning to visit the occupied homeland after decades of diasporisation. Many are contemplating a possible return and are exploring available options and possible avenues. That trend has to be encouraged. The addition of individual cases will transform it into a collective phenomenon. In this respect, I have to pay tribute to Professor Abu Lughod, who abandoned a brilliant academic career in the most prestigious American universities to come back and teach in the West Bank at Bir Zeit University. His highly appreciated decision has created a role model that will be emulated in the near future.

4. Jerusalem is so unique that it deserves the two-embassies solution. Peter Mansfield keeps reminding me that I do not need to have the word 'unique' preceded by 'so'. But I like the unnecessary emphasis. In future, Jerusalem can remain undivided. I deliberately avoid the word 'united' because it was perverted by the Israeli annexationists. It will be two cities, two capitals for two separate and sovereign political entities with freedom of access to everybody everywhere and each religious shrine will be run and managed by the relevant religious community. Embassies will be opened in East Jerusalem accredited to the Palestinian State and embassies will be transferred from Tel Aviv to West Jerusalem accredited to the Israeli State. After 1967, the American Consulate in Jerusalem tried to initiate a one-reception event for both East and West on the occasion of their Independence Day on the 4 July. A two-state solution, a two-embassies solution also mean a two-cocktails solution. The more receptions there are, the merrier it will be.

In answer to several questions by the audience:

I will single out one of the four points that Michael Dumper offered as factors for greater optimism, namely, the lure of Tel Aviv for West Jerusalem liberals. On the contrary, I find this phenomenon as a source for greater worry because we are left with right-wing and ultra-orthodox residents who are much more fanatical and less accommodationist. With settlement building around occupied East Jerusalem continuing with even greater acceleration, we have to note that the more recent the Jewish immigrant the more radical he/she is. During my visit to Jerusalem, I was harassed twice by settlers. One happened to be a recent immigrant from Latvia, the other from Brooklyn, New York. The most brutal coercers of the Palestinians today are the Falashas in the Israeli army.

The point raised by Leila Fanous concerns Palestinian return. I have just come back from a visit to Jerusalem after more than a quarter of a century. Of the thirty-six pupils of my class of 1966 in the College des Freres, only three are still in Jerusalem and the thirty-three others are scattered literally in the four corners of the world. The age category of the 30 to 50 year olds is almost non-existent in Jerusalem. It is as if society has simply skipped one generation. Most were in my case abroad to pursue university studies in 1967 when East Jerusalem was occupied, annexed and a demographic census conducted. We became legally non-existent. In 1968, I applied for family reunification but I was offered instead a tourist visa, for one month, non-extendable, on condition that I show my return ticket before I am allowed in Jerusalem. Involved in student politics – and then was the golden era of student politics – even a new tourist visa became impossible.

I personally believe that our struggle will grow increasingly non-military but will remain equally as challenging, if not more challenging, and demanding. Up to now we have paid the price of the peace process: Israel has rehabilitated itself internationally, it has renewed diplomatic relations with almost all countries, and funds and investments are pouring in. The peace process and the new ambience created allow us now to start visiting our homeland. Visiting is a first step. It can become an unstoppable bulldozer. Some say, 'I won't go back unless and until the situation has changed'. My answer is that the situation won't change unless and until we start going back. There is going to be a battle for Jerusalem. It is of a demographic nature, and of an institutional nature. We should practise our beliefs. We believe in the indivisible nature of the Palestinian people and, from now on, we should achieve enhanced Palestinian-Palestinian-Palestinian co-operation in all fields, meaning the Palestinians of the diaspora, the emerging Palestinian entity, and Israeli Palestinians. For example, a Palestinian publisher in London can have the books he publishes printed in Jerusalem. It has economic rationality – much cheaper – but also political and strategic significance; that of energising the Palestinian economy. The struggle in Palestine has been: 'Whose demography on whose geography?' and we should spare no effort in creating job opportunities for all those still there and, even further, to integrate returning Palestinians. Palestinian refugees now living in the periphery of Amman, Damascus, Beirut and Sidon should not be expected to come back and live in the periphery of Nablus and Hebron. Only a dynamic economy can integrate large numbers of returnees as full partners and participants in the new society and new political entity. I am personally very unhappy and unsatisfied with our political under-development. I believe we have neither the establishment or institutions we deserve nor the opposition we need. Working at improving both is a very worthy task. For better strategic planning we need better of both.

Michael Safier used a word I frequently resort to in my parallel discourse: cosmopolitan. Yet I am not sure we give the same meaning to that concept. The Palestinian people is an Arab people whose culture is Arab and Islamic. They include a small but dynamic Christian minority. At the crossroads of three continents it has been historically an outward orientated society. Having holy places for the three monotheistic religions has put it in daily contact with the outside world and the world daily comes to Jerusalem. For a variety of reasons, Palestinian society today is one of the best equipped to reconcile harmoniously authenticity and modernity, specificity and universality. Jerusalem has been, and should be, the centre of gravity of cultural cross-fertilisation and of the dialogue of civilisations. It is there that we can move beyond confrontation towards authentic reconciliation. Yet I do not believe that Zionism and settlement building have enriched the cosmopolitan tissue and texture of society in Jerusalem. Being exclusivist and expulsionist, it has rather impoverished Jerusalem.

Religion: I am totally foreign to any attempt to give this conflict religious connotation. I have always been exasperated by the use, misuse and abuse of religion in political struggles.

The intrusion of religion in political debates has always exacerbated tensions. Anyway God is usually innocent of the behaviours/misbehaviour of those who pretend to be guided or inspired by Him/Her.

Uri Davis addressed the issue of settlement and settlers. There are four categories of settlers: the security settlers, the ideological settlers, the ecological settlers and the economic settlers. The security settlers were put in place just after the 1967 war in what was designated as strategic locations. Military experts now consider them to be more a security liability rather than a strategic asset. The economic settlers are the ones who were enticed and attracted by economic incentives, cheaper housing, credit facilities etc. The ecological settlers are mainly yuppies, young professionals who were seeking unpolluted areas out of West Jerusalem or Tel Aviv and an 'apartment with a view' on the Dead Sea or the Judean Desert. The ideological settlers, the most aggressive of the four categories, are the religion-motivated settlers who believe that the Palestinians are the contemporary Amaleks of the Bible that God wishes to see expelled or exterminated.

I personally believe that leaving the settlers is a recipe for failure and disaster. They have settled in occupied territories in total defiance of the international community and of international law. Their continued presence is not only wrong legally and ethically but also pragmatically. They have declared openly that they are organising in an underground paramilitary organisation. They will have one of two types of behaviours, if not both, like the OAS and the French *pieds-noirs* of Algeria. They will either go into Palestinian neighbourhoods to provoke tension and friction, feeding the spiral of violence, or hope to be beaten so as to project of themselves the image of an endangered species re-inviting the Israeli army back if and when it had withdrawn. The Israeli society and leadership have to face the fact that the settlers do not represent the most adorable segment of Israeli society and they are hardly the best equipped to be the bridge for future harmonious relations. After the emergence of the Palestinian entity, individual Israelis can apply, through normal institutional channels, for residing in Palestinian territory. Yet I do not think that anyone who wants to pray in a shrine of religious significance has to settle beside it. My family, we go to Rome and to the Vatican and then we move along, without expressing any claim, though we believe we are the descendants of the early Christians, those who were sent to the circus to amuse the mob and feed the lions. I mention that because some invoke suffering as a valid argument for territorial claims.

Gayth Armanazi raised the issue of how to move from A to B. It is 'the question' still begging for an answer. Having taken part in a variety of diplomatic encounters or academic seminars, I have realised that diplomacy is not an exercise in intellectual seduction. It is a confrontation of wills within the framework of a certain *rapport de force,* where every advantage is taken of any disequilibrium of power. I believe if the local belligerent parties are left to themselves – as is the case now – they will never achieve an acceptable compromise. I have supported the Oslo Agreement *faute de mieu,* as the least unattractive of a set of very unattractive alternatives.

Mr Chairman, I belong to a minority school of thought that advocates an elegantly imposed solution – if need be inelegantly – from the outside that is mutually unacceptable. Bearing in mind the pathology of conflict and the psychology of the belligerents, I believe that 'mutually unacceptable' carries more potential than the concept of 'mutual acceptability'. Since both societies tend to believe that Mandatory Palestine is totally theirs, the two-state solution should be the solution aimed at hoping that both states will opt in the future for vertical expansion rather than horizontal expansions, one at the detriment of the other. This will not be a just peace, but it will be just acceptable. Anyway the Palestinians have resigned themselves to aim at possible justice rather than absolute justice.

I personally am in favour of an interventionist United Nations body. I believe that in our contemporary international system – and I prefer international system to world order because the concept of order has moral connotations that system totally lacks – UN supremacy is the only possible substitute to American hegemony. During the last three decades international pressure was exerted on the Arab side to reduce their demands. We had to discover that there were three layers in political expectations: the desirable, the possible and the acceptable. We had to discover that not everything desirable was possible, not everything possible was acceptable. As a consequence we had to reconcile our national rights with the international will.

The same pressures have now to be exercised on the Israeli side. I am revolted by the self-inflicted impotence of the major external actors when dealing with the Middle East. Palestinian decision-making has to take place in the most uncomfortable political environment. We have to constantly bear in mind: 1) Arab impotence; 2) the decline, then the demise, of the Soviet Union; 3) the abdication of Europe for a geo-strategic role; 4) the paralysis of the UN; and 5) the total alignment of the US on every capricious Israeli preference, priority or policy. External pressure will be most helpful to the most advanced or enlightened Israeli politicians who are now hostages to a public opinion that they have once helped to fanaticise. Anyway, peace in the Middle East is too important to be left to the Israelis alone to decide upon. But, for the moment, given the givens, they believe that they can set the ceiling of the possible and of the permissible. That they can dictate the pace of progress of the peace process: extremely slowly.

Notes

1. The study recently published by PASSIA (Palestinian Academic Society for the Study of International Affairs) in Jerusalem. *The Municipality of Arab Jerusalem* by Oussama Halabi (in Arabic) traces the history and the composition of the Jerusalem Municipal Council.
2. I have relied on data contained in Mr Ibrahim Mattar's very informative paper: 'To whom does Jerusalem belong?' which is an update of his article: 'From Palestinian to Israeli: Jerusalem 1948–82', published in the *Journal of Palestine Studies*, Summer 1983 no. 48.

XII

Those were the days[1]

Ladies and gentlemen,

Of the many duties I have had to undertake here in London during the last four years, your invitation today will probably be the one I will remember, in the future, with the greatest tenderness and affection.

Having been successively, some two decades ago, president of both the Belgian, then the French, sections of the General Union of Palestinian Students (GUPS), your invitation has plunged me in nostalgic recollections of what is supposed to have been the golden age of the international student movement, from Berkeley to Belgium and Berlin, from Paris to Prague.

Those were the days, my friends, when we reinvented the world and the future almost every day. Voracious readers, we used to engage in sleepless nights and endless talks about the ideal society. Some of us were ready to die in bringing about their ideals. Others wanted simply to live them. Schools of thought proliferated and they all revolved around the idea of social change and – yes, already then – a new international system. Some thought change in the centre would be decisive while others considered changes in the periphery to be the recommended course of action. Some regarded the working classes in the industrialised nations to be the major

---

1. Speech delivered on the occasion of the inaugural session of the Global Festival celebrating the Centenary Year of the London School of Economics at the invitation of the Student Union – 6 February 1995.

175

agents of change while others looked upon the peasantry of the Third World as the vehicle of social transformation. Some argued that the state, which had to become a neutral body based on meritocracy, would assume this function by being the guarantor, the regulator and the redistributor within society while Herbert Marcuse, one of my generation's favourite authors, flattered our egos with his theory that in our contemporary society, where we witness the embourgeoisement of the proletariat and the continuing conservatism of the peasantry, students, and only the students, were the sole agent of the desirable change. Students, those future intellectuals, were a topic Antonio Gramsci had addressed with great eloquence. Advocating a special relationship between the oppressed and the intelligentsia he called for 'an alliance between those who think because they suffer and those who suffer because they think.'

So we thought and thought and I am sure that our elders must have suffered when hearing us think aloud. But that is altogether another story.

Our slogans then reflected '*l'air du temps*': '*l'imagination au pouvoir*', '*le droit à la différence*' (the right to be different), '*il est interdit d'interdire*' (it is forbidden to forbid). A favourite among many was '*le droit à la pareses*', the right to be lazy, which incidentally referred to the legitimacy and desirability of general strikes rather than the appealing notion of *dolce vita* based on *fare niente*.

'*Il faut s'occuper de la politique sinon la politique s'occupera de vous.*' You should take care of politics or else politics will take care of you.

And the last that I will quote: 'Politics is too important to be left to politicians.'

Each of us had his or her heroes and *maitre(s) à penser*. Some became dogmatic and doctrinaire. But great intellectual diversity and tolerance was the major feature of those times. I was, what we used then to call, eclectic, belonging to no chapel, no clique or clan. Because of my historical and sociological background, Jesus and Mohammed had undeniable influence on my intellectual upbringing. The principles of *'liberté, fraternité, égalité'* and the French Revolution itself had exercised a great fascination on me. As a Palestinian who favoured Arab unity, I showed an early interest in Bismarck, Cavour and Garibaldi, Jamal Abdel Nasser but also in Jean Monnet. I read Marx, in depth, and never became a Marxist myself yet had often to protect him from frequent misinterpretations, distortions and mutilations of some of his disciples just as many of us have frequently to proclaim God's innocence of beliefs and behaviours perpetrated on His/Her behalf. Let us not forget that Jewish fundamentalists have transformed God into some sort of real estate agent.

I devoted much time to Lenin and Mao, finishing an MA thesis in the very Catholic University of Louvain in Belgium – in fact the oldest Catholic university in the world, established in 1425 – on 'Revolutionary Strategies and the Conquest of Power: A Comparative Study of the Bolshevik and Maoist Revolutions,' yet had a special weakness towards those who encountered a tragic fate (Che Guevara, JFK and Martin Luther King), or were maltreated by history and by their contemporaries (Leon Trotsky) or had gained power only to abandon it voluntarily (Emiliano Zapata).

To add to the irritation of some of my friends, I remained totally unseduced and unmoved by the Chinese Cultural Revolution and openly preferred Chou en Lai the statebuilder, the technocrat to the unattractive and constantly intriguing manipulative agitator Lin Piao.

This list would be incomplete if I were to omit my obsession with and admiration of Charles de Gaulle, this Western leader that Stanley Hoffman had called *'un artiste de la politique.'* He had had to struggle, brilliantly, against foes and friends alike to maintain the rank of France undiminished after its devastating defeat in 1940. The analogy with the Palestinian re-emerging national movement would not have escaped you. His tumultuous relationship with that other giant – Winston Churchill – would keep me awake night after night. Churchill had summarised this complex rapport by saying: 'Of the many crosses I have had to carry, the Cross of Lorraine was surely the heaviest' (the Cross of Lorraine being, of course, the symbol of the French Resistance). Again, regional analogies were obvious.

My fascination with de Gaulle was responsible for some of my most tormenting moments. I was, then, in total solidarity with the French student movement, but this movement was irreparably destabilising de Gaulle. Anyway, even his abdication was done with such grandeur that his place in history – undiminished and unstained – was preserved for posterity.

In 1972, I moved from Belgium to the Institut d'Etudes Politiques in Paris and got involved in discussions on the nature and the scope of Political Science itself. Some of you present here today would remember that as a relatively new discipline Political Science was still struggling to assert itself and its domain. So we still called it then 'Political Sciences', in the plural, seeing it as a sort of interdisciplinary field, it is true, dealing with the study of the state, of government and of power in general, but encompassing History, International Relations, Sociology and Economics with very unclear demarcation lines. In Anglo-Saxon countries, they had no problem describing students of and experts in political science, a political scientist – but in the French-speaking world, even that was subject for debate and dissent. Some called him/her a '*politiste*,' others preferred '*politoloque*,' yet others favoured '*politicoloque*.' The jokers would simply say '*les sciences poseurs*'.

Ladies and gentlemen, this was the flavour of those times. We were then young and audacious, questioning everything and everyone. We were the world '*en miniature*' with an experimental 'global village' mentality. We were one, yet, in every sense, plural. We shared values and dreams and were endeavouring hard to reconcile our respective cultural authenticities with what we thought was modernity, to reconcile our respective political specificities with what we hoped was universality. Universality for us was surely not the American way of life or Western hegemony but an elusive and yet to be defined constellation of ideas and values enriched by the many inputs of every culture and civilisation. I am sure that the quest for 'that universality' still goes on today in this university and elsewhere too.

Yes, we were one and plural: proud nationalists, profoundly internationalists, totally cosmopolitan. With the student movement on the ascendancy, catalysed by the Vietnamese tragedy, the 1967 war took place in the Middle East resulting in the humiliating defeat of the Arab armies and the Palestinian reawakening. Israel, in a continuing process of elastic expansion, dispossession and dispersion, occupied East Jerusalem, the West Bank and Gaza in addition to the Sinai and the Golan. A whole generation of Palestinian students were trapped abroad and when Israel conducted a demographic census, we all became legally non-existent. This student community became the new wandering Palestinians. Many of us were already active in resurrecting the Palestinian National Movement around Yasser Arafat and his colleagues. Now most joined in, becoming a major influence within the PLO.

Already in those days many of our friends were Jews. They were anti-Zionists or non-Zionists. The West, then, was a cemetery for those in politics, in the media or in academia who dared question Israel's intentions or dare condemn its policies and practices. Reputations were ruined, careers were shattered and character assassination was the name of the game. Israel felt immune to criticism and the most unacceptable intellectual terrorism prevailed, as a powerful deterrent. Philippe de St Robert wrote that he received a letter from one of his readers saying, 'You are an objective writer but when Israel is concerned, impartiality is unwelcomed.' So some of the best critical books or articles were then mainly written by Jewish scholars. But even they would not escape insults and abuse. 'Self-hating Jews' would be one of the mildest. The most radical among them would question the very legitimacy of the Zionist enterprise in Palestine while the more moderate believed that the creation of a Palestinian State was a Jewish moral obligation, a Jewish ethical responsibility. I still remember, with enormous political gratitude, Rabbi Elmer Berger, Alfred Lilienthal of *What price Israel?* and of course Naom Chomsky in the USA. In Belgium, Marcel Liebeman and Nathan Wienstock. In France, Ania Francos, Ilan Halevy and Maxime Rodinson and what was then the highly needed eye-opener in intellectual circles, his *Israel: a colonial settler State*. In the UK, Eli Lobel, Moshe Machover, Uri Davis and Isaac Deutscher. Deutscher, in his criticism of the 'Prussians of the Middle East', offered a parable of his own to make comprehensible the human dimensions of the Israeli-Palestinian conflict. Putting aside the calculations of politicians and the machinations of states, he said that this conflict was between a person who had to jump from a building on fire but landed on another person whose back he broke. Each time the second person moaned in pain or tried to stand up again, he would receive a beating for fear of revenge or claims for compensation.

A prominent French Jewish intellectual visited Israel during those years and returned profoundly disturbed by the arrogance and the macho military mentality he encountered. I will never forget his remark then: 'These Israelis are no more Jews.'

'These Israelis are no more Jews.' An interesting statement that deserves one day some further elaboration.

Rightly or wrongly, we were then considered a generation of

adorable or of exasperating dreamers. Rightly or wrongly, the generations who followed were perceived as more disciplined, more career-orientated. But there were a few exceptions, among others the Palestinian students of the West Bank and Gaza who played a leading role during the first years of the intifada. They were models of self-sacrifice to whom the entire nation is eternally indebted.

Some decades ago, Daniel Bell followed by Raymond Aron predicted 'the end of ideologies'. Years later, the end of history itself was announced to which Andre Fontaine, in a beautifully worded article in *Le Monde*, responded by saying, 'If it is true that we witness the end of history, then we are living the beginning of boredom.'

The way you have decided to celebrate the 100th anniversary of your Alma Mater, the theme – Globalism – that you have chose for the centenary festival, proves that we are not, definitely not, witnessing the end of idealism.

XIII

The role of third parties[1]

Secretary of State,
Excellencies,
My Lords, ladies and gentlemen.

It is a privilege for me to be invited to speak again at MAP's
annual dinner. A very successful British-Palestinian charity. To
us all, MAP is a constant reminder that politics is not only about
power, but mainly about people. Throughout the years, your annual
gathering has undeniably become a major social event for the Arab
community in London and for their British friends. Our presence
here tonight is a tribute to the remarkable work undertaken by
MAP's dedicated staff and volunteers. Allow me today to single out
one individual: the late Dr Riad Khreishi. Riad incarnated MAP's
spirit and philosophy. His love and devotion for his country and
his community were unparalleled and I will always regret that my
arrival in London coincided with his physical decline, depriving
me prematurely of his valuable advice and guidance. I can still
remember how during his last weeks he would frequently drag
himself painfully to my office to share with me in his own way his
political testament of lessons drawn from his active and eventful
life.

---

1. Speech delivered at the Annual Dinner, Medical Aid for Palestinians,
    Park Lane Hotel, London on 23 May 1996. The keynote speaker was
    Secretary of State the Rt. Hon. Malcolm Rifkind MP.

Today, all our wishes for success go to Saida Nuseibeh and I am fully confident that she will be faithful to a distinguished and long family tradition in public service.

Ladies and gentlemen, today's event takes place a few weeks after the outrageous aggression against the Lebanese people, a few days before the Israeli general elections, ten days before President Yasser Arafat's visit to the United Kingdom, and a few weeks before restarting decisive negotiations on final status.

For us Arabs, there will always be 'before Qana' and an 'after Qana'. From 1948 until April 1996, Arab casualties were at best simply figures, just numbers that would even sometimes go unmentioned as though they were faceless, nameless, fatherless, motherless, childless ... worthless. Whether there is one mankind or different kinds of men and women seems to be an issue that has not yet received an adequate answer. In interviews with the Israeli weekly, *Kol Ha'ir*, Israeli soldiers were quoted saying that they had no regrets over killing more than one hundred civilians sheltering in a United Nations base because the dead, they said, 'were just a bunch of Arabs.' To raise morale apparently, a commander gathered his troops after the shelling and told them, 'anyway there are millions of them,' 'them' being *Arabushim*, a Hebrew derogatory term which, fortunately, has no English equivalent.

How often have we heard, 'This time Israel has shot itself in the foot'? But it seems that Israel has many more than two feet to shoot at since miraculously it keeps getting away with almost anything.

Ladies and gentlemen, we should spare no effort in conveying the message that we are definitely not children of a lesser God and that our tears and blood do also count.

In the midst of horror in Lebanon, Prime Minister Shimon Peres, paradoxically our partner in peace, in his attempt to prove to the Israeli electorate that he is not unlike his predecessor Rabin, he started to resemble General Sharon. One is tempted to say 'With a dove like that, who needs hawks.' If I speak with passion, it is because we, the Palestinians, have a special bond with the Lebanese people. We are greatly indebted to Lebanon for having carried with us the burden of our national resurrection.

Ladies and gentlemen, I have no doubt that the Israeli political class left, right and centre – and the Israeli public at large – aspire to achieve peace, yet it seems to me that they still, to varying degrees, wish it to be a reflection of Israeli intransigence, American alignment, European abdication, Russian decline, Arab impotence and, as a result, Palestinian resignation. How this peace is expected to be lasting, durable, final, permanent, I have difficulties to comprehend. And I dare not utter the words brave, honourable, equitable, just, or even just acceptable.

Ladies and gentlemen, Israel will be ill-advised if it were to confuse Palestinian realism with resignation and it is high time that the Israeli society underwent a much needed soul-searching exercise, an ethical debate revolving around 'What price Israel?' – about the human and political cost paid by us the Palestinian people, individually and collectively since four generations.

Israel was supposed to be an answer to what was called the 'Jewish question'. As a result we became the Palestinian question, a problem that awaits an equitable and satisfactory answer. I have not despaired yet that one day, hopefully soon, our people will hear expressions of remorse that will help pave the way for authentic reconciliation. Such an ethical undertaking seems indispensable if we are to move away from power politics, military preponderance and regional hegemony.

Such a soul-searching exercise is today possible because Israel is in a strategically comfortable situation. It enjoys nuclear monopoly in the area with all that this exclusivity implies. It has overwhelming conventional superiority *vis-à-vis* any possible Arab coalition. And thirdly it enjoys an 'unwritten alliance' with the only remaining superpower which seems to be more advantageous than a formal written alliance since it does not require responsible behaviour from the junior partner that can freely operate as an 'undisciplined ally'.

Ladies and gentlemen, a sovereign independent state is undeniably a Palestinian right. It is also an Israeli duty, an Israeli moral obligation, a Jewish ethical responsibility.

Today the electoral victory of Shimon Peres seems to be an international concern. To that effect Peres was offered a spectacular summit in Sharm El-Sheikh which was diverted and hijacked from its initial purpose. He was offered excessive understanding towards the multiple closures inflicted on Palestinian areas literally strangling the society and the economy. He was offered embarrassed silence during the initial phases of aggression on Lebanon and, in spite of all that, he was offered a warm reception at the White House where shared values were again stressed. Some might even interpret my heavy-handed criticism of Peres as a modest but subtle contribution to help him rally right-wing undecided voters.

Ladies and gentlemen, I have my doubts on whether a policy aiming only at helping Peres translates necessarily into support of the peace we all aspire to see achieved. Shimon Peres has a tendency to believe that he can set the parameters of the possible and of the permissible. The transitional agreements were accepted only because of their temporary nature. I hope that after Israeli elections negotiations on final status will start in a new mood, a new environment, a new mentality.

I personally believe that the best way, today, to support the peace process is to have major actors of our contemporary international system send an unequivocal, unambiguous message to Israeli public opinion, preferably now in an election period that whoever they elect on 29 May is expected to comply with certain internationally accepted principles and abide by internationally adopted resolutions. Such an international attitude will help liberate the Israeli political class from a hostage situation *vis-à-vis* a public opinion that they helped fanaticize throughout the last decades. In that way, the Israeli voters will express their preference on 29 May on the basis of the experience or inexperience of the candidates, their charisma or its absence and socioeconomic policies and not on how much land and peace they are willing to condescendingly restore to their legitimate owners. Peace is too important to be left to the Israelis alone to decide upon. The Oslo Channel should encourage external actors to adopt a more decisive, visible and assertive role. If the Oslo connection has not yet put Palestine fully on the map, it has, for sure, put Norway on the map.

Secretary of State, we feel privileged to have you among us today. For us Palestinians, the United Kingdom is a very important interlocutor. You were the Mandatory Power in Palestine present, to say the least, at the creation of the Palestinian problem. You are a permanent member of the Security Council of the UN and we are not resigned to its total absence in our quest for peace. You are a major pillar of the European Union and enjoy special relations with Washington, where you have often played the role of an inspiring Athens to what seems frequently as an unsophisticated contemporary Rome. With all these factors in mind, President Yasser Arafat will come to London early next month.

Secretary of State, we have a dream. A dream only you can make come true. A dream of a Rifkind Declaration. A declaration that takes the lead in spelling out support for Palestinian aspirations and Palestinian rights. A declaration that addresses the principles, conditions and contours of the desirable peace.

I know some sceptics, some cynics, might say that Britain in this *fin de siecle* is not what it used to be at the turn of the century, but I am sure that British public opinion will 'view with favour' that Britain again 'punches above its weight'.

XIV

Historical or territorial compromise[1]

The Israeli government seems to believe that the peace process is the continuation of war by other means. The drive towards the rampant annexation of the occupied territories is pursued relentlessly making the coming negotiations on final status simply meaningless.

Land for Peace and UN Security Council Resolution 242 are the basis of the current peace process. For the Arab side, Palestinians included, the desirable historical compromise between the belligerent parties meant that in exchange of Israeli withdrawal from the 1967 expansion, recognition will be bestowed on Israeli existence in its pre-1967 boundaries. This is the historical compromise that is on offer and it meets all the requirements that were expected from the Arab side to establish a durable comprehensive peace.

Israeli successive governments prefer the concept of territorial compromise. With that concept in mind, they consider the West Bank (and the occupied Golan) as disputed land and propose to meet us half way, somewhere in between Jerusalem and Jericho. On the other hand, the Arabs consider Mandatory Palestine to be the disputed area and propose to meet the Israelis along the 4 June 1967 frontiers and nowhere else but in Jerusalem. The Israelis repeat constantly that all Jerusalem is their internal capital and that it is not negotiable because it is at the heart of the Jewish people. Real peace and authentic reconciliation necessitate the Israeli public

---

1. Preface to the booklet by Mr Ibrahim Mattar, *The Transformation of Jerusalem 1948–1997.*

opinion to admit finally that we too happen to have a memory, a history and a heart and that Jerusalem is at its centre.

Former Secretary of State Malcolm Rifkind, in a detailed speech on 23 May 1996 declared, 'as is well known, Britain made clear many years ago, as did the international community, that it considered Israel to be in military occupation of East Jerusalem and to have only de facto authority over West Jerusalem.'

His Holiness Pope John Paul II, the Archbishop of Canterbury Dr George Carey and the Secretary General of the World Council of Churches, Dr Conrad Raizer, all three have declared in the most responsible manner, that in Jerusalem there are two national aspirations to be satisfied and three religious rights to be respected, They are surely not intruding outsiders as a regrettable editorial of *The Times* seemed to imply in a very questionable article that endorsed blindly and vehemently, in the best (or worst) inquisitional tradition, a narrow Judeo-centred interpretation of the past and vision for the future.

The Palestinians and the Arabs, Islam and Christianity will never accept Jewish monopoly and hegemony in and over Jerusalem. Sharing Jerusalem is our goal and that of the international community. It is not the international community that has aligned itself on our position, but we were the ones who have moved gradually, since 1973, towards the international consensus.

XV

From breakthrough to breakdown?[1]

Deciding on titles for lectures is an interesting and intriguing affair. Speaking at MIT in 1986, at a moment of diplomatic stagnation, the title I gave to my talk then was 'Dead ends?' A friend later told me that the question mark after dead ends was my only concession to optimism. Years later, in May 1994, lecturing in California at the invitation of the World Affairs Council, I opted for: ' Palestine: A State in the making?' and then the question mark seemed as my only reluctant concession to pessimism.

During the Napoleonic wars which devastated Continental Europe, the Swiss had a wise saying: '*Les peuples heureux n'ont pas d'istoire.*' Happy peoples have no history. Well in Palestine/Israel, both peoples concerned are blessed or burdened and plagued with too much history. I still remember when Fukuyama wrote his article and then published the book *The End of History*, Andre Fontaine, the editor-in-chief of *Le Monde* in Paris, wrote in his regular column, 'If we really live the end of history, then we are witnessing the beginning of boredom.' Bearing in mind that 'may you live in interesting times' is a curse in China, you can imagine how often and how hard we sometimes yearn for a boring moment.

Chou en Lai, China's Prime Minister for decades, was extremely worried by the then widely acclaimed detente of the late sixties/ early seventies. He feared both American-Soviet collision but also American-Soviet collusion that might result in a world

---

1   Transcript of a lecture given at Harvard University in April 1997.

condominium. In his own inimitable way, he, the blasé statesman would warn, 'Detente is like a bed but where each makes a different dream.' Today the same could be said of the Middle East peace process. Everybody is in favour of peace of course. Majorities in each constituency support the peace process, but, like in Chou en Lai's detente, each player has a different finality in mind, where visions for end-results are competing and incompatible and the dreams of one side can be a nightmare for others.

When Labour was still in power in Israel, I often repeated that it seemed to me that in this peace process, we, the Palestinians, were interested in peace but that the Israeli side seemed more interested in the process itself. Today, with Netanyahu and the Likud presiding over an extreme right-wing coalition, I believe that we have neither peace nor a process anymore.

Let me retrace briefly important landmarks. After the end of the Gulf war in 1991, the USA could not remain inactive towards what former British Secretary of State Douglas Hurd had called the 'unfinished business', namely the unresolved Israeli-Arab conflict.

From March to October, 1991, Secretary of State James Baker undertook multiple trips to the area in what I called then negotiating pre-negotiations leading to pre-negotiating negotiations. It was an exercise of shuttle diplomacy dealing with talks about talks about talks.

Years earlier, both at the think-tank in Washington close to the Israeli lobby AIPAC and in the American magazine *Commentary*, abundant literature on conflict resolution in the Middle East was produced with the following recommendations emphasised:

1. With the decline of the Soviet Union and of communism, Islam and fundamentalism were the new global threat and in those new changing realities, Israel maintains an important strategic function as the regional ally;

2 The Palestinian question should not be given centrality in any quest for peace. The Arab countries should not be invited as a block to negotiate with Israel but as individual actors with different sets of priorities and concerns;

3. Israel should be enticed into a peace process by carrots – normalisation with non-neighbouring Arab countries, economic dividends etc – rather than the stick. Israel was to be encouraged by rewards rather than sanctions;

4. The UN and other third parties should have as limited a role as possible leaving the diplomatic outcome to emanate from the interaction of the local belligerent parties that would become negotiating partners. The international ramifications of the conflict were to be sized down to regional proportions and, even further, to a local dimension.

The team around James Baker had all worked in that think-tank, the Washington Institute for Near East Policies, and their motto was, 'We should make an offer to Israel that it cannot reject.' So they simply adopted Israel's preferred negotiating strategy and made it their own. The choreography of negotiations starting in Madrid, end of October 1991, was to be extremely complex with multiple bilateral tracks coupled with several multilateral talks.

In the aftermath of the Gulf War, the Orient was literally disoriented. Advantage was to be made out of Arab disarray. Minimum levels of co-ordination were lacking and Israel did not hesitate to take advantage of the difficulty in synchronising positions and progress in the different tracks.

In any negotiation, the nature of the forum, the nature and the number of the participants, determines the possible outcome. Instead of an international conference under UN auspices, we all were invited to a 'Peace Conference' with the USA and the rapidly vanishing USSR as co-sponsors. The UN was expected to be and to remain a silent observer. The European Community, that hoped – and the Arabs supported that aspiration – to be a co-sponsor playing a decisive role in the birth of a future Middle Eastern constellation, was relegated to a financial-economic role on the margin of the geo-strategic sphere kept jealously as the *domain reservé* of the Americans.

As we all remember, the Palestinians were offered to be half a delegation, representing half the people and seeking half a solution. Taking pretext that the Israeli government would not negotiate with the PLO and that it was also opposed to the emergence of a Palestinian State, the Palestinians were offered to sit in a joint Jordanian-Palestinian delegation. The Palestinian participants were supposed to be recruited from the West Bank and the Gaza Strip only, but no Jerusalem residents or diaspora Palestinians or PLO officials could be admitted in the negotiating room. The fact that it was the PLO leadership which selected the Palestinian negotiators and gave them legitimacy and instructions made former Israeli Foreign Minister Abba Eban say, 'Whether he likes it or not, Shamir is negotiating with the PLO, but he prefers to adopt the ostrich posture which is neither a comfortable nor an elegant posture.' By seeking half a solution I mean that, unlike the other tracks, we were expected to negotiate a five-year interim transitional period of Palestinian self-government on the road to final status. The more difficult issues – Jerusalem, the refugees, the settlements, boundaries and sovereignty – were deferred to a second phase starting no later than the beginning of the third year.

I have often described the Palestinian attitude then as being unreasonably reasonable and that not only because we are angelic but because peace, and peace now, corresponds to our enlightened national interest. Any loss of time is extremely detrimental for us. We are the ones whose land is being confiscated, whose water is being plundered, whose individuals are being deported, whose houses are being demolished, whose trees are being uprooted, whose universities and schools are being closed, whose economy is being strangled. Yet we went to Madrid with great expectations in spite of all the flawed and humiliating conditions, since we were led to believe that this was the only game in town. From March to October 1991, we carried all the burden of momentum, all the burden of flexibility, because we wanted to give peace a chance, hoping that Madrid would trigger a snowball process.

On the other hand, Israeli Prime Minister Shamir had to be dragged reluctantly and grudgingly to the negotiating table. He had difficulties understanding and adhering to the principles of 'land for peace', the basis and foundation of the entire exercise and his political 'generosity' and 'magnanimity' never went beyond offering peace for peace, and the perpetuation of the territorial *status quo*. In Madrid, he looked as though he had been ambushed and trapped. He sounded anachronistic and out of place. Months later, in June 1992, Madrid resulted in the electoral Waterloo for Shamir who, back in opposition, admitted and confessed that he intended to play delaying tactics at the negotiating table for ten years while accelerating settlement building and accomplished facts on the ground, creating thus an irreversible situation that even the peace process would not overcome.

From Madrid, the bilateral talks moved to Washington and the multilateral talks (arms control, economic development and integration, water, environment and refugees) literally to the four corners of the world. In Washington, resorting to 'corridor diplomacy', the Palestinian team succeeded in imposing an Israeli recognition of the gradual decoupling of the Jordanian and Palestinian tracks, while the composition of the different layers of the Palestinian team – PLO coordinators, diaspora advisors, Jerusalem spokespersons – reflected more and more the different categories of Palestinians that Israel wanted to see excluded.

But in Washington, the talks quickly stagnated and the change of Israeli government, from Likud to Labour, did nothing to reinvigorate them. The head of the Israeli negotiating team was confirmed in his functions signalling more continuity rather than change and Israel amused itself, but not others, by sometimes giving the semblance of an impression that it might shift the emphasis from the Palestinian to the Syrian track or back to the Palestinian without any tangible achievement anywhere.

In the meantime, the level of support among public opinions started to be seriously eroded. In Palestine, on their return from Madrid, the Palestinian team were welcomed by massive and spontaneous demonstrations where a new subversive weapon, the olive branch, was brandished proudly. But, by now, disenchantment and scepticism prevailed and radicalism was again on the ascendancy.

It is at this juncture that a secret channel was opened in Oslo by the Israeli government and the PLO and when, in August 1993, the breakthrough was announced, it took almost everybody by surprise, including the official negotiators in Washington. I keep saying, maybe impertinently, that if the Oslo channel has not yet put fully Palestine on the map, it has put Norway on the map. I usually offer this thought as an additional incentive to third parties with a potential for a decisive role in peacemaking.

The Declaration of Principles agreed upon in Oslo was signed on the White House lawn on 13 September 1993, with the world as witness. Even the reluctant hand extended by Rabin after an encouraging nod from Clinton to Arafat's enthusiastic availability did not ruin the mood or alter the general perception that history was in the making. It must be said here that Israel was finally negotiating with the Palestinian national movement as such representing the totality of the people as an indivisible unit.

Yet the magic, the spell, the charm were of short duration. Again at the negotiating table in Taba, the Palestinians were stunned to discover that Israel intended to keep forty percent of the Gaza Strip during the interim period. After laborious negotiations only twenty-eight percent remained under Israel's exclusive control and those were twenty-eight percent too many, knowing the Palestinian need for every single square inch in overcrowded Gaza. Also, the Israelis interpreted the 'Jericho area' they were meant to withdraw from as close as possible to the city limits, far beneath Palestinian expectations for freeing the 'Jericho province'. Again 'constructive ambiguities' in diplomacy proved to be a dangerous recipe.

Israel should be aware that redeployment out of Gaza was a Palestinian gift to Israel, and not the other way round, bearing in mind how unmanageable Gaza was for the occupying authorities. For the Palestinians, the test of Oslo, the credibility and the believability of Oslo, resided in further redeployment in the West Bank. If the process became static, the very pillars of its legitimacy would be seriously shaken. Yet Rabin was in no hurry, repeating that 'dates are not sacred', even though in the often unsatisfactory Oslo Agreement, the only precise area was the calendar of events. I believed and often repeated then that a territory that was occupied in 1967 in less than six days could be also evacuated in less than six days, so that Mr Rabin could rest on the seventh.

The assassination of Rabin by a fanatic right-winger sent shock waves through Israeli society. Peres, his successor, decided to move fast towards redeployment from the urban centres of the West Bank so that the Palestinians could go ahead with their presidential and legislative elections. Yasser Arafat had, in the meantime, obtained from the Islamic tendencies, through persuasion and also better control, several months of an unproclaimed ceasefire. During this period, it was the Israeli government and their secret services who were provoking the Islamists and not the Islamists provoking Israel. Dr Fathi Shikaki, leader of Islamic Jihad, was assassinated in Malta in October 1995, and Yehya Ayyash was exploded by telephone in

Gaza early in January 1996, in the midst of Palestinian territory and an election campaign.

Retaliation was to be predicted and, as expected, happened in March 1996 both in West Jerusalem and in Tel Aviv. Israel immediately resorted to its customary policy of closures and collective punishments that totally crippled Palestinian society and suffocated the Palestinian economy. The date of Israeli elections having been already advanced to May 1996, Peres decided to out-Likud Likud in his campaign message, to the extent that observers commented, 'With a dove like that who needs hawks. With a left like that, who needs a right?' He even waged an unnecessary war on Lebanon, and then succeeded in failing again in the Knesset elections.

Today, there is a tendency to view the Labour-led era with nostalgia. In a way, this is simply the prolongation of the undeserved praise and positive media coverage Labour usually got, whether right or wrong. History will record that, when Netanyahu assumed power, the Palestinian side already had thirty-four legitimate grievances on agreed upon issues that were left unimplemented during the interim period: freedom of movement for people and products, the management of the passages towards Jordan and Egypt, and through them to our Arab hinterland, the free passage along the corridor linking the Gaza Strip to the West Bank, the port, the airport, the freeze on settlement building. But now Netanyahu carried away by his victory, his ideological inclinations, his demagogic promises and a successful first trip to Washington, where senators and congressmen shamelessly gave him several standing ovations, simply declared war on the peace process, which he viewed as the continuation of war but by other means. The battle for Jerusalem was immediately waged, first with the opening of a controversial tunnel, then by the bulldozers in Jabal Abu Ghoniem. The mounting pressures, local and international, resulting from the tunnel crisis forced Netanyahu to implement an eighty percent redeployment in Hebron city. This was applauded, maybe too enthusiastically, as an indication that the pragmatic Netanyahu was prevailing on his more ideological nature. For the first time, Likud negotiated with the PLO and Likud was seen withdrawing within the West Bank. That victory was short lived, since he immediately rewarded or compensated his indispensable extreme right-wing coalition partners with bulldozers in Jabal Abu Ghuniem. The settlement there would be innocently repackaged as a 'suburb'. A week earlier, few Israelis had ever heard of Har Homan. Now, abandoning the site became equivalent to 'national suicide'.

I personally believe that, had Labour been in power, we would also have had a deadlocked situation. We have now finally reached the moment of truth: final status issues, and the gaps, if the parties are left to themselves, are simply unbridgeable.

In spite of all the diplomatic agitation, the local parties are left to themselves. And the overwhelming military superiority Israel enjoys encourages its insatiable appetite, making impossible an acceptable compromise. In the absence of decisive external input by third parties, this process is doomed to failure. Yes, it is true, the European Union have nominated a special envoy, yet his mediating efforts need a clearer mandate and, surely, more muscle. In the meantime, the Russians were busy managing their decline and occupied in occupying Chechnya. Warren Christopher and/or Dennis Ross, though frequent visits to the area, project the image of messengers with no message. The USA, a superpower all over the globe, seems to have abdicated this particular role in the Middle East in favour of its regional ally Israel. The American Congress is even more supportive of Israeli extravagance than the Knesset itself, validating the perception of Capitol Hill as that other Israeli occupied territory that needs to be liberated if we are to have a successful peace process.

American decision makers, but also other Western capitals, better realise soon that unlike the fifties, the sixties and the seventies, when Israel marketed itself as a bastion against militant Arab nationalism, Israeli intransigence today defies, destabilises and delegitimises a profoundly pro-Western Arab regional state system. In this context, is Israel a strategic asset or a liability? Awaiting the storm that will inevitably come, one wonders whether there is a convergence or rather a divergence and a bifurcation between Israeli ambitions and Western interests.

XVI

Out of Jerusalem?[1]

«في عام ١٩٤٨ ضيّعنا بلادنا وفي عام ١٩٦٧ ضيّعنا أولادنا».

'In 1948, we lost our country and in 1967 we lost our children.'
That was the observation made by my father, Emile Safieh, at the
end of June 1967. East Jerusalem had been conquered a few weeks
earlier by the Israeli 'defence' forces, then 'annexed' by the Israeli
occupying authorities, which immediately conducted a census as
a result of which my older brother Hanna and myself – abroad for
our university studies – became 'legally non-existent' in Jerusalem.
An entire generation of Palestinian students were trapped in foreign
countries in what was one more manifestation that Israel wanted
the geography without the demography.

Before 1948, my family lived in Upper Baqa'a, a residential
neighbourhood in West Jerusalem. In May 1948, days after the
massacre perpetrated by Jewish terrorists against the Deir Yassin
village (in the immediate vicinity of Jerusalem, in which 254
villagers were savagely butchered), they took shelter, like many
others, in the old city, where they shared half a classroom for four
months, in the St Joseph Girls School near Jaffa Gate. They then
left Lebanon and stayed in Broumana in the Hotel Freiha for
several months before moving to Damascus on their way back to
East Jerusalem in September 1949.

I arrived in May 1950. In my early teens, I had the first of
many existentialist crises. Reading books available at home, on

---

1.   From the booklet with the same title published by the Palestinian General
     Delegation/London in December 1997.

the 'absurdity' of life (Camus), brought back by my sister Diana, who had studied in England and Strasbourg, and flirting with the idea of suicide (Durkheim), I remember complaining to my parents that procreation was a very undemocratic exercise when the concerned party cannot be consulted on whether interested or not in coming to Planet Earth (Abu Ala'a al-Ma'arri). We all settled for the flattering explanation, for me of course, that I was, for the family, the 'consolation after the catastrophe'.

Having finished high school in 1966, I left for Belgium to the University of Louvain, the oldest Catholic university in the world, in existence since 1425. The 1967 war made me the 'wandering Palestinian' I still am. From Belgium, I moved to Paris to pursue my studies, then lived and worked in Geneva, Beirut, Belgium again, Harvard/Boston, The Hague, London ...

November 1989, I had called for a big public meeting in the conference centre of The Hague. The pro-Israelis, demonising the PLO, waged a three-week battle to sabotage the event and openly pressured my guest speakers to withdraw. I was interviewed on TV, saying, 'This meeting has become a test between courage and cowardice.' At the entrance of the conference centre, around fifty right-wing supporters of Likud and a few Dutch fundamentalist Christians were shouting anti-Palestinian slogans. To my surprise, one of the slogans was, 'Safieh–Satan'. I had thought that the usage of such concepts was restricted to the Third World. I sent a friend to tell them (half) jokingly, 'Please do not compare me to Satan, you risk making Hell look less unattractive than it was intended to be.' And in front of a packed room I started, 'I do not know what they are shouting down there but I hope it is, "Safieh go home!" This will be the beginning of a convergence in our respective positions.' Going home, that is what it was all about.

December 1992, in the House of Commons, marking the International Day of Solidarity with the Palestinian People, I started my introductory remarks, 'My mother from Jerusalem happens to be here with us this evening. Allow me to tell her, and through her to all the mothers of Palestine, please try to wait, your children are coming back home.' Her eyes filled with tears. I was told that she was not the only one.

In September 1993, I welcomed the Oslo breakthrough enthusiastically and, after an absence of more than a quarter of a century, I was the first PLO official to visit Palestine, in a private capacity, with my wife and daughters, months before the Palestinian National Authority was established. With obvious Hollywoodian inspiration, we called it 'Home Again I'. In November 1994, during 'Home Again 3', and accompanied by a Franciscan father, I went to the Israeli office in East Jerusalem to present an application for 'family reunification'. The governmental official who received me was an Ashkanazi Jew and his secretary an Ethiopian Falasha who had probably arrived in the country the day before yesterday. An unforgettable and extremely painful moment. 'They' were to decide whether I had the 'right' to reside again in Jerusalem. Yet, I was optimistic. At the time, all my political friends were hoping to move up. I was dreaming of moving ... out, away from what de Gaulle had called *la politique politicienne*. I intended to go back, not as an official, but simply as a 'project of a citizen'. I reproduce at the end the document I circulated to friends and acquaintances around the world. It reflects accurately the mood prevailing then.

In February 1995, my mother, Odette Batato Safieh, got a letter from the Israeli Ministry of Interior. One line and a half. In Hebrew, with an Arabic translation beneath it, said: 'Concerning the above-mentioned, we have studied the case and unfortunately could not give a positive response.' Later, to friends who wrote to inquire or to protest, a standard letter was sent saying that they 'process in priority cases of minors and spouses'. I was obviously no longer a minor and it was, it seems, a distant relative who had filled in my application – my mother.

Theoretically, the 'good guys' were in power in Israel then. The late Prime Minister Rabin was also a Minister of Interior and many international and influential personalities lobbied him and Foreign Minister Shimon Peres personally and directly concerning my application. The *nyet* I got for an answer reinforced my belief that it was the Zionist left that had historically made Palestine unliveable to us Palestinians. The novelty is that the Israeli right, secular and religious, makes Israel also unliveable to many Jews.

April 1996, I was invited by my friends Dr Roger Williamson and Revd Garth Hewitt to address 150 workers in the field of international development from the different dioceses around the UK. Shimon Peres had just launched an unnecessary war in Lebanon and the Qana massacre was only a few days old. I was revolted, angry, emotional and, I believe, moving. During the coffee break, an elderly lady, obviously a pro-Israeli, angrily approached and shot at me, 'Since when are you a Christian?' I could read through her. She probably believed that one day Yasser Arafat and his colleagues met in clandestine underground and decided that I should convert to Christianity so that I would sensitise audiences who might be more sympathetic if they were to learn that there are also Christian Palestinians. She – and I – knew that Western audiences could have that type of un-Christian attitude. Very quietly, I answered, 'Madam, I was born a Christian. My family goes back in Jerusalem as far as the archives exist. Do not forget, Christ and the Christian faith were born in Palestine. So I am a historic Christian. You can even say, a prehistoric Christian.'

August 1997, my brother, a university professor, invited us all to a family gathering to his home in Brazil. The happiest days of my life. Around my mother, four generations assembled with great love and tenderness. A fact could not escape us – the numerical centre of gravity of the family had shifted out of Jerusalem. We are fifteen in total: two are still in Jerusalem, four in London and nine in Brazil. The case of every Palestinian family, Christian and Muslim alike.

End of November 1997, Bibi Netanyahu has just visited London, where Tony Blair, Robin Cook and even Madeleine Albright 'firmly' reminded him of Israel's obligations. He then appeared on every TV channel to announce that given a choice between keeping (East) Jerusalem and peace, without hesitation, he would opt for Jerusalem. Writing quickly this article to meet the printer's deadline, I have to admit that I am again passing through one more existentialist crisis about the 'absurdity' of life, its purpose and its meaning. A diplomat, I have to confess that I increasingly find the diplomatic avenue of the peace process to be an unamusing farce. But I can assure you, this time I am no longer thinking of suicide.

The Palestinian – a weekly[1]

Introduction

Afif Safieh, the Palestinian General Delegate to the United Kingdom, is planning to return to Jerusalem, his hometown, in the middle of next year. He initiated the process of family reunification in November 1994. Once back in Jerusalem, he intends to start an English weekly that will cover political and economic current affairs, news and analysis, feature stories, as well as cultural and social issues.

This new weekly is intended to become a unique forum for Palestinians to debate issues, a vehicle of communication between

1. Written in 1994. This is the document I circulated to friends in Palestine and around the world, a sort of mission statement that attracted much interest. The refusal by the Israelis to grant me 'family reunification' in Jerusalem terminated the dream.

the 'Palestinians of the inside' and the diaspora communities, as well as the link between Palestinian society and the outside world. Totally independent, this weekly will mirror Palestinian pluralism.

Readers

This English weekly will aim at reaching five different audiences:

Locally

1. The English-speaking Palestinian intelligentsia, decision-makers, the civil servants, the business community, as well as the academic community.
2. The foreign community in Palestine/Israel: diplomats, consulates, journalists, United Nations personnel, non-governmental organisations personnel and volunteers, churches, tourists, etc.
3. Israeli institutions and individuals who are interested in trends and evolutions within Palestinian society.

Abroad

4. Middle East research centres in universities around the world. NGOs interested in Third World issues and the Middle East, the solidarity network in every country and every city, etc.
5. The Palestinian diaspora around the world, Arab diaspora communities and many Jews interested in a Palestinian point of view.

Strategy for Promotion

There are markets in Palestine, Israel and Jordan through various distribution networks available for around 5,000 copies. Over 100,000 addresses, from Scandinavia to Australia, all Palestine-related, have been assembled from a variety of mailing lists. A supplementary mailing list is also being compiled from the Chambers of Commerce of Western Enterprises dealing with the Arab world. The objective is to irrigate this network with promotional issues hoping to get seven percent positive responses. Given the nature of these mailing lists, 7,000 subscribers from such a promotion campaign is not an over-ambitious goal. From the very first week onwards 10,000 copies will be printed of each issue: 3,000 for the local market and 7,000 for promotion and/or subscribers.

The quality and diversity of such a readership should attract a wide range of advertisers. The fact that the Middle East is undergoing profound transformations at a great pace, together with the fact that Palestinian society is in the process of institution-building and, hopefully, state-building, will be seen as an added incentive for the construction, modern office equipment and tourist industries, as well as for banks, insurance companies etc to choose *The Palestinian* as their advertising and publicity conduit towards potential clients.

The Team

In addition to a deputy editor, four writers/journalists will be based in Jerusalem. At least one will be an economist by training. To ensure efficient and professional management of the institution, five management staff will be required who will provide subscription services, marketing and distribution, advertising and secretarial assistance. The weekly will also have foreign-based American, European and Israeli correspondents.

The Palestinian will contain forty pages plus cover. It will aim to be global in its coverage and distribution.

The project of launching this English-language weekly has triggered immense support within the intellectual Palestinian community. Six eternal contributors will be invited each week to address a variety of issues relevant to the debates of the moment.

The world has heard of Palestinian talent and sophistication.

This weekly will prove it. *The Palestinian* will mobilise the best brains and will make use of their expertise to raise the awareness of both decision-makers and public opinion. It will also aim to inform, give cohesion and a sense of purpose for the Palestinian diaspora communities in the Unites States and elsewhere. It will endeavour to raise the level of public debate by injecting new ideas and introducing new approaches. Agitators of ideas will be an accusation for which we will willingly plead guilty.

Possible Extensions

A successful weekly is a powerful vehicle that can help promote cultural events because of the visibility it provides and the coverage it ensures. The weekly will seek to cooperate with the British Council and the Centre Culturel Francais to organise film festivals with the participation of film directors and leading actors. It will sponsor local theatrical groups, singers, athletes of Olympic standard ...

The Palestinian monthly lecture could become a highly appreciated *rendezvous* with distinguished visiting speakers.

After the initial six months needed for the launch, the weekly will consider starting a publishing house so that interesting manuscripts can find their way to the readers, local and foreign, without the usual quest for a publisher who often hesitates confronted with what might be too controversial a subject.

As a modern and dynamic institution, this English weekly magazine will contribute significantly to the much-needed revitalisation of the political and cultural life in Arab Jerusalem and beyond. During the last decades, Arab Jerusalem – Muslim and Christian – was plunged into historical decline. This magazine will be one of many initiative needed to help Jerusalem regain its political and intellectual centrality.

History – as always – is in the making. The difference now is that *The Palestinian* will be part of it.

XVII

Fifty years on:
achievements and challenges[1]

I feel honoured and privileged to have been invited for a third time in eight years to address MAP's annual dinner, the major social event in London for the Arab community and for our British friends. MAP has undeniably become the pride of us all who yearn to enhance British-Palestinian cooperation.

Secretary of State, I wish to convey to Prime Minister Tony Blair and to yourself President Yasser Arafat's deep appreciation for your constructive contribution during our multiple recent talks here in London with the Americans and indirectly with the Israeli side. Allow me to express my respect and admiration to all the officials in the Foreign Office that I deal with. They have always shown immense professionalism and profound decency. Allow me also, to welcome my British counterpart and friend, HE Robin Kealy, the British Consul-General in Jerusalem and his wife, Annabel, who represent Britain in Palestine with great distinction and dedication.

This year, the Israelis celebrated the fiftieth anniversary of the birth of their State. This year the Palestinians commemorated the fiftieth year of the loss of our homeland. I do not see this MAP dinner as another Wailing Wall or as an opportunity for

1. Speech delivered on 9 July 1998 at the Annual Dinner of Medical Aid for Palestinians (MAP). The keynote speaker was Secretary of State, the Rt. Hon. Robin Cook MP.

self-flagellation. Fifty years on, it is time for an evaluation of the achievements accomplished. Fifty years on, it is time for an assessment of the challenges that still lie ahead.

Achievements:

I believe that there are four achievements of historical significance:

1. Years ago, those who chose to be our enemies, many analysts and commentators predicted that, shattered and scattered to the four corners of the earth, the Palestinian people were destined and doomed to evaporate into historical oblivion.

2. Having been the Jews of the Jews, the victims of the victims of European history, we the Palestinian people were denied in 1948 our legitimate share of sympathy, solidarity and support. But successive eye-openers created conditions for an improved perception of our unacceptable fate and an improved awareness of our desirable future. Those eye-openers were the brutal occupation policies that followed the 1967 war, the accession of Likud to power in 1977, the invasion of Lebanon in 1982, our cry for freedom out of captivity and bondage represented by the intifada, our peace strategy. Today – unlike yesterday – in the Western world, it is no more politically suicidal to be pro-Palestinian. Today – unlike yesterday – it is no more electorally rewarding to be anti-Palestinian.

3. I have always believed the PLO was at the same time an institution and an idea. The idea was simple yet inspiring and immortal: our sense of identity and our ceaseless quest for independence and sovereignty. For the last four years, this idea has started to become a territorial reality. In political science, a state is defined as 'an authority on a demography on a geography' and history will prove that the emergence of the Palestinian entity has been a historical and irreversible turning point.

4. Already for many years the international community has recognised the legitimacy of our quest for Palestinian statehood.

Now unsympathetic yet extremely influential personalities like Henry Kissinger in the United States and General Ariel Sharon in Israel admit, yes reluctantly but unequivocally, 'the inevitability of Palestinian statehood'. That is a major achievement that we owe to decades of Palestinian sacrifices. Yet we should always bear in mind how Nahum Goldmann once defined diplomacy. He said, 'It seems to me that diplomacy in the Middle East is the art of delaying the inevitable as long as possible.'

Secretary of State, I believe it to be the noble task of British and Palestinian diplomacy to disallow the attempts at delaying the incvitable and, even better, to usher in the historical shortcuts needed to end unnecessary protracted injustice, unnecessarily prolonged suffering and unending belligerency.

Challenges:

1. Economic success or failure: when the peace process was initiated, knowing how devastating the notion of a 'divine mission for a chosen people on a promised land' was, we rebaptised Palestine as 'the promising land'. Today, because of the unconvincing nature of the process, because of the policy of closures that result in the strangulation of the Palestinian society and economy, we are witnessing dramatic reductions in per capita income, rocketing levels of unemployment and hardly any significant investment. Yet, for every possible reason, we are condemned to succeed in the economic arena.

2. The territorial dimension: today's diplomatic *impasse* that has shattered the little credibility left to the process does not stem from what percentage of withdrawal is required for the long overdue first and second and even third redeployments. It is already the battle for final status. Bibi Netanyahu does not conceal his 'vision' of returning around forty percent of the occupied West Bank. Ladies and gentlemen, I have news for Netanyahu. I fully agree with 'his' principle of reciprocity and since the peace process is

based on the concept of 'land for peace' and since we are in favour of one hundred percent peace, he should not be surprised at all that our expectation is the return of one hundred percent of those territories occupied in 1967.

With Netanyahu and most of the Israeli establishment, we seem to have a conceptual difference. They tend to prefer the concept of 'territorial compromise', consider the West Bank as 'disputed territory' and generously offer to meet us halfway between Jerusalem and Jericho. We, on the other hand, operate on the basis of the search for a 'historical compromise', consider Mandatory Palestine to be the disputed territory and offer to meet them along the 4 June 1967 boundaries in Jerusalem and nowhere else but in Jerusalem.

It seems that Arab realism was misunderstood as resignation. Since the Arab Summit meeting in Fez, Morocco in 1982 and the adoption of the peace proposals of the Crown Prince Fahd of Saudi Arabia, the message from the Arab world was, 'In exchange for Israel's withdrawal from its 1967 expansion we are ready to recognise Israel's existence in its pre-1967 boundaries.' That is the only game in town form Morocco to Muscat. That is the only deal in town, from Rabat to Riyadh.

In the Israeli-Palestinian conflict, the victim has moved faster than the oppressor beyond double negation towards mutual recognition, mutual recognition between Israel and Palestine. I hope Bibi Netanyahu has not misread our intentions again. We were not in favour of a Palestinian unilateral recognition of Israeli existence. Recognition should be two-way traffic. Recognition can only be a double-way traffic. Secretary of State, if the diplomatic avenue continues to be obstructed, I fear that many from the realist school of thought will be reduced to say 'Radicalism is too important to be left to the radicals alone any longer.'

Former Israeli Prime Minister Itzhac Shamir, in his speech at the Madrid Peace Conference of 1991, spoke of 'Israel's hunger for peace'. Secretary of State, we can satisfy Israel's hunger for peace, if Israel abandons its appetite for territory.

3. The need for an improved performance: there is undeniably room for improvement in the Palestinian performance. By the way,

Helmut Schmidt is known to have said that 'The largest room on earth is precisely the room for improvement.' I still believe that we, the Palestinian people, have still neither the authority we deserve nor the opposition we need. There is ample room for improvement in both. The criticism also extends to the performance of the Palestinian intelligentsia, the Palestinian business community and the Palestinian diaspora.

4. Alienation of segments of our society: with great lucidity, we should admit that the way the peace process was approached, great anxieties surfaced among certain segments of our society. The Palestinian refugee community, still living in sub-human conditions on the periphery of the homeland, feels abandoned, ignored, neglected. We should do our utmost to keep their dossier, which the PLO reluctantly had to accept to see deferred to final status negotiations, on the forefront of our agenda. The Palestinians who have succeeded in staying in what became the State of Israel in 1948 also feel that they have been dropped from any vision for the future since we adopted the two-state approach. A dynamic strategy based on a triangular Palestinian-Palestinian-Palestinian cooperation, among the Palestinians of the state in the making, diaspora Palestinians and the Palestinians of Israel, should be initiated. A multi-faceted cooperation, a multi-dimensional interaction, with political economic, commercial and sociological components that will strengthen our social tissue, our national fabric.

5. Redefinition of roles: during the last years, the centre of gravity of Palestinian nationalism has moved back home to Palestine. That was the logical and inevitable evolution in any rational strategic thinking. The re-emerging Palestinian national movement was a diaspora phenomenon. It all started in the university campuses of Cairo and Beirut. Its constituency was in the refugees camps, its financial backing was provided by the Palestinian communities in the Gulf. But this development, the shift from the periphery to the centre, from outside to inside, invites us to quickly undertake a redefinition of the respective roles of the different components of our society, not least the more than ever decisive role of our diaspora communities, mainly in the USA, but also in Europe and elsewhere.

Global Tribes

There is a new concept in contemporary international relations, fashionable yet fully relevant to our Palestinian experience: the concept of 'global tribes'. The Jews are the global tribe *par excellence*. But so are the Anglo-Saxons, the Scots, the Chinese, the Indians, the Armenians – and the Arabs and the Palestinians. We can and should transform our geographic dispersion, from Scandinavia to California, the symptom of our tragedy, into a major source for influence and empowerment. We often diagnose as one of the major causes of our underdevelopment, our inclination to clannish and tribal patterns of behaviour. The challenge and the opportunity for us is to succeed in operating from now on as a tribe, as a modern tribe, as a global tribe. While maintaining and cultivating our intimate interaction with the homeland, we should better integrate and fully participate in the political life of our host countries. The day will come, soon, when here in the United Kingdom we will witness the birth of the British-Arab Liberal Association, the British-Arab Conservative Club and of course, Secretary of State, the British-Arab Labour Movement, becoming no longer an alien phenomenon or a foreign factor, but a domestic actor. Ladies and gentlemen, this distinguished gathering tonight can make any Western political party blush with envy.

Ladies and gentlemen, not only in Palestine, but all over the world, we live today in a transitional period. I have never belonged to a fatalistic, a deterministic school of thought, but to the voluntarist school that emphasises the importance of the will, individual and collective. Yes, today, and on a variety of issues, history is undecided. We should shed the psychology of failure, the mentality of defeat, the feeling of impotence and be confident that we can make a difference.

XVIII

On Sabeel[1]

Institution-building under duress has been the Palestinian response to the challenge of decades of statelessness, military occupation and forced diasporisation. In an environment of proliferating NGOs of unequal importance and durability, one of the most interesting has been undeniably Sabeel. Around the inspiring leadership of Canon Naim Ateek, dozens of individuals have proven unwavering dedication and impressive competence in meeting the tasks they had assigned to themselves.

Sabeel's agenda was both ambitious and long overdue:

1. To shake away an ideology of determinism and defeatism, and to install a belief that we are not doomed to be mere objects of history, but can be decisive subjects of our own history, capable of making a significant difference in shaping our future and destiny. While religious-oriented endeavours usually tend to be more focused on rewards in the after-life, Sabeel in Jerusalem, just like Christian Aid here in the UK, asserts the importance also of their belief in 'life before death'.

2. To help articulate the political expression of the Christian communities in Palestine, enhance their social and political consciousness and refine their collective and individual contributions in public life.

3. To engage in dialogue with pilgrims visiting the religious sites in the

1.   Foreword for the book *Quissatouna: our story*, published by Al Sabeel, Jerusalem, in 1999.

Holy Land, thus helping them depart from the previous pattern of the traditional tour devoid of any encounter with the communities – those Living Stones – whose lives, for generations, have been affected, often negatively, by their proximity and intimacy with a land burdened by history, theology, as well as mythology.

4. To undertake through the network of 'Friends of Sabeel' a global effort, of advocacy and campaigning for Palestinian rights, mainly raising awareness within Christian churches and Christian communities around the world, hoping to influence thus foreign policy decision-making in their respective countries in favour of justice and peace in the Middle East.

The publication of *Quissatouna: our story*, in addition to the quarterly newsletter, *Corner Stone,* is one of many initiatives that tend to serve this purpose. Having been the victims of the victims of European history, the Palestinian people never got their legitimate share of sympathy, solidarity and support. The debate around their ordeal was more characterised by passion than compassion. Fortunately, but at great human cost, the intifada, our cry for freedom out of captivity and bondage, was an eye-opener for Western public opinion.

Today, the Palestinians are no more demanding absolute justice but possible justice: the two-state solution and the sharing of Jerusalem. The Israeli political establishment – left, right and centre – still seems to want a diplomatic outcome to the peace process that would reflect Israeli intransigence, American alignment on the Israeli preference, Russian decline, European abdication, Arab impotence and, as a result, Palestinian resignation. How this peace is expected to be lasting, durable, final and permanent, I have difficulties in comprehending. And I dare not utter the words brave, honourable, equitable, just or even just acceptable.

To usher in the twenty-first century, we had hoped that peace in the Holy Land would be our gift to the world. But if the local belligerent parties/negotiating partners prove to be incapable of achieving it, peace should be the gift of the world to us in the Holy Land.

Let us hope that Bethlehem 2000 will also be Palestine Year One.

XIX

Diplomacy:
The art of delaying the inevitable[1]

In the last ten months, the Palestinians have been blamed in certain influential circles for having missed a historical opportunity by rejecting the most generous offer by the most dovish Israeli government, and that our intifada allowed Likud and Sharon back to power. This perception stemmed from the undeserved good reputation that the Israeli Labour Party enjoys in the West, but also from statements made by former President Clinton that Ehud Barak was bold, courageous, audacious, generous, magnanimous, constructive, creative, imaginative and innovative. English is not my first language. It is not even my second, but I have never seen those concepts used in such a questionable manner. As for the favourable prejudice that Labour benefits from, I keep telling my numerous Israeli interlocutors that historically it was Labour that made Palestine unliveable for the Palestinians. What Likud does also makes Israel uninhabitable for many Jews. As a result of this misperception, unlike the 1970s when European governmental positions were far better informed when compared to their respective public opinions, today public opinion is more sympathetic towards Palestinian suffering and more supportive of Palestinian aspirations than European official positions.

---

1. Edited transcript of a lecture delivered at the Royal United Services Institute for Defence Studies, and published in *RUSI Journal* in August 2001 (Volume 146, No 4).

It was General Sharon's visit to the Aqsa Mosque that inflamed the situation and triggered the second intifada. It was only the straw that broke the camel's back. We had warned Barak and Clinton not to permit this. In retrospect, there were obvious Machiavellian calculations which allowed that visit to occur. This coincided with the day that the Israeli Attorney General cleared Binyamin Netanyahu from an investigation he was conducting because of insufficient evidence. Every commentator foresaw that Netanyahu would be able to capitalise politically from this decision and stage his comeback in the political arena. At the time, it was in Barak's interest that Sharon remained the leader of Likud precisely because he thought he was beatable in a national election, while Netanyahu's flashy and charismatic character was seen as a more formidable challenge to Barak's re-election efforts. Barak wanted to provide Sharon with an advantage over Netanyahu by not allowing the latter to steal the limelight. Once again, however, Barak, a supposedly excellent chess player, miscalculated. As it turned out, even Sharon beat him electorally.

In my opinion, the intifada has three explanatory factors. First, the Palestinians have witnessed fifty-three years of forced diasporisation and thirty-four years of endless occupation. Forced diasporisation does not only include the Palestinian refugees who happen to be in Lebanon, Syria or Jordan. Two out of every three inhabitants of the Gaza Strip are refugees in refugee camps and one out of every three inhabitants of the West Bank is a refugee in refugee camps. So it's not an external phenomenon; it's also an internal factor. One also has to bear in mind that the occupation of the Gaza Strip, the West Bank and East Jerusalem is the longest military occupation in modern history, with humiliation and harassment of an entire people on a daily basis.

The second factor is the ten years of an unconvincing peace process. When we went to Madrid in 1991, I qualified our attitude as being 'unreasonably reasonable'. We then accepted to function as half a delegation, representing half the people, and seeking half a solution, just because we wanted to give peace a chance. In Oslo in 1993, we were promised a five-year transitional period for the Accords to be implemented. By 1998, we were supposed to have achieved final status. It is useful to recall Yitzhak Rabin's maxim that 'dates are not sacred', yet if there was anything precise in the Oslo Agreement, it was precisely the timetable for its implementation. There was no need for an unnecessarily protracted peace process. A territory that was occupied in 1967 in less than six days can also be evacuated in six days so that we could all rest on the seventh.

After ten years of negotiations and agreements, we have received only sixty-five percent of the Gaza Strip with thirty-five percent still under Israeli exclusive total control, since there are twenty illegal settlements and five thousand illegal settlers in the area. In the West Bank, arrangements are even more complex. At present, we have three zones: A, B, and C. We control totally or partially forty percent (Zones A and B) whereas sixty percent remain under Israel's exclusive control. What we have witnessed during the last ten years can only be described as an accelerated expansion of the settlements. Hence an expansion of the occupation rather than real withdrawal. This was more real during Labour governments, including Barak's, than during the Netanyahu years. The total number of illegal settlers rocketed up to 400,000. In a way, throughout those years of 'theoretical' peacemaking, there was an intifada in the making.

The third factor is the failed nature and the content of the Camp David talks that took place in July 2000 – talks which undoubtedly poisoned the diplomatic and political environments we are currently operating in. Why is this the case? Because for the first time since we had reached the moment of truth, Palestinian public opinion discovered what was the ceiling of the possible and the permissible in this particular peace process. Barak, with

Clinton's help, succeeded in projecting the image that Israel offered us ninety-five percent plus one or plus two in the territorial swap. It was never the case; the Israeli maps offered at Camp David excluded four areas: expanded East Jerusalem, the Latroun Salient, the no man's land around the West Bank between 1948 and 1967, and the shores of the Dead Sea. What Barak was offering was ninety-five percent of ninety percent which is close to eighty-five percent. Barak, recently, published an op-ed piece in the *New York Times/ International Herald Tribune* where he explicitly stated that Israel should keep fifteen percent of Judea and Samaria, plus a security zone in the Jordan Valley. In spite of that, prominent commentators like Thomas Friedman, continue to write, with a vengeance, about the ungrateful Arafat who rejected ninety-five percent as though Barak 's article was never written or published.

What was the Israeli offer at the Camp David talks? Israel wanted to keep a security zone in the Jordan Valley and the settlements that are scattered in this valley, although some serious Israeli generals noted that this would give Israel only one additional second of earlier warning in case of a missile attack. This is an insignificant advantage. The same generals have also made it clear that these settlements, in the case of belligerency, would become a military burden and a liability. At Camp David, Barak asked for major territorial rectifications to absorb and annex to Israel eighty percent of the settlers and since those settlements were deliberately built on the aquifers of water they would, *en passant*, swallow our rare hydrological resources. The West Bank would end up as several dislocated, disconnected Bantoustans.

Thirdly, in the Camp David talks, Israel refused to acknowledge any historical, moral, or legal responsibility on the refugee issue. During informal talks, they were only accepting back a maximum of 100,000 refugees, but in instalments of 1,000 to 5,000. We would have needed the entire Third Millennium to bring back a significant number of refugees.

Anything dealing with Jerusalem can hardly be seen as a minor territorial rectification. Last but not least, Barak explored the possibility of returning one out of every three neighbourhoods in occupied East Jersualem, maintaining control of almost half of the old city of Jerusalem: the Jewish quarter, the Armenian quarter (I wonder why), the Wailing Wall (50 metres) and/or the entire Western Wall (450 metres) and wanted shared sovereignty on the Islamic shrines. This came as a shock to the Palestinian leadership and society. The Palestinian State will have control neither of its airspace nor of its frontiers.

A word on the Taba talks that occurred two weeks before the Israeli elections. The Israeli proposals were undeniably more advanced than in Camp David, but everybody knew that it was, by now, too late. The Israeli negotiating team did not have any legitimacy to speak on behalf of a government which was deserted by most of its coalition components and which, it was predicted by all opinion polls, was going to perform lamentably in the forthcoming elections.

Often the Israeli territorial appetite is disguised in terms of security needs and requirements, even though we, and others, have told them repeatedly that security comes from regional acceptance and not from territorial aggrandisement and that we are the key to Israel's regional acceptance. Israel's doctrine towards its regional environment is better described by the concept of compellence than deterrence. Deterrence is a policy aiming to dissuade a neighbour from undertaking policies seen as detrimental or damaging to one's national interests. On the other hand, compellence, an under-exploited concept of Thomas Schelling, is a policy that tends to coerce, compel and re-order the environment in a way that is seen to suit better one's own national interest. In spite of that, some commentators still write as though it is Palestine that occupies Israel and not the other way around.

What kinds of lessons can be drawn from ten years of diplomatic failures? The major flaw in the peace process is the fact that the local belligerent parties and negotiating partners were left to fend for themselves. The international community only played the role of facilitating the dialogue and financing the process. We need a decisive input from third parties. If we are left to 'sort it out' by ourselves, we will not achieve an acceptable peace. We will continue to have talks about talks and engage in negotiations *ad nauseam*. An acceptable peace with durability, without external support, is not achievable. What is democratically acceptable to the Israeli people is simply unacceptable for the Palestinian people. And *vice versa*. In matters of war and peace, the international will should have primacy and should prevail over the national whim.

The issue of democracy in Israel is often mentioned and used as an argument to improve Israel's public image abroad. I adhere to the school of thought which argues that Israel is a democracy for its Jewish component but I also maintain that the fact that Israel is a democratic state is not an extenuating factor, but an aggravating one. There is nothing more morally disturbing than a democratic oppression supported by the informed consent of the voter and the citizen. At present, negotiations in the Middle East are taking place in a total imbalance of forces. Peace is too important to be left for the Israelis alone to decide upon, yet we are constantly told that we should always rally the Israelis to any pursuit of peace. Israeli public opinion will always maintain that Israel needs to withdraw as little as possible.

I was in London when Saddam Hussein invaded and occupied Kuwait and was unequivocally vocal in condemning his occupation of Kuwait. At the time, nobody argued for a referendum in Baghdad to see if they wanted to withdraw and, if yes, how far. Saddam

Hussein was simply asked to withdraw. International law and oil were both invoked then as an explanation for external intervention. I have news for you. We too happen to have oil: olive oil. The Palestinians crave for international intervention and have appealed for it on numerous occasions. There is a need for international protection and constructive intervention on the part of external actors. At the moment, we are negotiating and suffocating at the mercy of a balance of power which is not favourable to achieving our recognised legitimate aspirations.

Israel has three military and strategic advantages over the Palestinians. First, the Israelis maintain a nuclear monopoly in the region. Secondly, they have an overwhelming conventional military superiority *vis-à-vis* any possible coalition of Arab forces. Thirdly, Israel maintains an unwritten alliance with the only remaining superpower, the United States. An unwritten alliance with the only remaining superpower is even more important than a formal alliance since it allows Israel to benefit from all the advantages such an alliance can offer without having the responsibility and the restraint that alliances imply for the junior partner. An unwritten alliance also allows the senior partner to look unaccountable *vis-à-vis* the behaviour of its protégé and its protégé can act as a sort of 'undisciplined ally'.

The Israeli political establishment – left, right and centre – was hoping for a diplomatic outcome that would reflect Israeli intransigence, American alignment on the Israeli preference, Russian decline, European abdication, Arab impotence and what they hoped to be Palestinian resignation.

This is the framework within which we are operating. Where do we stand today? Today, Israel is incapable of suppressing the intifada, but the intifada by itself is incapable of terminating the occupation. We have a deadlock which can only be solved by bold diplomatic initiatives. Until now, we have witnessed the failure of diplomacy, specifically preventive diplomacy, in achieving a breakthrough in our negotiations with the Israelis.

Now is the time for a major diplomatic initiative. If not now, I wonder when? I often joke with my Norwegian friends by telling them if the Oslo channel has not put yet Palestine fully on the map, it has put Norway on the map. I usually offer this thought as an incentive to European interlocutors by telling them that Europe is still perceived as an actor in search of a role and that we in the Middle East have a role in search of an actor. A merger of the two would be beneficial for all concerned. We share the desire in Europe to transform its role from merely being a 'payer' into becoming a 'decisive player'.

The US remains a decisive player and I for one believe that the battle for Washington is winnable. A serious strategic debate will inevitably soon surface in Washington on the nature of the American-Israeli relationship. Is Israel still a strategic asset or is it gradually becoming a strategic burden and a liability? Today, after the demise of the Soviet Union and the end of Arab militant regimes, the Arab regional system is profoundly conservative and pro-Western. Israel, by its insatiably territorial appetite, is defying, de-legitimising and destabilising the network of friendship America enjoys in the region. Arab public opinion, from Morocco to Muscat, is boiling. Islamic public opinion, from Nigeria to Malaysia, is angry at the perceived American complacency over and complicity with Israel's endless occupation of Palestinian territory. Israeli regional expansion, if perpetuated, can disrupt and endanger American global interests.

... I am in favour of a policy of linkages and hope that one day the Americans will be converted to this idea of linking aid and advice, since I believe this policy has worked twice in the last decades. Once, in 1957, when Eisenhower asked the Israelis to withdraw from the Sinai after the Suez War and once for six months in 1991, during the tenure of Bush Senior and former Secretary of State James Baker, when they linked the issue of the loan guarantees to the freezing of settlements. Consequently, the Israeli leadership went reluctantly to Madrid and enforced a six months freeze on building or expanding settlements. Establishing the link between American advice and aid is critical.

We are witnessing a new phenomenon in international relations: global tribes. The Jews are the global tribe par excellence. But so are the English, the Irish, the Scots, the Indians, the Chinese but also the Armenians, the Palestinians and the Arabs. Today, the Palestinians are no longer the 'small kid on the block', but because we are the Jews of the Jews we were scattered to the periphery of Palestine and beyond. The Palestinians are not only a local phenomenon, but are also a regional factor and an international actor. One encounters Palestinians all over the world. The same applies for Arab communities. I believe that in any future strategic thinking these diasporas will function as important actors in international politics. We should concentrate on maintaining the links between these communities and their countries of origin and, in a parallel manner, help and encourage their further integration in their countries of adoption. This is a source of political empowerment that we have somewhat neglected.

I am very encouraged by the fact that the Arab and Muslim-American communities in the United States are becoming better integrated and better equipped with political institutions to express aspirations and preferences. In the past, many of our failures were attributed to our pattern of tribal behaviours. Tomorrow, the challenge for us is to behave like a global and a modern tribe – a challenge for all Arab communities scattered mainly in Western societies.

During the last thirty-four years, we Arabs have reduced our levels of expectation and have aligned ourselves with what was then called the international consensus in the UN, which was mainly formulated by European states and favoured the adoption of a two-state solution and the implementation of relevant UN resolutions. Years ago, it was Kissinger who dwarfed a potential European role by stating that Europe would be unhelpful in any peace process because 'it would raise Arab expectations.' Europe has not aligned itself with Arab preferences. On the contrary, it is the Arab world that has aligned itself with the way Europe and the international community want to see the conflict resolved. The responsibilities of the international community have increased. We have respected our commitments to the international community and it is now to up to the international community to respect its commitments to us. The Israelis need to be made aware of what is expected from them in the peace process. If this is achieved in the near future, the Israelis will vote for their leadership not as a function of how much territory they are ready to condescendingly concede. Instead, they will frame their choices based on how much experience or inexperience a candidate enjoys, charisma or its absence, and the nature of their economic policies. With the absence of such an unequivocal message, the Israeli voter believes that he or she has the ability to choose a leader whose programme for the future coincides with their preference on how much territorial concessions they are ready to tolerate.

I am politically very nostalgic of Charles de Gaulle. After the 1967 war, President de Gaulle suggested '*la concertation à quatre*' – the co-ordination of the major four countries (China was not yet in the Security Council) – to help solve the Arab-Israeli conflict. The idea never really got off the ground because the Americans seemed comfortable with the Israeli victory of 1967 that compensated for their humiliations in Vietnam. The Soviets, short-sightedly, were unenthusiastic because they preferred a bipolar international system and didn't see why they should recognise equal status to lesser countries like Britain and France. The British were not supportive because it was initially a French initiative. A few meetings of the permanent representatives at the UN in New York took place; the idea then vanished into historical oblivion. Thirty-four years later, the conflict remains unresolved. Rather than leaving both societies 'to sort it out' in search of an elusive 'mutually acceptable solution', maybe an elegantly imposed solution by the international community – 'a mutually unacceptable formula' – would have been the only way out of this vicious circle. In the meantime, instead of a durable peace, we now have a permanent peace process.

XX

The end of pre-history[1]

We are the coalition: the coalition for peace and justice. We are gathered here today because of our firm belief that the best retaliation is justice. Our firm belief that in our constantly shrinking world, the highest standards should be required and applicable to all. Our firm belief that there is only one mankind, and not different kinds of women and men. Our firm belief in a necessary, respectful and cross-fertilising dialogue of cultures, civilisations and religions. Our firm belief that the Palestinian people are not, definitely not, children of a lesser God.

Today, in the USA, there are three schools of thought. The first is the 'minimalist school' that is against the elastic extension of the designated targets of this campaign. The second is the 'maximalist school' that advocates expanding the theatre of operations to engulf more countries in a devastating war with unpredictable repercussions. And a third school of thought, represented by Cardinal Egan of New York, who lucidly and courageously invited his compatriots, in the tragic days that followed the horror of September 11th, to initiate a soul-searching exercise on the role of America in the world.

Unsurprisingly, the pro-Israeli lobby in Washington operates as the hawk of the hawks. That lobby has grown accustomed to use one muscle too many and to go one pressure too far. I happen to have lived in the USA in the mid-80s when the imminent

1. Peace Rally, Trafalgar Square, Saturday 13 October 2001.

downfall of the Soviet Union was being predicted in academic and political circles. While, in the Third World and within the left, some were worried by the implications of the loss of 'a friend and ally', the pro-Israeli lobby in Washington was even more worried by the possible repercussions of the loss of the 'enemy'. Magazines like *Commentary* and *The New Republic* were 'studying' how the demise of the Soviet Union might affect the *raison d'être* and the strategic function and utility of Israel in Western strategies. It is in those magazines that an alternative global enemy was ideologically fabricated: Islam and the Muslim world in confrontation with the Judeo-Christian world. A frightening scenario that could become self-fulfilling.

Two weeks ago, Israeli Prime Minister Sharon, in between two massive bombings of Palestinian cities, villages and refugee camps, plaintively declared that Israel was the Czechoslovakia of 1938, abandoned by the policy of appeasement. General Sharon will be well advised to read Jewish historian Isaac Deutscher, who wrote, already in 1967, that Israel was rather the Prussia of the Middle East. Thirty-four years later, Israel still occupies territories of three neighbouring countries: Lebanon, Syria and Palestine and, in the most ferocious manner, tries to crush our cry for freedom out of captivity and bondage.

We support the third school of thought, soul-searching. Soul-searching in Israel, where they should finally become aware of the human cost paid by the Palestinian people – individually and collectively – for the creation of the State of Israel. Israel was supposed to be the answer to the Jewish Question. As a result we are now the question – the Question of Palestine, yearly on the UN agenda since 1949 – awaiting a convenient and equitable answer.

The issue of Israeli democracy is constantly used as an argument to improve Israel's public image abroad. I believe that the fact that Israel is a democracy for its Jewish component is not an extenuating factor but an aggravating one. There is nothing more morally disturbing than a democratic oppression supported by the informed consent of the voter and the citizen. They ought to remember what Rabbi Abraham Heschel stated during the Vietnam War: 'In a democracy, if a few are guilty, all are responsible.'

So far Israeli society has been insensitive to the ordeal it inflicted: the geography occupied, the demography dispossessed and dispersed on the periphery of our ancestral homeland. We were victims of four successive denials: the denial of our mere existence, then the denial of our rights, followed by the denial of our sufferings coupled with the denial of their responsibility for our suffering. There constantly were attempts to banalise and trivialise the tragedy that befell us.

I have never compared the Palestinian Nakba of 1948 to the Holocaust. My conviction has always been that there is no need for historical analogies and comparative martyrology. No one people has a monopoly on human suffering and every ethnic tragedy stands on its own. If I were a Jew or a Gypsy, Nazi barbarity would be the most atrocious event in history. If I were a Black African, it would be slavery and apartheid. If I were a Native American, it would be the discovery of the New World by European explorers and settlers that resulted in near-total extermination. If I were an Armenian, it would be the Ottoman massacres. If I were a Palestinian, it would be the Nakba/Catastrophe of 1948. Humanity should consider all the above morally repugnant and politically unacceptable.

I do not consider it advisable to debate hierarchies of suffering. I do not know how to quantify pain or how to measure suffering but I do know that we are not children of a lesser God.

Dear friends, I believe that a Palestinian State is not only a right for the Palestinian people. It is the ethical duty, the moral obligation of the Israeli and Jewish communities.

In Washington, a serious debate has started on whether Israel is a strategic asset or a strategic burden and a liability. The USA is committed to Israel's existence, a message we, in the Arab world, have understood for decades. Does it also need to be perceived as endorsing Israel's expansionist inclinations and its territorial appetite? Isn't it this perception of constant alignment on the Israeli policy that has antagonised Arab public opinion from Morocco to Muscat and Muslim public opinion from Nigeria to Malaysia?

American society is a nation of nations. In today's monopolar international system, nonalignment in regional conflicts should be what characterises American foreign policy, because alignment on the preferences of one belligerent actor results, not only in antagonising other regional players, but also in alienating one component of its own domestic American national fabric. For over half a century, it has not been easy to be an Arab-American, seeing that your country of adoption was unfriendly to your countries of origin.

In his memoirs *Present at the Creation*, former American Secretary of State Dean Acheson writes that the UN Charter was a condensed version of American political philosophy. All I can hope for is that America will reconcile tomorrow its power with its principles.

Both President Bush and Prime Minister Blair have recently pronounced the 'P' word – Palestine – that General Sharon would like to purge and censor out of the vocabulary of Western leaders. Tony Blair was very enthusiastically applauded by the delegates of the Labour Party Conference when he said 'justice to the Palestinians, equal partners of Israel,' proving again that we are no more marginal but mainstream.

It is now almost ten years to the day since the peace process was triggered in Madrid in October 1991. In the peace process we were interested in peace. The other side seemed more interested in the process. This is why, ten years on, instead of durable peace, we have a permanent peace process made of talks about talks about talks, negotiating pre-negotiations and pre-negotiating negotiations.

Peace in the Middle East, justice for the Palestinian people, implementation of all relevant UN resolutions, is the unfinished business of international diplomacy. The unfinished business left over by the Republican administration of Bush Senior and two Democratic administrations of Bill Clinton. It is a noble and worthy cause for a decisive bipartisan endeavour.

I personally believe that a territory that was occupied in six days can also be evacuated in six days so that some can, at last, rest on the seventh and we, the Palestinian people, can start the fascinating journey of state building, reconstruction and economic take-off. We have so much suffered from the notion of Palestine 'the Promised Land' that we intend simply to turn it into 'the promising land'.

Francis Fukuyama wrote brilliantly and very controversially about 'the end of history'. We in Palestine, we have been blessed or burdened by several millennia of history, theology and mythology. The end of occupation will be for us the end of pre-history and the beginning of a new era of constructive contributions in the concert of nations.

XXI

The international will and the national whim[1]

Friends,

At the same moment when French public opinion massively coalesced to inflict a resounding defeat to the racist and xenophobic Jean-Marie Le Pen, here in London, on 6 of May, a rally was organised to express support to the Sharon Government, even though Sharon is by far a more dangerous, a more racist, a more xenophobic politician, who disposes of one of the most powerful armies in the world and is in illegal occupation of territories of three neighbouring countries: Palestine, Syria and Lebanon. That demonstration was totally hijacked by an even more extreme, a more unscrupulous Israeli politician: Bibi Netanyahu, the come-back kid, who upstaged, dwarfed and eclipsed all the other speakers at this event. While his fans described his intervention as 'Churchillian', according to the *Jewish Chronicle,* there were 'rumblings of criticism' over Bibi's speech. Maureen Lipman commented that 'perhaps Bibi went a little far for a peace rally.' The chief Rabbi, Dr Sacks, later observed that 'Bibi's remarks had been inappropriate to the occasion,' while Andrew Gilbert, the vice-chair of the Reform Movement, described Bibi's speech as 'a low note rather than keynote'.

The day after, Norman Lebrecht, a frequent columnist in the

---

1.   Solidarity Rally, Trafalgar Square, Saturday 18 May 2002.

Jewish Chronicle, wrote in *The Evening Standard*, 'yesterday's solidarity rally for Israel was, for me, a march too far ... It succeeded only in exposing weakness in numbers and a vacancy of ideas ... This was a rally without a definite object. Participants were asked to show support for Israel without necessarily endorsing the policies of the Sharon Government ... Communal celebrities and even some prominent rabbis were notably absent ... No member of the Cabinet was free to speak ... and where last month's pro-PLO march attracted visible support from the liberal left, the pro-Israel rally drew groups of evangelical Christians.' End of quote.

But, friends, how Christian are those evangelical fundamentalist Christians? Here in the UK and mainly there in the USA, as a Palestinian Christian, born in the land where Jesus Christ and the Christian message were born, I find, to say the least, their understanding of God's will extremely disturbing.

Having started by being nauseatingly anti-Semitic, Christian fundamentalists then converted to unconditional, unquestioning support to Israel because, supposedly, Jews assembling in the Promised Land will simply accelerate 'the end of time', doom's day and the return of the Messiah. Their depiction of the Divinity is so alarming, so frightening, so delirious that I have often had to defend 'the innocence of God'. Being in regular contact with the Vatican, with the World Council of Churches in Geneva, with Lambeth Palace, with the Anglican communion and the Patriarch of Jerusalem who, by the way, all support the end of occupation and Palestinian Statehood, I simply thought that Christ had never left us and did not need to have His return to earth accelerated by such questionable means.

So, Friends, who are we, we who are assembled here today in Trafalgar Square?

We are the coalition for Justice. The coalition for Peace. We are the coalition of Muslims, Christians, Jews and non-believers who stand for the UN Charter and international law. We firmly believe that there is only one mankind, and not different kinds of men and women. We obviously believe that the Palestinian people are not, definitely not, children of a lesser God. And as recent opinion polls demonstrated, we are no more a marginal minority, but mainstream.

We stand against any racial discrimination, against all racist prejudices. We are equally against anti-Semitism, against Arabophobia, against Islamophobia.

Just as we were horrified by the month-long Israeli siege of the Church of the Nativity in Bethlehem during the re-invasion of the occupied territories, we unambiguously condemn any attack on any synagogue. We unequivocally condemn any desecration of any Jewish cemetery, whoever are the perpetrators.

Anti-Semitism is morally repugnant and politically unacceptable. Its victims are the Jews and its victims are also the Palestinians. It was the Dreyfus Affair in Paris at the end of the nineteenth century that resulted in an assimilated Austrian Jewish journalist, Theodore Herzl, starting the Zionist movement. And until the accession to power in Berlin of Adolf Hitler, Zionism was a struggling minority tendency within the different Jewish communities in Europe.

While the Jews and the Palestinians are the direct victims of anti-Semitism, Zionism, Israel and General Sharon are its immediate beneficiaries. And let us face it, today's anti-Semitism is the oppression, the persecution of the Palestinian people by the Israeli State. And the xenophobic tendencies manifesting themselves in Europe are mainly aimed at the Arab and the Muslim communities.

Friends,
The argument of anti-Semitism is constantly and Machiavellically invoked to silence legitimate criticism of Israeli misbehaviour. In a shameless exercise of intellectual terrorism, journalist Melanie

Philips tried to explain that the mounting criticism was the result of the deeply rooted historical hatred of Jews in Christianity itself reinvigorated, according to her, by 'Palestinian Christian revisionism', only to attract more than 500 letters to the *Spectator* signalling to her that intellectual terrorism, that the pro-Israeli inquisition, will work no more. These days, the pro-Israeli lobby in the USA, accustomed to using one muscle too many and to going one pressure too far, is waging a campaign against Europe itself, including advocating a boycott of the Cannes Film Festival. On that one, I align myself with my favourite New Yorker. Not Rudolph Giuliani. I meant Woody Allen.

Friends,

The events of the last six weeks have proven that the Nakba catastrophe was not a frozen moment in history that happened sometime in 1948. It is, also, still an ongoing process until today, from Deir Yassin to Jenin. Ariel Sharon and his army have behaved again in a manner that makes Genghis Khan and Attila the Hun look like choir boys but we, the Palestinian people, remain unbowed and undefeated. We have always believed that the PLO was at the same time an institution and an idea. Each time the institution is under attack, the idea gets stronger. The idea is simple: it is our sense of identity. It is our ceaseless quest for independence and sovereignty. It is our unwavering determination to rid ourselves of the chains of our captivity and bondage. This idea is immortal because the eight to nine million Palestinians, in Palestine and all over the world, are the powerful vehicles of this historical drive.

Friends,

Since we are at a walking and hearing distance from Downing Street, I wish to say that it is not up to Barak, Bibi or Sharon to decide how much occupied territory they are 'generously' available to withdraw from. Peace is not a compromise formula, half way between the different poles of the Israeli domestic debate, half way between Shamir and Sharon, half way between Bibi and Barak, half way between Labour and Likud. In international relations, in matters of war and peace, the international will has primacy and should prevail on a national whim.

XXII

Rome and its belligerent Sparta[1]

As a peace enthusiast, I was heavily involved, at the end of the eighties and early nineties, in Israeli-Palestinian dialogue when every university, think-tank and political party around the world was organising a seminar of its own to contribute to a rapprochement they saw as desirable and inevitable. In all those encounters, every possible scenario in peacemaking, and its opposite, was explored *ad nauseum*. This led many to believe, naively, that when a peace process would finally be triggered, it would be of short duration, since much of the preliminary homework was already done in these fora which, though unofficial, were high powered.

Posted in London, a very demanding and time-consuming assignment if any, I was mercifully not engaged in the negotiating process started in Madrid in October 1991. But in 1998, I attended three meetings here in London between Yasser Arafat and the American Secretary of State, Madeleine Albright.

After one of those encounters, retiring to our hotel depressed because of the absence of any tangible progress, I told Yasser Arafat, 'Abu Ammar, we, the Christian Palestinians, are two percent of society in Palestine and we were two (Nabil Abu Rudeinah and myself) out of eight in the Palestinian delegation: that is twenty-five percent. The Jewish community in the USA. are also two

1. This article was published in the Royal United Services Institute for Defence Studies (RUSI) *Newsbrief* in August 2002 (Volume 22, No 8).

percent of society, yet they constituted eight out of eight of the American delegation: that is one hundred percent. We are either under-represented or they are over-represented.'

Before objections start flooding in, I wish to remind readers that, when in any analysis of the French and British domestic scenes, it is said that the Corsicans and the Scots play a disproportionate role, there is no avalanche of expressions of indignation and outrage. Yet their role and status are modest in comparison.

The loss of an ally and the loss of an enemy

Between 1985 and 1987, I spent two years as visiting scholar at Harvard University. Two memories stick out:

1. It was obvious then, in academic and political circles, that the collapse of the Soviet Union was a matter of years away. Within the Third World, and in some leftist Western circles, there was a certain disquiet about the possible global and regional repercussions of such a major alteration in the international system. To my surprise, within pro-Israeli circles in America, a worry of a different nature was manifesting itself. Contrary to those who were assessing the possible impact of the loss of 'an ally', their worry was about the loss of 'an enemy', what it might signify for the *raison d'être* and the strategic function and utility of Israel in American foreign policy as a bastion and strategic asset to contain Soviet expansionism. It was precisely during this period that the ideological construction of an alternative global threat, the peril of Islam, took shape. This self-fulfilling theory/prophesy/ideology gained a momentum of its own, rendered more plausible by the shallowness, irrationality and extremism of some Oriental responses to Occidental challenges.

2. In magazines like *Commentary* and *The New Republic,* there was an acute awareness that one day a peace process would have to get started and a number of serious articles explored the avenues that might suit Israeli interests best. The architecture and the choreography of negotiations, it was said, had to reflect the

'non-centrality' of the Palestinian problem in the Middle East and there was a need to de-couple the different negotiating tracks to make it difficult to link and to synchronise progress. The American role had to be limited to convene the parties to the negotiating table, but not to be decisive towards achieving a certain finality. The outcome would be 'as agreed upon by the local negotiating sides' as though the USA had no international commitments in the United Nations, no international responsibilities necessitating leadership and guidance, no regional interests and friendships that such a complacent attitude towards the Israeli territorial appetite might jeopardise.

When after the Gulf War of 1991 the American administration felt the need to invite for a Peace conference (out of fidelity to the Arab members of the coalition, to confer retroactive respectability to the war in the Gulf by showing sensitivity also to the endless ordeal of the Palestinians etc), that was the model of negotiations suggested. It was considered to be an offer Israel could not refuse precisely because it corresponded to its preferred negotiating strategy. It was called 'the only game in town', 'the only deal around'. Negotiations started in Madrid at the end of October 1991 and then predictably stagnated in Washington until August 1993 when a parallel and secret track witnessed a breakthrough the Americans were not involved in.

The decline of the Arabists

Henry Kissinger has had an enduring impact on American foreign policy beyond his years of service. He was, as National Security Advisor, the one who undermined in 1970 the Rogers Plan, by repeating to whoever cared to listen that it was precisely only that: a Rogers Plan. Once dear Henry succeeded in supplanting Rogers at the State Department, he proceeded to purge the Arabists because, for him, they were infected by 'localititis', and gradually replaced them by staff who had acquired their political experience working in the many organs of the pro-Israeli lobby. Their influence varied depending on the personality of the Secretary of State. It was immense during the time of George Schultz, Warren Christopher, Madeleine Albright, who were after all employees of the President, not belonging to the inner circle, but contained with James Baker, who was a close friend and behaved as a partner to George Bush Sr.

A messenger without a message

Dennis Ross emerged as the most influential of the pro-Israelis among the senior civil servants, no thanks to his powerful intellect, but because of his survival capabilities, and hence his durability. For twelve years, he was a frequent visitor to the area. He incarnated the self-inflicted impotence of the only remaining superpower. He was the most distinguished representative of the strategy outlined in *Commentary* magazine.

He advocated this approach tirelessly. He practised it unwaveringly. I called him on BBC World 'a messenger without a message', since he never came with any original idea or any American proposal not cleared in advance with the Israeli government, but always conveyed and explained the Israeli position. The USA, the only global superpower, thus neutralised, had abdicated its role and status in favour of its regional protégé, Israel. History will record that if Dennis Ross had nothing to do with the diplomatic breakthrough of 1993, he was heavily guilty of the breakdown in 2000. His name will always be associated with bias, partiality and the absence of American even-handedness in the quest for peace in the Middle East. The way Dennis Ross conducted himself, the Palestinians were reduced to negotiate at the mercy of a very asymmetrical balance of power. He allowed the Israeli side to indulge in the illusion that the diplomatic outcome would reflect

Israeli power and American alignment on the Israeli preference. Israeli 'generosity' would decide the territorial contours of the agreement.

Rome and its belligerent Sparta

The study of American-Israeli relations has fascinated, intrigued, occupied and pre-occupied two generations of scholars. Two competing schools of thought addressed the 'who wags whom' debate. The first school spoke of 'an American Israel', with the United States dictating to the local ally what should be its regional policy in accordance with the American global vision. Noam Chomsky had written, two decades ago, that Washington was the contemporary Rome and Israel its regional belligerent Sparta.

The second school projects the image of 'an Israeli America', a complex relationship where the global superpower simply adopts the regional policy of its client state and integrates it in its global strategy. This is seen as a result of the powerful pro-Israeli lobby that succeeded in turning 'Capitol Hill into another Israeli occupied territory'. I have always believed that both schools of thought were correct but at different moments in history, depending on a variety of considerations like the strength – electoral and intellectual – of the American president, on how comfortable he is in the country and in Congress and how comfortable the United States is in the world.

After the horror of 9/11, when the predictable retaliation was being discussed, the pro-Israeli lobby immediately emerged as the 'maximalist school', which wanted to elastically expand the theatre of operations beyond Afghanistan to engulf more countries. America now prepares itself to wage an attack against Iraq that nothing justifies except Israel's regional hegemonic inclinations. The lobby has really grown accustomed to using one muscle too many and to going one pressure too far. The satisfaction among the right-wing Israeli establishment is immense now that the USA appears to be Israel's regional belligerent Sparta.

The Two Americas

In today's administration the pro-Israeli lobby, in alliance with the Christian fundamentalists and their delirious theology, has totally dominated and confiscated the debate around American foreign policy in the Middle East. During a recent quick visit to America on the 3rd and 4th of July, I was dazzled to watch on all TV channels the artificially imported Israeli discourse on insecurity and terrorism, giving the impression that the USA was under massive attack on Independence Day. Colin Powell and the State Department still represent a pocket of resistance, aided occasionally by the distant voices of Jimmy Carter, Brent Scowcroft and Zbigniew Brzezinsky.

When Ariel Sharon waged his reinvasion of the occupied territories, I believe that President Bush expected the withdrawal to take place 'now', 'immediately' and 'without delay', but had to retract because of massive pressures in Washington. Bush was defeated even before Powell departed for his slow-motion trip to the area. Again, it turned out that the lobby does not suffer from 'dual loyalty'. When, on the rare occasion, the president happens to differ with an Israeli Prime Minister, the lobby sides not with the president.

Both Bushes, the father and the son, experienced that in less than a decade. When Vice-President Cheney passed through London in March on his way to the region, I published in *The Guardian* an open letter in which I wrote that the Arab world has no ideological dispute with the USA. Our belief is that there are two Americas, two political cultures, two historical memories.

There is the America of the early settlers who, on discovering the New World, clashed with the indigenous population and almost totally terminated them; the America that established slavery and had an elastic conception of its frontiers expanding shamelessly at the expense of Mexico. This is the America that Ariel Sharon always seeks an alliance with. When 'the shared values' are invoked, it is in this national experience that the common traditions are deeply rooted.

But there is another America. The America of the War of Independence against the colonial power; the America which took the painful decision to undergo a Civil War to abolish slavery; the America of Woodrow Wilson which came to the Versailles Conference upholding the principle of self determination; the America of the civil rights movement and Martin Luther King's dream. It is this America that we Palestinians appeal to and seek an alliance with.

These two Americas do not coincide with Democratic America and Republican America. The two historical memories cross this political divide. I could have added the America of Dwight Eisenhower who in 1956–7, just after the Suez War, obtained, through 'friendly persuasion', Israel's withdrawal out of the occupied Sinai in twenty-four hours. Israel then was governed by Ben Gurion and, unlike President Bush, Eisenhower obtained Israeli acquiescence, without having the 'reward' of the Saudi initiative, which enjoys Palestinian blessings and now has been endorsed by the Arab Summit of Beirut.

Choices

Decision-makers in Washington had always a choice between a foreign policy that will make America loved and respected around the world or a policy that will make it feared and hated. They now have to decide what is the unfinished business on the international agenda: disciplining Israel diplomatically or crushing Iraq militarily. In the meantime, Dennis Ross, after a twelve-year stint in the State

Department, is back home in the pro-Israeli lobby as Director of the Washington Institute for Near East Policy. In the new administration, the centre of gravity of the pro-Israeli lobby moved from the State Department to the Department of Defence. He frequently appears on all TV channels on both sides of the Atlantic as the peacemaker *par excellence* pontificating in the most irritating fashion as though he was an equidistant third party. He indulges in the character assassination of Yasser Arafat, trying to politically demolish what the military campaigns of Ariel Sharon did not succeed in achieving.

In a very gloomy situation, the birth of the new structure of the Quartet (US-UN-EU and Russia) is the only source of optimism in the immediate future. It has the double advantage of reintroducing important players who were deliberately excluded or marginalised because, as Kissinger had written, their presence might 'raise Arab expectations', and of strengthening the more reasonable and decent school of thought within the American administration.

With the vision of the two-state solution, we now have the light. The Quartet could be the missing tunnel. I have always believed that the Arab-Israeli conflict was a test between moral courage and political cowardice. Having encountered cowardice so frequently, I still hope that we may soon have a *rendez vous* with history.

XXIII

Letter to Prime Minister Blair

London, 11 July, 2003
Dear Prime Minister

I am writing to you, Prime Minister, a few days before you receive in Downing Street Israeli Prime Minister Sharon to express some grave worries I have concerning the implementation of the Road Map, a document in whose adoption and publication you have played a deservedly recognised and significant role. Mr Sharon might want to capitalise internationally on his reluctant verbal acceptance of the Road Map while, on the ground, the situation leaves, alas, much to be desired.

The major reason why the Road Map was welcomed in Arab and Palestinian circles was the involvement and the commitment of the international community through the Quartet and the clarity of their expectations, of both sides, who were called upon to undertake precise measures simultaneously and mutually. It seems to me that the last weeks, on the Israeli side, were far from convincing. Prime Minister Sharon should not be allowed to drag the peace process into the familiar path of the previous oriental bazaar during which successive Israeli governments thought they could get away with setting the ceiling of the possible and the permissible, as well as dictating the pace of progress.

I believe, Prime Minister, that your discussions with Mr Sharon can help pre-empt and prevent a predictable impasse if no external stimulus is injected. The peace process will be again in your debt, Sir, if you were to raise the following issues:

1. The Road Map demands that Israel abandons its policy of repeated incursions in Palestinian territories and its practice of targeted killings. Alas, we have witnessed incursions, assassinations, with 'collateral damage' and massive arrests.

2. The Road Map demands that Israel dismantles all the settlements/ outposts, authorised and unauthorised, built since March 2001. The Americans have informed the Israeli side that their intelligence-gathering shows ninety-four such outposts. The Israeli government started, timidly, dismantling less than ten uninhabited outposts, and have allowed several new ones to crop up. More dangerously, settlement expansion is underway in occupied East Jerusalem in the Beit Iksa and Abu Dis neighbourhoods.

3. The Israeli military checkpoints continue to suffocate the Palestinian people and strangle our economy. Paradoxically, the proliferation of those checkpoints accompanied the peace process triggered by Madrid, Washington and Oslo. The freedom of movement of people and products still awaits its materialisation on the ground.

4. The Wall being erected deep in the 1967 occupied territories is another issue that needs to be urgently addressed. Already tens of thousands of Palestinian villagers in addition to the city of Qalqylia are trapped by the monstrous and controversial Berlin-like fence. The Israeli political establishment has to become aware that their entire security doctrine is erroneous and counter productive. Security comes not from territorial aggrandisement, but from regional acceptance. And we, the Palestinians, are the key to regional acceptance from Morocco to Muscat, from Rabat to Riyadh.

5. The issue of release of prisoners was already mishandled by the Israeli side after Oslo. We kept telling them, and we were not alone, that there should be a massive release of detainees, so that every city, village and refugee camp will have cause to celebrate the return back home of loved ones, helping to create a new mood,

a new atmosphere and shaping a new positive and constructive environment. The Israeli behaviour on that issue is not only unwise, it is simply sadistic.

6. The Road Map calls upon the Israeli government to allow the reopening of the Palestinian institutions that were closed in occupied East Jerusalem. Maintaining and respecting the *status quo* in religious sites in Jerusalem, is also of capital importance. The breaches that are occurring, with greater frequency in the last weeks, on the Holy Sanctuary, seriously threaten to inflame the situation again, in and beyond Palestine.

7. It would be extremely helpful, Prime Minister, if you were to raise with your guest the issue of facilitating the process of voter registration. This will tremendously accelerate the path leading to the second phase of the Road Map which deals with Palestinian elections. Since the publication of the Road Map was unnecessarily delayed, it would be wise to do some catching up. Palestinian presidential, legislative and municipal elections need not be delayed because of acrobatic conditions inflicted on the teams undertaking the indispensable registration of voters.

8. Last but not least, the siege imposed on President Yasser Arafat in what remains of his office in Ramallah. This siege is perceived by the Palestinian people as a collective national insult that mirrors the siege imposed on our entire society. Mr Arafat is the democratically elected President and remains the embodiment of Palestinian legitimacy and the pillar and cement of central authority. Yasser Arafat has always been, in Arab politics and Arab summits, one of the major leaders of the pragmatic school of thought. His freedom of movement regained will be a major factor in the emergence of the perception that the Road Map is not a trap, but a very credible path guided by the international community towards peace and reconciliation.

Please accept, Prime Minister, the expression of my highest consideration.

Afif Safieh, Palestinian General Delegate to the United Kingdom

XXIV

On Edward Said[1]

Edward was profoundly Palestinian. Edward was totally cosmopolitan. Edward was the universal intellectual *par excellence*.

I still remember his devastating critique of Samuel Huntington's *Clash of Civilisations*, in which he argued that even the city-states of Ancient Greece owed a lot and borrowed much from those they considered 'barbarians'. That the Roman Empire was, by its very nature, a pluri-ethnical, multi-cultural society. On the basis of this vision of the constant cross-fertilisation of cultures and civilisations, I believe that Edward Said was our Palestinian contribution to the international intellectual landscape, our Palestinian input in contemporary political thought.

Edward was a charming, private person. Edward was an immensely charismatic public figure. For Christ'l and I, Edward was a very close and dear friend since 1978 when we met in Beirut. He had just published *Orientalism,* which was hailed more as an event, rather than simply one more book. In academic circles, there will always be 'a before *Orientalism'* and 'an after *Orientalism'*.

Is there a contradiction due to the fact that Edward was a severe critic of the Palestinian National Authority and my being here to pay tribute to his legacy and to his memory? Not at all. Edward and I agreed, years ago, that the Palestinian people had neither the authority they deserve, nor the opposition they need.

1. Memorial Event, Friends House, London, 6 November 2003.

248

We agreed, years ago, that the PLO was at the same time an idea and an institution. I happen to represent the institution. I hope with dignity. He was the powerful vehicle of the idea. And ideas are immortal.

One of Edward's favourite thinkers, Antonio Gramsci, wrote brilliantly about the special relationship between intellectuals and the oppressed: 'those who think because they suffer and those who suffer because they think.' An opinion as though tailored specially for Edward. The fact that today supporters of Palestinian aspirations are no more a marginal minority, but belong to the mainstream in Europe, owes much to Edward's prolific writing and his tireless lecturing. Edward would have been delighted by the results of the opinion poll conducted by the European Commission, which showed that fifty-nine percent of European public opinion considers Israeli policies and practices to be the greatest threat to world peace. Of course the pro-Israeli inquisition will try, through their usual intellectual terrorism, to drag in the mud those who undertook the poll and those whose opinions it expressed, yet the message from European public opinion is clear:

1. Anti-Semitism today is the persecution of Palestinian society by the Israeli state;
2. It is the constant American alignment on the Israeli preference that is poisoning international relations;
3. It is the collusion between the Israeli and the American agendas that has put America on a collision course with the Arab and the Muslim world;
4. The European governments are too timid, insufficiently assertive, too complacent in their dealings with an Israel that daily violates international law and defies the international will.

All through his life, Edward denounced both Judeophobia and Islamophobia. He never indulged in comparative victimology or martyrology. He never volunteered mechanisms and methods to measure pain or to quantity suffering.

The last time I met Edward was at his keynote speech at SOAS (School of Oriental and African Studies) on 29 January 2003. It was followed by a small dinner, in his honour, nowhere else but in the British Museum. Knowing that the end was near, I felt that the place was extremely well chosen to pay tribute to a living monument, a roving encyclopaedia. If ever we the Palestinians were to have, like in Paris, a Pantheon of our own 'for those to whom the nation is indebted,' it is undeniably there that Edward Said would belong.

Bing Crosby, the singer, said of Frank Sinatra, 'Such a voice happens only once in a lifetime. Why the hell did it have to happen during my lifetime?'

Edward, we are all proud, we all feel immensely privileged that you 'happened' during our lifetime.

XXV

Which way is forward?[1]

I

I would like to thank Professor Eugene Rogan and St Anthony's College for organising this series of lectures: 'Palestinians on Palestine: The way forward.' Let us hope that this initiative will result in obliging the speakers, myself included, to think deep into that important topic and thus help elevate a necessary debate that is long overdue.

The title of this lecture is followed by a question mark which, with me, is not unusual. A lecture I gave in 1986 at MIT was titled 'Dead ends?' and a friend told me then that the question mark was my only concession to optimism. Lectures I gave in 1994 in California at the invitation of the World Affairs Council were titled 'Palestine: a state in the making?' Then the question mark was my only concession to pessimism. Today, it is there as a sign of humility, a recognition that there are other avenues offered to Palestinian public opinion, an admission that we are in a realm where there are hardly any certainties.

II

I will start with Israel, since after all, it is Israel that occupies Palestine and not the other way around. The first President of the

---

1.   Transcript of a lecture given at St Anthony's College, Oxford University, Friday 23 January 2004.

State of Israel, Chaim Weizman, wrote, 'I am certain the world will judge the Jewish State by how it will treat the Arabs' (*Trial and Error*, London 1949, p. 566). Today, the 'we did not know' attitude by Israelis is as unbelievable and as unacceptable as it was decades ago in other circumstances. Palestinian historians, confirmed by Israeli revisionist colleagues, have shown how the demographic upheaval was orchestrated in Mandatory Palestine, how the majority was reduced to a minority and how the minority was propelled to become a majority. The events of the last three years show us that the Palestinian Nakba/Catastrophe was not a frozen moment in history that occurred some time in 1948, but is an ongoing process, deploying itself until this very day with great savagery, aiming at acquiring as much of Palestinian geography as possible with as little of Palestinian demography as possible. It is interesting to note that the oppressors seem to hate their victims much more than the victims hate their oppressors, and that the victims have moved faster than their oppressors beyond double negation towards mutual recognition.

The Israeli Labour Party has enjoyed internationally an undeserved good reputation. I have often told Israeli interlocutors that it was Labour that made Palestine unliveable to Palestinians. What Likud does is make Israel also unliveable to many Jews. The ethnic cleansing of 1948, the Suez War of 1956, the initiative for the 1967 war, the beginning of the illegal settlement building, the idea for a separation wall – it was Labour, Labour and Labour.

When Barak faded away in 2001 and Sharon won by a landslide, most analysts put the blame on Yasser Arafat, the absence of a partner and Palestinian untrustworthiness since they responded to the most 'generous' offer with an armed intifada, proving that the Palestinians had a hidden agenda – total liberation, not just the two-state solution.

I personally attribute the repeated defeats of the Labour Party to three major factors:

1. The Israeli Labour movement has been in constant decline since 1948. If one looks at the successive compositions of the Knesset, one would notice that the Labour contingent in Parliament was regularly shrinking, even in the elections they won. They lost their dominance and centrality in 1977 with the first Menachem Begin victory. This was mainly due to sociological, anthropological, tribal reasons. Labour never succeeded in attracting a significant number of Oriental Jews. And Oriental Jews were by 1990 over sixty percent of Jewish Israeli society. Yes, in the decade of the nineties, a million Russian Jews and Russian non-Jews flocked into the country, but few joined Labour. This massive immigration changed the balance between the Sephardim and Ashkenazi Jews but it further plunged Labour into its historical decline. Then there was the loss of the Palestinian Israeli voters, fifty percent of whom used traditionally to vote Labour. That was due to the multiplication of Palestinian Israeli lists, compounded with repeated Labour blunders, such as the war on Lebanon in 1996, the Qana massacre and the ferocious repression of October 2000 when peaceful demonstrators were showered, not with water, but with lethal bullets resulting in thirteen fatalities. A party that does not appeal to the Oriental Jews, that does not attract the Russian vote and has repelled its Arab supporters, is surely heading towards its electoral Waterloo. Especially if it is led by the Israeli Bonaparte/Barak, who had already succeeded in antagonising his Labour colleagues and alienating his coalition partners.

2. The political price paid for the unequal partnership of the Likud-Labour coalition between 2001 and 2003 produced the lamentable results in 2003 by Amiran Mitzna, a decent, but underwhelmingly charismatic leader. Labour accepted the humiliating treatment of a junior partner with no say on policy and strategy, yet was there to offer more domestic acceptability and international respectability. A mere fig leaf for Sharon, simply because Ben Eliezar and Shimon

Peres were both afraid that, in opposition, they would move from the 'who is who?' to become the 'who is he?' of Israeli politics.

3. The ephemeral passage of Ehud Barak at the helm of the Labour Party. The emergence of Ehud Barak on the political scene was internationally boisterously welcomed. He was hailed as the most decorated Israeli officer, a strategic thinker, a mathematician, a gifted pianist, a *dégustateur* of classical music.

Rabin had been elevated to sainthood after his martyrdom. Barak was elevated to sainthood even before his election. Analysts forgot to observe that he was too young to have played a significant role in the conventional Arab/Israeli wars, that all his decorations were earned for his responsibility in hit-teams and death-squad operations, which inevitably affects one's psyche and one's *modus operandi*. His complex and tortuous personality was best demonstrated just after his comfortable electoral victory when he spent all of the forty-five days of coalition building finding ways to humiliate, diminish and dwarf his colleagues in Labour by giving them each the ministries they did not want. Commentators did not explain enough his unprincipled nature. When he terminated his career in the army and was preparing his entry into politics he hesitated between joining Labour or Likud. Only assurances that Rabin might favour him as his *dauphin désigné* swayed him to opt for Labour.

Conflicting perceptions of what really took place during the Camp David talks will continue to plague international relations for some time. Aided by President Clinton himself, media reports spoke of Barak as having been not only bold, audacious, courageous, magnanimous and generous but also constructive, creative, imaginative and innovative. Now English is not my first language. It is not even my second, but I have never heard so many words used in such a questionable manner. Yes, Barak went further than other Israeli leaders had ventured. But he had to. His predecessors had dealt with transitional arrangements for the interim period while, at Camp David, with inexcusable delays, final status issues were at last in discussion. He made a generous offer? Bearing in mind the history of dispossession, dispersion and domination, the mere usage of the word 'generous' is offending or tactless to say the least. Ninety-five percent? Since the West Bank, East Jerusalem and the Gaza strip together are only twenty-two percent of Mandatory Palestine, a hundred percent offer can hardly be described as a generous offer. But was it really ninety-five percent? Robert Malley, an American official who took part in Camp David, believes that it was ninety-one percent (*The New York Times*, 9 July 2001) while Barak advocated keeping 'about fifteen percent of Judea and Samaria' and wanted 'to ensure a wide security zone in the Jordan Valley' (*The New York Times*, 25 May 2001). The differences over what was really proposed stem from the chaotic, informal, poorly choreographed encounters in Camp David.

At Taba, a few months later, the Israeli team 'offered' territorially around five percent more, which is sufficient proof that the Palestinians were justified in their rejection of the Camp David deal, whatever that really was. But why did Taba fail? Mainly for two reasons. First, Barak, his coalition in tatters, had unwisely called for anticipated elections. The prediction of opinion polls was that he was heading for a poor performance to the extent that Attorney General Rubenstein declared that the Israeli team had no legitimacy to conduct diplomacy on behalf of the State. The second reason was equally significant. Within the Barak camp, there were two schools of thought, both related to how to win the coming elections. The first school of thought advocated moderating the Israeli negotiating posture so that an agreement would be reached with the Palestinians which would bring back into the fold the disenchanted Jewish peace camp and the Palestinian Israelis. The other group, which importantly included Barak himself, considered that both those categories would anyway vote for Barak as Prime Minister, *faute de mieux*, took them thus for granted and favoured a radicalisation of the Israeli stand. For them, this strategy would allow them to recapture the central ground, the floating votes, the undecided who were tilting in favour of Sharon. Needless to say, the Barak school prevailed, the Taba talks ended inconclusively, and the rest is ... history.

In 1982–3, an Israeli Commission of Inquiry had ruled that Ariel Sharon was 'not fit for public office', yet today, he is not in jail, but in power, with high approval ratings, a large majority and a coalition of right-wing and extreme right-wing parties, settler networks and Jewish fundamentalists whose common denominator seems to be annexation and the 'tranferist' ideology. The Palestinians, not only in the Occupied Territories, but within pre-1967 Israel, are constantly referred to as 'a demographic threat', a 'time bomb', a 'fifth column'. An expert who was invited to speak recently at a Likud Herzilia Conference shamelessly advocated 'enforced family planning'. In other words, the collective sterilisation of the Palestinian population.

What reveals best the prevailing and dominant political culture in Israel is a recent interview with Benny Morris in *The Haaretz* on 8 January 2004. Displaying a fascinating dual and schizophrenic personality – Historian Benny Morris and Citizen Benny Morris – a sort of Dr Jekyll and Mr Hyde, Morris explains, in great detail, that his research during the last decade confirms the results of his previous publications. Working on newly declassified documents, he states that he has discovered even more massacres, also twelve cases of rape which he admits are 'just the tip of the iceberg' since the Palestinian traditional society tends to hush-hush such occurrences, and that the units of the Haganah (not only the Irgun of Menachem Begin) were given 'operational orders that stated explicitly that they were to uproot the villagers, expel them and destroy the villages themselves.' All this is said in a clinical fashion, with no emotion and where ethical considerations are totally absent. For him, 'there are circumstances in history that justify ethnic cleansing' and 'you can't make an omelette without breaking eggs.' It was 'inevitable' if Israel were to be created.

Anyway, all this we knew already. That was the Historian Morris speaking. The frightening part is when he gives way to Citizen Morris. His grievance, and he has one, is the unfinished business of 1948. He says, 'Ben Gurion made a serious historical mistake in 1948 ... he got cold feet during the war. In the end, he faltered' and 'because he did not complete the transfer in 1948, he left a large and volatile demographic reserve in the West Bank and Gaza and within Israel itself.' Morris continues, 'Had he carried out a full expulsion – rather than a partial one – he would have stabilised the State of Israel for generations.'

Today, the unfinished business left by Ben Gurion, Sharon hopes to address by the accelerated building of the Wall of Shame snaking through the West Bank. All those who will be trapped outside the Wall and many of those who will be caged within the Wall will be actively 'encouraged' to emigrate'.

III

It is obviously the Palestinians who have no partner for peace. The Israeli side wants a diplomatic outcome that reflects Israeli power and intransigence, American total alignment on the Israeli preference, Russian decline, European abdication, Arab impotence and what they hope to be Palestinian resignation.

De Gaulle, a statesman like they make them no more, because of his familiarity with the psychology of belligerents and the pathology of conflict advised in 1967 in favour of an elegantly imposed solution through what he called *la concertation à quatre* (the coordination of the four major powers; China was not yet in the Security Council). This idea never really took off. The Americans were not unhappy with the Israeli military victory since it compensated the humiliations of Vietnam. The Soviets, short-sighted as they often could be, preferred the bipolar constellation and did not want to give equal status to lesser countries like Britain and France. And London was unenthusiastic simply because the idea was French to begin with. Since then, instead of a durable peace, we have had a permanent peace ... process.

The peacemaking approach adopted, mainly because it suited Israel's preferred negotiating strategy, left it all to the local belligerent parties/negotiating partners to 'sort it out' amongst themselves. Today, it is clear that what is democratically acceptable to the Israelis is unacceptable to the Palestinians, and *vice versa*.

What is to be done?

I have always observed a certain self-restraint when dealing with domestic Palestinian issues. I believe this is the proper pattern of behaviour for civil servants. This code of conduct is not always respected and, at moments, one believes that civil servants should not refrain from injecting their input into the national debate.

One cannot study Palestinian strategies in isolation from the regional Arab state-system, its natural political environment. These last decades, the Arab world has become a regional grouping where no advantage is reaped by befriending it, nor any risk is taken by antagonising it. In addition, the Arab world suffers from a double crisis: the crisis of regimes and a crisis of the oppositions. Pan-Arab nationalism is still, thirty-three years later, orphaned by the death of Abdel Nasser. The Arab left has not yet recovered from the collapse of the Soviet Union and the Soviet model. The liberal school of thought never really existed as an organised trend. We are left with only the Islamic parties who, for a majority of public opinion, do not seem to be the desirable appetising alternative to the unrepresentative, incompetent and corrupt governments in place and thus, paradoxically, result in prolonging their durability.

The PLO, it has to be recognised, has always functioned as a multi-party system. In spite of external pressures and internal 'opportunities' there was never an attempt to crush or eliminate a party, a trend or an opposition. At least not by the leadership. On the contrary, Tripoli 1983 was an attempt by an insurrection backed by a regional power to eliminate the legitimate leadership. But the democracy and pluralism were often chaotic and the usual quest for consensus among the factions could result at crucial moments in the paralysis of decision-making. I have always believed that, like all other societies, differences of opinion were not only healthy, but simply normal. And like any other society, we are condemned to have either unity/unanimity or a strategy. At times, I have to say, we seem to have neither unanimity nor a strategy.

Let me, first of all, wave away what I consider to be an optical illusion: the one bi-national state. This is not a new strategic vision, but a recycled, reheated old dish. In the late sixties, the resurrecting Palestinian national movement formulated the proposal of a unitary democratic bi-cultural, multi-confessional, pluri-ethnic state. That was genuinely a 'generous offer' from those who believed to have become 'the Jews of the Israelis' yet did not want those who chose to be their enemies to become 'the Palestinians of the Palestinians'. This project emerged at a moment in history when we believed – naively – that we were on our way to victory. Today, those who speak of the bi-national state do it out of resignation that the occupation is irreversible and suffer from a psychology of failure and a mentality of defeat. Besides my doubts about the feasibility of this proposal, I have serious reservations about its desirability. A fanaticized Israeli Jewish community is hardly a partner one would seek with relish as co-citizens. The disparity between both societies – and the qualitative gap is widening – makes the one-state formula a mechanism for the perpetuation of the domination of one community by the other. In addition to that, I personally believe that many more refugees can exercise their right to return to their homes and hometowns, but mainly to their homeland – the nascent Palestinian State – within the framework of the two-state solution rather than the one-state solution. Those who see this slogan as a tactical tool, a sort of scarecrow, to convince and frighten the Israeli society in favour of withdrawal must have realised that its deterrent value is limited because of a belief in Israel that the apartheid reality can be prolonged the way it operated in South Africa for decades, in spite of the huge numerical imbalance. The Israeli government wants a one-state solution – a Jewish State – and a no-state formula for the Palestinians.

The two-state solution has been adopted by the Palestinian national movement since the October/Ramadan/Kippur War of

1973, which was the real demarcation line in strategic thinking in the Arab world. With self-confidence restored, a political maturity manifested itself distinguishing the desirable, the possible and the acceptable. Differentiating between absolute justice and possible justice. The huge aerial bridge by the American administration to the Israeli army was proof enough that the USA will never allow Israel to be defeated militarily. Since then, the absence of an Arab arms industry, the collapse of the Soviet Union, the 'loosening' of relations between the Arab military actors and the de-linking of any serious coordination between those actors and Arab oil-producing countries – all were contributing factors to the absence of a credible Arab military option.

In the absence of an Arab military option, is there a credible Palestinian military option? I think not and have never thought so. During our presence on the Lebanese theatre, our aim was to remain a military actor so that we could be recognised as a diplomatic factor. In the diplomatic arena, during those years we were not a rejectionist force but the rejected party. The first intifada of 1987, which operated on the Palestinian scene as the October War did for the Arab State system, allowed us both to proclaim our national existence (Independence – Algiers, 1988) and to demonstrate our availability to coexistence.

The Mitchell Report admits that the first weeks of the second intifada were mainly non-violent, at least from the Palestinian side. It was the brutal and ferocious nature of Israeli repression – over one hundred Palestinian fatalities in the first two weeks – that pushed a few in our ranks to use – unwisely – the few weapons they disposed of, thus allowing the Israelis to further escalate. I wish we all had remembered the wisdom of the late Faisal Husseini: 'If you want to defy Tyson, don't invite him to the boxing ring, but to the chess board.' The genius of the first intifada was its non-violent nature which neutralised most of Israel's military arsenal.

This time, they had no restraint in using their Merkava tanks, their Apache helicopters and their F16s. Very few people, especially not pro-Israelis, are morally qualified to give us lessons in political ethics, but it is high time we all realised that suicide bombings are counter-productive. At least in two moments in recent history, they had devastating effects on the national interest.

It is not true that 9/11 had an immediate effect on changing American foreign policy in the Middle East. Preparing to wage war in Afghanistan, the American administration, along with several European countries, was then keen to be perceived as pursuing an active role in the pursuit of peace in Israel/Palestine. Ariel Sharon was complaining publicly that Israel was being treated like the Czechoslovakia of 1939, abandoned to the territorial appetite of its neighbours. It is a public secret that Bush, still interested in winning hearts and minds in the Arab and the Muslim world, was growing increasingly impatient with a reluctant Sharon and had banged the telephone, interrupting a difficult and unpleasant conversation. Bush then designated General Zinni as his special envoy, which was good news because that envoy for once was not from the American Jewish community, was a general himself and would not be impressed or intimidated by the physique or the personality of Sharon, and was a former Commander of the American forces in the Gulf, hence fully aware of the burden of Israeli intransigence on American-Arab relations. In brief, for us the ideal envoy. Bush furthermore summoned – not invited, summoned – Sharon to Washington. That was at the end of November 2001. On the eve of Sharon's difficult visit to Washington and of the arrival of Zinni to Palestine/Israel, two suicide bombings occurred, making the Zinni visit a failure by shrinking its purpose to the security dimension instead of the political horizon and saved Sharon's visit to Washington, making it a major success. In Washington, Sharon, and with the help of influential circles within the administration, convinced Bush that his repression of our people was part of the global war against terrorism.

The second moment when suicide bombing inflicted strategic damage on our national interest was in March 2002 when the Arab Summit in Beirut adopted the Saudi initiative which had Palestinian blessings. Sharon had a choice: either responding to a collective diplomatic invitation, or retaliating to a military provocation. We could have predicted his preference.

Today, clinically, Israel has to become aware that it cannot terminate the intifada. Today, clinically, we have to be aware that by the intifada alone, we cannot terminate the occupation. The fact that we remain undefeated, unbowed, untamed, undomesticated is our victory. We should never forget the primacy of politics. In the final analysis, battles and wars are won politically, not militarily. Most national liberation movements won politically, not militarily. If the aim is the two-state solution, and it is, we have already won diplomatically and politically. UN Security Council resolution 1397, the Road Map, the 'Bush vision', all recognise a need to end the occupation that started in 1967 and for a two-state solution. Our remaining challenge is to translate this victory geographically, territorially.

The choice for Palestinian society is not, like it is sometime superficially presented, between resistance and non-resistance – intifada or no intifada – but the choice is between different means of expression of our rejection of occupation. Bearing in mind all the factors mentioned above, I hope and advocate, with great conviction, a total conversion in favour of a confrontational strategy of popular non-violent resistance. This is not the option of the naïve or of those who suffer from struggle fatigue. It is an efficient and a very convincing vehicle for Palestinian empowerment. For the different factions, it will constitute a formidable challenge. It is by far more difficult and demanding to organise, channel and choreograph the struggle of 3.5 million people than to manage fifteen cells of three persons. Such a strategy will involve all strata of society. Women will play the prominent role they aspire for. The Israeli Palestinians and the Palestinians of the diaspora will find it easier to contribute and complement such a struggle. The Israeli peace camp would welcome and join such an approach, propelling it again on the ascendancy trend. The international NGO network could become a partner, physically, in our daily struggle. A popular non-violent strategy would promote the question of Palestine as the universal battle for justice in our time.

In a Brecht play on Galileo, there is an interesting scene where a disciple says, 'Unhappy are the people who have no heroes,' to which Galileo responds, 'Unhappy are the people who still have a need for heroes.' We are obviously still in need of heroes. I bow in respect for the Palestinian collective hero – the people themselves – for their steadfastness, their endurance, their capacity to absorb unimaginable pain and suffering. And I firmly believe that there is today a need to define or redefine heroism.

XXVI

On Yasser Arafat[1]

Ladies and gentlemen,

No, he was not infallible – but who is? – yet he was a great man, undeniably one of the greatest of the second half of the twentieth century.

Throughout his political career, Yasser Arafat was the object of relentless campaigns of character assassination – not because of what he was but because of what he represented: the Palestinian people whose mere existence was a monumental nuisance for those who coveted Palestine. With the Palestinian people threatened by historical oblivion, with our geography occupied and our demography dispersed, Yasser Arafat was the architect of the resurrecting Palestinian national movement in the mid-1960s and was its engine and locomotive for almost forty years.

He was our own Palestinian de Gaulle, and, like de Gaulle, he has had to struggle against foes and friends alike to maintain the rank and status of Palestine and of the Palestinians undiminished. All throughout those decades, the tragedy was the absence of an Arab Churchill and an Arab Roosevelt. But that is another story.

Ladies and gentlemen,

Making history is extremely important. So is interpreting history and disseminating one's own version of history. We still suffer an uphill battle because of the travesty of history concerning Barak's

1. Memorial service, Friends House, London, 7 December 2004.

pseudo-generous offer. We should never again lose the battle of the different versions of history.

Today we are being told that because Yasser Arafat is out of the way, there is a window of opportunity to revitalise the peace process. Today we are being told that because Yasser Arafat is out of the picture, the Palestinian people will finally familiarise themselves with democracy and elections.

Ladies and gentlemen,

History will record that Yasser Arafat has led and preserved the multiparty system that is the PLO; history will record that, in spite of tremendous pressures, regional and international, Yasser Arafat always stood firmly against the elimination of the pluralistic nature of the national movement. And history will record that Yasser Arafat, besides his revolutionary and historical credentials acquired also, in 1996, democratic legitimacy in an internationally monitored and competitive presidential election in which Mrs Samiha Khalil, the director of the biggest NGO in Palestine, was the contender.

As for the peace process reactivated, we, here in London, still remember Tony Blair's speech at the end of September to the Annual Conference of the British Labour Party: 'Come November,' he said, 'I will make it my personal priority ... ' Yasser Arafat was not even sick then. 'Come November' simply meant when we will have the American presidential election behind us. There was then in the air, in the pipeline, the idea of a joint visit to Ramallah of the three major foreign ministers of the European Union – Jack Straw, Yoshka Fischer and Jacques Barnier – in order to help us regain the freedom of movement of President Arafat out of his captivity in the *Muqata' a*.

History will record that the reactivation of the peace process today is not due to the death of Yasser Arafat but is the result of the convergence of three factors:

1. Now that President Bush has secured his place in the White House for a second mandate, he might also want to secure his place in history;

2. There is immense European and international exasperation – mildly and moderately expressed by Tony Blair – with the self-inflicted impotence of the American administration for the last four years which has resulted in the irresponsible deterioration of the situation in Palestine/Israel;

3. There is a growing awareness around the world from Paris to Pakistan that what is poisoning international relations and creating a rift with the Arab and Muslim worlds is the unresolved Palestinian tragedy and the perceived American complacency and complicity with the Israeli territorial appetite.

Yasser Arafat, an obstacle to peace? History will record that we need an Israeli 'obstacle' of a similar kind in order to make further progress in our elusive quest.

Ladies and gentlemen,
Reform they said. No, reforms we say. Reforms are not going to be a pre-condition imposed on us by the outside world. Reforms are a Palestinian expectation, a Palestinian aspiration, a Palestinian right and even a Palestinian duty.

Reform they said. No, reforms we say. The American political system is increasingly turning into a mediocracy, rather than an appetising democracy, where lobbies can hijack American foreign policy and where interest groups have totally domesticated and tamed an undignified political establishment.

Reform they said. No, reforms we say.

Ladies and gentlemen,
These last weeks, most commentators, knowingly or unknowingly, repeatedly referred to, quoted or invoked Max Weber who, more

than a century ago, wrote about the three phases of leadership and legitimacy:

1. the traditional leadership;
2. the charismatic leadership;
3. the institutional leadership.

We had, prior to 1948, a traditional leadership. We have just witnessed the end of the charismatic era. Now begins the institutional phase. With the world as our witness, we have had a very smooth transition and the Palestinian people have demonstrated enormous maturity and a great sense of responsibility.

I once asked Yasser Arafat: 'Abu Ammar, which was your happiest day?' To which he answered, poetically, 'My happiest day? I haven't lived it yet.'

Abu Ammar, you were, at the same time, an individual, an idea and an institution. The individual is perishable, but the idea will prove to be immortal and through the institutions that you have helped create, your people will soon live that happiest day that you devoted and dedicated your whole life for.

XXVII

Anatomy of a mission:
London 1990–2005[1]

I feel privileged to have been invited to address such a distinguished audience at such a prestigious forum. Speaking today, almost a week before the end of my official duties in London, I cannot but recall that I started my assignment in London with a Chatham House lecture in September 1990, when I had to step in at the last moment to replace Hani al-Hassan in a session chaired by the late Sir John Moberly. Let me first give a short history of the Palestinian diplomatic representation in London. Location: From the early 1970s until 1986, the Palestinian diplomatic representation was part of the Arab League office in 52 Green Street. In 1986, it moved to independent premises in South Kensington at 4 Clareville Grove. For austerity measures, in 1996 we moved again to a smaller but more modern office in a lesser neighbourhood – Hammersmith at 5 Galena Road.

Appellation: From the early 1970s until 1988, the mission was called the PLO Information Office. Then, in 1988, because of our peace initiative based on our acceptance of the two-state solution, and in agreement with Her Majesty's Government, the Delegation was upgraded to PLO General Delegation. In 1993, just after the Oslo breakthrough, the delegation was renamed the Palestinian General Delegation, representing the PLO and the PNA at the same

---

1. Transcript of the farewell speech at the Royal Institute for International Affairs at Chatham House on 13 July 2005.

time. We were then authorised to fly the Palestinian flag, which we did at a very moving ceremony attended by William Ehrman, the head of NENAD, the Near East/North Africa Department, on behalf of the Foreign Office, and the members of the Council of Arab Ambassadors.

Representation: The first PLO representative was the late Said Hamami, from the early seventies until he was assassinated in 1978. I never met Said, but he was undeniably a very effective representative, and I still feel the impact of his passage in London. He was succeeded by Nabil Ramlawi, from 1978 to 1983, who was then transferred to the UN in Geneva. He is now in our Foreign Ministry in charge of the unit for diplomatic training. Faisal Oweida followed from 1983 till 1990 and from here was transferred to Austria. Unfortunately, he died two years ago from cancer.

I am the fourth Palestinian representative in London. I do not know if there were any assassination attempts. Anyway, if there were, they passed totally unnoticed by me. Concerning my health, yes I suffer from diabetes, cholesterol, high blood pressure and I am over weight and a chain smoker. My doctor, every time she sees me, tells me, 'Bravo, Afif, for still being with us.'

Size: In 1990, I inherited an office with twelve employees, including the secretary, the receptionist and the driver. Then, because of budgetary constraints, the number was brought down to five, to rise again gradually up to eight.

In those fifteen years, I have dealt with three Prime Ministers: Margaret Thatcher, John Major, and Tony Blair. With four Secretaries of State: Douglas Hurd, Malcolm Rifkind, Robin Cook and now Jack Straw. With ten Ministers of State: William Waldegrave, Douglas Hogg, Sir Jeremy Hanley – during the Conservative period, then with the late Derek Fatchett, Peter

Hain, Brian Wilson, Geoffrey Hoon, Ben Bradshaw, Baroness Symons and now with Dr Kim Howells.

During these fifteen years, I have arranged and organised ten Arafat visits to London, three of them mainly connected to meetings with Madeleine Albright. We have more recently arranged a visit for our Prime Minister Abu Ala'a last year, and this year for President Mahmoud Abbas for the London conference on 1 March.

The upgrading was gradual. Landing in town in September 1990, it was prohibited for me to have any ministerial level contacts. Since then, I have become familiar to 10 Downing Street, to the Foreign Office and to Westminster-Whitehall in general. Christ'l and I started being invited to the Tea Garden Party by Her Majesty the Queen, first with the crowd, then we were upgraded to the diplomatic tent, which is for junior diplomats, and then to the Royal Tent itself. We have been invited to a Royal Banquet in Buckingham Palace for a visiting Head of State. We are also yearly invited to Trooping the Colour, the Lord Mayor's Banquet and to Ascot, only to discover that I am not particularly enamoured with horse racing. Without forgetting the annual invitation to the prestigious Diplomatic Dinner by De La Rue, who hope to be contracted to print one day, hopefully soon, our national currency.

Job description: What does a Palestinian representative do? We have all the responsibilities, burdens and expectations of an embassy. Yet we have neither all the privileges, nor the immunities, nor the financial capabilities of a normal embassy. We are still a national liberation movement, still struggling for independence and statehood. How do I define my job description? Wherever I am posted, I consider that there are ten layers of work that we have to handle:

1. government
2. Parliament
3. political parties

4. the diplomatic corps
5. the media
6. the NGOs
7. the Palestinian community
8. the Arab community
9. the Muslim community
10. the Jewish community

This, in addition to the regular reports to the leadership and some consular duties. We issue neither passports nor visas, but we authenticate documents, power of attorney etc ... In moments of optimism, we do have some commercial duties with companies consulting us about potential for economic transactions.

Let me go through those different 'layers' of work:

1. The government: at the very beginning, it was mainly the Foreign Office and at a sub-ministerial level. Now it is the Foreign Office at all levels, but, beyond it, we have to deal with many other departments, including the Prime Minister's office and different ministries.

2. Parliament: I really gave great importance to my dealings and interactions with both Houses of Parliament. I was invited three times for hearings by the Select Committee for Foreign Affairs, the first time in April 1991.

   In the House of Commons, we have five institutional interlocutors and channels of communication. The first is CAABU, the Council for the Advancement of Arab British Understanding, that has a triple chairmanship now from the three major parties: John Austin, Crispin Blunt and Colin Breed. The second is the Britain-Palestine All Party Parliamentary Group, that was presided over first by Ernie Ross, then by Dr Phyllis Starkey, and now by Richard Burden. Then we have the Labour Middle East Council, the Conservative Middle East Council – which was created by Lord Gilmour and Sir Dennis Walters, then was presided over by Nicholas Soames

– and the Liberal Middle East Council that was presided over by Lord David Steel and now by Sir Menzies Campbell.

3. Relations with political parties take place throughout the year, and each time I have a dignitary or a delegation, I make sure that they meet the leadership of the opposition parties as well. But the busiest period is during the season of the annual party conferences in late September and early October. I usually have one or more fringe meetings. Those fringe meetings are extremely important because they help shape perceptions, policies, projections and predictions.

4. The diplomatic corps: in a lesser capital, relations within the diplomatic corps are more horizontal: a bridge club, a tennis players' network, frequent gastronomic trips from The Hague to Brussels etc ... Such leisurely pursuits are unthinkable in London. Because of the intensity of bilateral relations, the volume of visiting delegations, ministerial, parliamentary etc, the size of the community, relations are more of a vertical nature. But the Council of Arab Ambassadors remains an extremely important forum and the resulting joint activities are of great value. I have always drawn the attention of our British interlocutors to the exceptional importance of this Council composed 'of former ministers and those who never wanted to be ministers'.

5. The media: beside the importance of the British media, its pool of sophisticated and knowledgeable journalistic community and the heavy presence of international media outfits, London is also the media capital of the Arab world. It hosts all the pan-Arab dailies distributed from Morocco to Muscat, as well as many weeklies and monthlies, without forgetting the proliferating TV satellite stations, many of whom were born in London or have their second most important offices located here.

6. The NGOs: this is the largest 'layer' and to which I devoted much time. It includes Churches, trade unions, university campuses, think-tanks, human rights institutions, solidarity groups etc ... On the lecturing circuit, this is the most demanding category. To take the Churches as an example, I have had the privilege to address

the Annual General Assembly of the Church of Scotland and of the United Reform Church, to lecture twice at Wesley Chapel of the Methodist Church, and stayed regularly in touch with the Archbishop of Canterbury and the Cardinal Head of the Roman Catholic Church.

7) The Palestinian community: it might not be as big as our communities in the USA, Chile, Canada, Australia or even Germany, but it is an extremely important community, concentrated mainly in the London area and is in more intense contact with the homeland and the region than other diaspora communities.

For example, because London is such an important Arab media centre, we probably have here more than one hundred Palestinian journalists, second numerically only to Palestine itself. Throughout the years, many institutions were established in London. The Association of the Palestinian Community, of which I am the patron, has a constitution, a general assembly every two years, democratic elections and already seven successive presidents. In addition, there are charities like Medical Aid for Palestinians (MAP), Welfare Association, and Interpal, or organisations dealing with lobbying and raising awareness, like The Return Centre or Arab Media Watch.

We the Palestinians, we have become the Jews of the Israelis and today, because of our geographic dispersal, we are 'a global tribe'. With the right approach, we could turn that into a source of empowerment.

8) The Arab community: we possess no accurate figures because in the national census, there is no such category for 'Arab', but 'Muslim' and 'Other'. A conservative estimate would be of over 400,000 British-Arabs. Politically speaking it is still an invisible community, the last ethnic minority to be totally unrepresented in both Houses of Parliament. This is due to a combination of factors; absence of any governmental encouragement and insufficient assertiveness by the community itself. The Arab Club and national associations are regular interlocutors of the Palestinian delegation.

9) The Muslim community: now close to two million, with already

five members in the House of Lords and four elected members of the House of Commons. Their electoral weight is increasingly being felt. Since my arrival to London, I am in regular contact with the Union of Muslim Organisations (UMO), and the Muslim Council of Britain (MCB), and have lectured at the invitation of City Circle, a network of second and third generation Muslims who work in the City ...

10) The Jewish community: wherever I happen to live or work, I devote a lot of time interacting with the Jewish community and many of its institutions. I have frequently lectured in the Liberal Synagogue in St John's Wood, always kept close relations with the Jewish Socialist Group, Jews for Justice, Friends of Mapam, Friends of Peace Now, Neturai karta, etc ... June Jacobs, Rabbi David Goldberg and many others are personal friends of both Christ'l and myself.

Some years ago, the *Jewish Chronicle* published, unaltered, a long letter of mine, where I said I never compare the Palestinian Nakba/Catastrophe to the Holocaust. Each tragedy stands on its own. I never indulge in comparative martyrology. If I were a Jew or a Gypsy, Nazi barbarity would be the most horrible event in history. If I were a Native American, it would be the arrival of European settlers that resulted in almost total extermination. If I were a Black African, it would be slavery in previous centuries and Apartheid during the last century. If I were an Armenian, it would the Ottoman/Turkish massacres. If I were a Palestinian – and I happen to be one – it would be the Nakba. Humanity should condemn all the above. I do not know of a way to measure suffering or how to quantify pain, but what I do know is that we are not children of a lesser God.

The broader picture: evolution of European perceptions

1948: European public perceptions of the Palestinian problem passed through a variety of phases. European anti-Semitism was decisive in the birth, then the success, of Zionism in Palestine. Without the Dreyfus Affair, there would not have been Theodore Herzel's manifesto, *The Jewish State*. Without Hitler's accession to power in the early 1930s and Nazi atrocities, Zionism would have remained a minority tendency within Jewish communities. Both Abba Eban and Nahum Goldmann wrote in a variety of books that the 'exceptional conditions' of the birth of Israel wouldn't have been possible without 'the indulgence of the international community' as a result of World War II. 'Exceptional conditions' meant the atrocious conditions in which the majority in Palestine became the minority and the minority a majority.

Alas, the Palestinian dispossession and dispersion, the Nakba, took place with Europe ... applauding. We were the victim of the victims of European history and were thus deprived of our legitimate share of sympathy, solidarity and support.

1956: I do not think that the tri-partite aggression against Egypt in 1956 made much of a fracture in the political establishment here in the UK. Yes, it shortened Anthony Eden's premiership. Yes, the late Lord Christopher Mayhew committed political hara-kiri when it was predicted that he had prime ministerial potential. Yes, the late writer Peter Mansfield resigned from the Foreign Office, but there was no major crack in society. In France, its impact was by far more serious. It helped terminate the Fourth Republic and the political careers of Gaston Deferre and Guy Mollet, brought back de Gaulle to power in 1958, and thus contributed to the reorientation of French foreign policy.

1967: If one reads the book of Livia Rokach, the daughter of the first Mayor of Tel Aviv, on the diaries of Moshe Sharett, one learns that Ben Gurion had two strategic doctrines. One was the periphery theory: since our environment is hostile, we have to make an alliance with the environment of our environment, meaning Turkey, Iran and Ethiopia. The other doctrine could be summarised thus: we should know how to provoke the Arabs into provoking us, so that we can expand beyond the narrow boundaries we have had to accept in 1948–9. That model applies perfectly to the escalating crisis that led to the 1967 war. General Matti Peled was known to have said, 'Believing that Israel was in danger in 1967 is an insult to the Israeli army.'

1967: is important because Israel starts to be perceived as an occupier. The facilitation of mass Palestinian departures to get rid of undesirable demography, the illegal annexation of expanded East Jerusalem, the beginning of settlement building … all start to tarnish the Israeli image.

1973: That was an important strategic moment and undeniably a demarcation line. Europe shows understanding towards the Arab military initiative to reawaken a dormant diplomatic front. The oil crisis that followed revealed the depth of interdependence, economically and on the security level between Europe and the Arab world and the risk of regional overspills. The Euro-Arab dialogue is initiated and the need for an equitable solution for the Palestinian problem emphasised.

1977: The first electoral defeat by Labour liberates more segments of Western public opinion anaesthetised by the soothing discourse of the Labour leadership and their *savoir-faire* in matters of public relations. The raw discourse of Likud, their vociferous and vehement statements, reflect better the reality of oppression. The Kibbutz movement, this 'paradise on earth' used to seduce public opinion, is discovered as a fading phenomenon that never represented more that three percent of society and of the Israeli economy, anyway mainly built on confiscated Palestinian land. Under Israel, Palestine. A very stubborn Palestine indeed.

1982: The invasion of Lebanon was an eye-opener. An unprovoked war. Analysts said then that it was a war out of choice, not out of necessity. Many Jewish and Israeli writers announced 'the end of the purity of arms'.

1987: The first Palestinian intifada. Mainly non-violent, coupled in 1988 by the PLO peace initiative of a two-state solution, and ushers in a new era in which the media starts to better balance its coverage, giving more time and space to Palestinian spokespersons carrying our version of history.

My term of duty in London

Let me first say that London, for an Arab or a Palestinian diplomat, is an emotionally difficult posting, from the Balfour Declaration to the Gulf Wars. Yet I have to commend all my interlocutors for their profound decency and extreme professionalism.

1990: I landed in town in September 1990 and it was not a soft landing, coinciding with the first Gulf crisis and Saddam Hussain's occupation of Kuwait.

We were accused then to having bet on the wrong horse. My major concern was not to get politically marginalised. I detested Saddam, the occupation of Kuwait, the rapid deployment of foreign troops and the preparations for war. I kept my adherence to the diplomatic option that I favoured. On a *David Frost on Sunday* programme I stated, 'You have seen Yasser Arafat kiss the cheeks of Saddam but you did not bother to ask what he was whispering in his ear.'

1991: With the end of the Gulf War, James Baker started his shuttle diplomacy. From London, we played an important role to project the image of the indivisible nature of the Palestinian people and of its national movement. In London, several publicised meetings took place between PLO officials, Palestinian personalities from the occupied territories and diaspora intellectuals like Edward Said and Ibrahim Abu Lughod. The British Government offered us facilities so that Faisal Husseini and Hanan Ashrawi could 'slip' through London to Tunis for consultations. My position was: the PLO is, at the same time, an institution and an idea. If ten thousand people work in the institution, the nine million Palestinians are the powerful vehicle of the idea. The PLO has represented the Palestinian people for over twenty-five years. Now it will be the Palestinians representing the PLO. I frequently repeated then that the PLO had become 'unreasonably reasonable', having accepted that in the Madrid Conference the Palestinians were 'half a delegation, representing half the people seeking half a solution.'

1992: While negotiations are stagnating in Washington, the Oslo process starts ... in London. On 2 December, the steering committee of the multilateral talks held its meetings in London. Abu Ala'a was the coordinator of the Palestinian negotiating teams but could not – the PLO was still excluded – attend himself. While the formal official event was taking place in Lancaster House, Abu Ala'a and myself met at the Ritz Hotel with Yair Hirshfield, an assistant of Yossi Beilin, with Terry Larsen, the Norwegian, hovering on the sides.

1993: The Oslo breakthrough and the White House signature. History in the making, I kept repeating. The specificity of the Palestinian situation: 'A leadership in exile, a demography dispersed, a geography occupied' could move towards normality or the semblance of normality of 'an authority over a demography over a geography.'

1994: My application for Family Reunification in East Jerusalem submitted by a distant relative – my mother – was rejected by the occupation authorities. I had planned to abandon politics and diplomacy and start an English weekly in Jerusalem, *The Palestinian*.

The beginning of disenchantment with the peace process. My message was: Israel seeks a diplomatic outcome that would reflect: 1) Israeli power and intransigence; 2) the American constant alignment on the Israeli preference; 3) Russian decline; 4) European abdication; 5) Arab impotence; and 6) what they hope to be Palestinian resignation. My advice was: do not confuse realism with resignation.

1995: All Palestinian factions abide with an unproclaimed ceasefire. Assassination of Rabin by a Jewish extremist. The Israeli Government provokes the Islamic tendencies by the assassination of Shikaki in Malta and the 'Engineer' in Gaza.

1996: Successful Palestinian presidential and legislative elections. Retaliation of the Islamic tendencies in response to Israeli assassination policy. Peres wages war in Lebanon, ending with the Kana massacre. 'Retaliation' of the Palestinian Israeli voters through abstention and election of Netanyahu, whom I described as 'a pyromaniac on a power keg'. My lectures are often titled *From breakthrough to breakdown?* – still then followed by a question mark.

1997: Diplomatic stagnation. Instead of a permanent peace, we live through the farce of a durable peace process.

1998: Three meetings between President Arafat and Madeleine Albright in London. Increasing irritation of the American administration with Netanyahu's rigidity. His damaging of

American-Israeli relations is one of the factors that lead in 1999 to his electoral defeat opposite Barak.

1999: Barak a monumental disappointment. A complex individual, he alienated his colleagues within Labour and antagonised his coalition partners. Freezes the Palestinian track and flirts with the Syrian track.

2000: Barak wants to jump over the interim phases and move directly to final status talks. Arafat makes known that he believes that to be premature, because insufficient homework was done. The American side restricted itself to conveying to us Israeli proposals. David Aaron Miller, in a recent candid op-ed in *The Washington Post* titled 'Israel's lawyer', writes that had the American side presented the 'Clinton Parameters' in Camp David in July rather than, too late, in December, we would have had an agreement then.

The failure of Camp David heightens tensions. The provocative Sharon visit to the Dome of the Rock ignites the situation. The Mitchell Report, some time later, admits that the second intifada started by being non-violent and that the ferocious repression by the Israeli side, causing more than a hundred fatalities the first two weeks, pushed a few on our side to resort, unwisely, to using arms.

2001–2: In the internal debate, I lobby for a unilateral Palestinian ceasefire. Clinically, I believe that the Israelis should be aware that they cannot terminate the intifada and that we should be aware that by the intifada alone, we cannot terminate the occupation. There is a need for a diplomatic initiative.

2002: The diplomatic initiative occurs when the Beirut Arab Summit adopts the Saudi peace initiative. It is, alas, followed by a Hamas suicide bombing in Netanya. Sharon, offered a choice between reciprocating to a diplomatic overture or a retaliating to a military provocation, chooses the latter. The world, suffering from self-inflicted impotence, watches the reinvasion of the already occupied territories. The Nakba is definitely not a frozen moment in history that occurred sometime in 1948.

2003: The previous September, Tony Blair, at the Labour Annual Conference, is very warmly applauded when he announces that he will convene an international conference to help resolve the conflict. The conference convened turns out to be more modest than expected: 'on Palestinian reforms'. Even that displeases Sharon who tries to sabotage the London gathering by preventing Palestinian ministers from travelling. Fortunately modern technology and video-conferencing salvage the day. Here in London, I have to carry the burden. The Message: Reform, meritocracy, transparency are not conditions to be imposed on us by the outside world. They are a Palestinian expectation, aspiration, a right and even a duty. Yet I warn: the issue of Palestinian reforms should not be the tree that hides the forest, and in this case the forest is an ugly spectacle of occupation and oppression.

2004: Again, during the Labour Party Conference at the end of September, Tony Blair gets the loudest applause for his passage, 'Come November ... I will make it my personal priority ...' I have, since then, often invoked this Blair speech to prove that Yasser Arafat was not the obstacle to peace. End of September, Arafat was not dead. He was not even ill. By 'Come November,' Tony Blair meant when we have the American presidential elections behind us.

2005: With the disappearance of the founder of the contemporary Palestinian national movement, I frequently refer to Max Weber, who spoke of the phases of leadership and legitimacy: 1) the traditional phase, 2) the charismatic phase, 3) the institutional phase. The successful presidential elections, competitive and internationally monitored are a good omen for the future. Having witnessed the end of the charismatic era, a managerial revolution should now be on the agenda. We all know Sharon's intention. How the world and the Quartet will carry the peace process beyond the unilateral Israeli disengagement from Gaza remains to be seen.

In Conclusion

We have an excellent working relationship with Her Majesty's Government and with the entire political establishment. In Parliament, it is the pro-Israeli lobby which is on the defensive, more comfortable in supporting an Israel run by Labour, rather than the internationally embarrassing Likud.

All opinion polls in Britain, but also across Europe, show that the trend is overwhelmingly in favour of ending the Israeli occupation that started in 1967, and the establishment of a Palestinian State. It is no more a left-wing phenomenon, but we enjoy comfortable majorities among the voters of the Liberals and also the Conservative.

Unlike 1973, when European governmental positions were more advanced than their public opinions, today public opinions are more sensitive and supportive of Palestinian aspirations than their governments. The future looks promising. It is no more politically suicidal to be pro-Palestinian. It is no more electorally rewarding to be anti-Palestinian. Quite the opposite.

Index